Caring for Families in Court

In many US courts and internationally, family law cases constitute almost half of the trial caseload. These matters include child abuse and neglect and juvenile delinquency, as well as divorce, custody, paternity, and other traditional family law issues.

In this book, the authors argue that reforms to the family justice system are necessary to enable it to assist families and children effectively. The authors propose an approach that envisions the family court as a "care center," by blending existing theories surrounding court reform in family law with an ethic of care and narrative practice.

Building on conceptual, procedural, and structural reforms of the past several decades, the authors define the concept of a unified family court created along interdisciplinary lines — a paradigm that is particularly well suited to inform the work of family courts. These prior reforms have contributed to enhancing the family justice system, as courts now can shape comprehensive outcomes designed to improve the lives of families and children by taking into account both their legal and non-legal needs. In doing so, courts can utilize each family's story as a foundation to fashion a resolution of their unique issues. In the book, the authors aim to strengthen a court's problem-solving capabilities by discussing how incorporating an ethic of care and appreciating the family narrative can add to the court's effectiveness in responding to families and children. Creating the court as a care center, the authors conclude, should lie at the heart of how a family justice system operates.

The authors are well-known figures in the area and have been involved in family court reform on both a US national and an international scale for many years.

Barbara A. Babb is an Associate Professor of Law and Director of the Sayra and Neil Meyerhoff Center for Families, Children and the Courts at the University of Baltimore School of Law, US.

Judith D. Moran was an Adjunct Professor of Law at the University of Baltimore School of Law, US.

Caring for Families in Court

An Essential Approach to Family Justice

Barbara A. Babb and Judith D. Moran

Routledge
Taylor & Francis Group
LONDON AND NEW YORK

First published 2019
by Routledge
2 Park Square, Milton Park, Abingdon, Oxon OX14 4RN

and by Routledge
605 Third Avenue, New York, NY 10017

First issued in paperback 2021

Routledge is an imprint of the Taylor & Francis Group, an informa business

Publisher's Note
The publisher has gone to great lengths to ensure the quality of this reprint but points out that some imperfections in the original copies may be apparent.

British Library Cataloguing in Publication Data
A catalogue record for this book is available from the British Library

Library of Congress Cataloging-in-Publication Data
Names: Babb, Barbara A., author. | Moran, Judith D., author.
Title: Caring for families in court : an essential approach to family justice/ Barbara A. Babb and Judith D. Moran.
Description: Abingdon, Oxon ; New York, NY : Routledge, 2019. | Includesindex.
Identifiers: LCCN 2018033537 | ISBN 9781138684119 (hbk)
Subjects: LCSH: Domestic relations courts–Social aspects–United States. | Juvenile courts–Social aspects–United States.
Classification: LCC KF505.5 .B33 2019 | DDC 346.7301/5–dc23
LC record available at https://lccn.loc.gov/2018033537

Typeset in Galliard
by Taylor & Francis Books

ISBN 13: 978-1-03-224169-2 (pbk)
ISBN 13: 978-1-138-68411-9 (hbk)

DOI: 10.4324/9781315544144

B. A. B.: To Peter, Harrison, Jordan, and Marin—my loving family.

J. D. M.: To Sam, Nate, Franny, Thomas, Stella, and Sophie and their caring parents.

Contents

Preface

This book is an outgrowth from our many years of involvement with the family justice system. We have represented family law litigants, have participated in family court administration, have advocated for and have facilitated family justice system reform initiatives, and have taught various family law courses in law school. We also have written about aspects of family justice system reform. We have observed the landscape of the family justice system through the lens of our own experiences, those of our clients and colleagues (law professors, lawyers, judges, and court personnel), and those of our law students. We now aim to consolidate the sum-total of what we have learned, along with what we believe is a vital new perspective on how family courts and those who work within them must approach their work.

We have worked with and have thought about courts and the families who seek their assistance for decades. It is not only our experience in family law that prompts us to engage in justice system reform. Each of us also has engaged in professions that have exposed us to families and children in need during our careers as a high school teacher, a social science researcher, a nurse, and a counselor. We have seen families struggle, and we understand that meeting their needs is a complicated affair. What is more, our desire to care for those with whom we have come into contact in these professions represents a significant part of the work. The family justice system and those who work within it, including judges, lawyers, court personnel, and service providers, are challenged similarly. They must respond with care and concern if courts are to function responsibly. We write this book as a call to action to create family courts founded on principles of justice *and* care, because caring also is required if courts are to respond effectively to families' needs.

Notions of care and caring are concepts that date back to ancient philosophers—the idea that we owe a duty to care for and to care about one another. Several generations of theorists have pondered and have refined these concepts over time. Feminist scholars recently have resurrected ideas of care and caring as they have described women's different approach to the world. The feminists have attributed the divergence in perspective to the female penchant for embracing the relational and contextual aspects of human endeavors—care theory at its essence. Others have followed suit, suggesting that caring is not the sole province or unique capability of women. The care movement has evolved, leading to its application in politics, medicine, and law, with the intention to extend the province of care to both genders and to all human endeavors. Our proposal, to incorporate an ethic of care as an animating principle of the family justice system, ensues. It is an essential ingredient in order to fully realize a holistic approach to justice for families. Otherwise, family justice is incomplete.

Our expectations for a more comprehensive view of family justice stem from the premise that each family is unique and that the problems that lead families to seek help from the courts are correspondingly distinct. Laws governing families are designed to address their legal difficulties, but the application of the law to the facts of each family's life requires a nuanced perspective that considers the family's particular circumstances. So, too, does the recognition that legal relief is not the sole solution to most family law cases. Other issues come into play, such as economic hardship and medical and mental health difficulties. They need resolution, as well. This requires the court to care about such issues.

Care and caring must undergird both the structure and the operation of family courts. In many of our nation's courts, family law cases constitute almost half of the state's trial court caseload. These cases include child abuse and neglect and juvenile delinquency matters, as well as marital dissolution and related issues, such as child custody and visitation. In fact, some view the scope of family law as anything that pertains to an issue involving families and children. Owing to the high volume of family law cases and to their complexity—often due to associated non-legal problems, such as poverty and its accompanying issues—courts and those who work in them are faced with litigants plagued by distressing circumstances. Much like hospital emergency rooms, family courts deal with people in crisis. In these instances, caring for and about litigants must supplement the traditional mechanisms for processing cases and rendering decisions.

The audience for whom this book is intended represents a wide range of individuals. We direct our discourse to those who work in family courts—the judges, lawyers, court personnel, and service providers who confront the panoply of human needs exposed daily in our nation's family courts. We also hope this book interests our colleagues in legal education, because we believe law schools must teach the principles and practices associated with the ethic of care as part and parcel of a law student's professional development. Lastly, we wish to reach specialists in other fields of endeavor, whether policymakers, physicians, nurses, psychologists, social workers, teachers, or even architects or designers. We maintain that the work of the family justice system must interest the entire community, for it is in this arena that families and children function. The effects of the family court process can affect their participation in community affairs and institutions. With this ecological model in mind, along with the requisite attributes that define the ethic of care, court outcomes can become the best of what is possible under the law. We hope that our book prompts those who read it to heed our call for reform and to join in the effort to enact our caring agenda.

Our goals for the readers of this text are several. First, as we contend that family problems are complex, our prescription for court reform involves, in addition to incorporation of the ethic of care, an understanding of four intersecting perspectives on families and courts. We hope to present to our readers a comprehensive overview of these concepts—the unified family court, the ecology of human development, therapeutic jurisprudence, and narrative—and the rationale for their relevance to our proposal.

Second, we wish to illustrate our vision for applying these constructs to the operation of the family justice system—the manner in which court actors interact with litigants, how lawyers represent their clients, how judges consider their decisions, how the physical structures that house family courts are designed and maintained, and how certain court policies and practices can promote our vision.

Third, we understand that some readers may approach our reform agenda with apprehension, believing that family court systems are so beleaguered that they are beyond repair. It surely is an undeniable fact that the scope of problems confronting family courts, wherever they exist, is fraught with obstacles. These problems are global, and they are daunting to contemplate. We offer a ray of hope by including an overview of innovative approaches some courts have adopted, demonstrating that reforms undergirded by care are possible.

Acknowledgments

Barbara A. Babb

The support of so many has contributed to this publication (please forgive me if I do not mention you by name, but please know how grateful I am for your friendship). I am especially grateful to several extraordinary faculty members at Cornell University. In graduate school at Cornell, the late Dr. Urie Bronfenbrenner was my teacher and cheerleader, urging me to attend law school in order to influence family policy. At Cornell Law School, Professor Judith Younger fostered my passion for family law, and Clinical Professors Robin Masson and Barry Strom taught me what it means and how to be a client-centered lawyer. Discovering the concept of therapeutic jurisprudence, which comported with how I practiced law and which made the implicit explicit for me, introduced me to what has become a decades-long friendship with "the Ws," Professors David Wexler and the late Bruce Winick, both of whom personify the meaning of "mentor." The Honorable Robert Bell, Former Chief Judge of the Maryland Court of Appeals, proved to me that even those at the highest levels of the judiciary truly can care enough about families and children to bring about needed change to the family justice system. My dear friend Judge Peggy Hora (ret.) from the Alameda (California) Superior Court is a pioneering reformer in her international work with drug treatment courts and has served as a role model for me since we met. At the University of Baltimore School of Law, for three decades I have been a member of a wonderful community of administrators, faculty, staff, and students. I am so fortunate to work on a daily basis with my colleagues at the Sayra and Neil Meyerhoff Center for Families, Children and the Courts, especially the center's exceptional Senior Fellow, Gloria Danziger, with whom I have traveled many miles in the name of unified family courts. While the law students who have assisted me with my scholarship over the decades are too numerous to name, I remain indebted to each one. In particular, while finalizing this book, I acknowledge the outstanding assistance of Blake Wheeler, Steffanie Langston, Marleigh Davis, and Andrew Berg. I cannot thank enough my husband Peter Toran and my children Harrison, Jordan, and Marin Kobb, for their encouragement and enduring belief in the work I do. I conclude by acknowledging my ongoing gratitude to my dear friend Judy Moran, for again collaborating with me on yet another venture. Onward.

Judith D. Moran

I am grateful to family, friends, and colleagues for their interest and support as I wrote this book. Thanks are due to Professors Anthony Amsterdam and Jerome Bruner, posthumously, New York University School of Law, and to Professors Rita Charon and Maura Spiegel, Columbia University, all of whom inspired my thinking about narrative. I also acknowledge the Jesuits of Georgetown University, who introduced me to the ethic of care. I wish to pay tribute to the Honorable Kathleen O'Ferrall Friedman (Ret.) and the Honorable Albert J. Matricciani, Jr. (Ret.), who embody caring family court jurists and who gave me the opportunity to work with them in the Family Division of the Circuit Court for Baltimore City, Maryland. I thank His Honor, Justice Michael J. Keehan, The Family Division of the High Court of England and Wales, for his specific contributions to this book reflecting the care ethic he practices as a family court judge. Also, I extend my appreciation to Caroline Ackerman and Adela Hurtado for their able research assistance and to Joseph Baviello and Mark Wiltshire for their technical assistance in producing the manuscript for this book. Finally, I thank my husband Ned Moran, for his enduring patience and my co-author Barbara Babb, teacher, colleague, and friend.

Barbara A. Babb
Judith D. Moran
June, 2018

1 The family justice system

What it is, how it works, and an ideal unified family court model

Introduction

> [W]hile the challenges of a contemporary . . . family court docket may be fierce, we can unquestionably find ways to meet them and do better. I am simply unwilling to adopt a despairing and defeatist attitude that "nothing works" or—put another way—"everything stinks," but don't change a thing.[1]

> [W]orking to devise a system that will better serve the needs of the public need not affect a court's ability to judge the merits of an individual case fairly. . . . [T]he goal is to improve outcomes within the framework of the rule of law . . . .[2]

Many societies assert that families, however variously defined, are their foundation, without which the societies would not exist.[3] "The family is one of the most important social and political institutions."[4] "Parents who raise happy, healthy, and successful children create an especially important public good. Children themselves are not the only beneficiaries. Employers profit from productive workers. The elderly benefit from Social Security taxes paid by the younger generation . . . . Fellow citizens gain from having productive and law-abiding neighbors."[5]

1 Judith S. Kaye, *Delivering Justice Today: A Problem-Solving Approach*, 22 Yale L. & Pol'y Rev. 125, 147 (2004).
2 Judith S. Kaye & Susan K. Knipps, *Judicial Responses to Domestic Violence: The Case for a Problem-Solving Approach*, 27 W. St. U. L. Rev. 1, 10–11 (1999–2000).
3 Daniel Engster & Tamara Metz, *Introduction: Justice and the Family in Western Political Thought, in* Justice, Politics, and the Family 1 (Daniel Engster & Tamara Metz eds., 2014); Mona Harrington, Care and Equality: Inventing a New Family Politics 97 (1999); Gilbert A. Holmes, *The Conversations About the Intersecting Institutions of Marriage*, 4 Tex. Wesleyan L. Rev. 143, 144 (1998); *see also* Bret Bogenschneider & Karen Bogenschneider, *An Evidence-Based Approach to Family in Tax Policy*, 51 Gonz. L. Rev. 283, 297–304 (2015–2016) (arguing for the importance of the family from an economic perspective); Herbie DiFonzo & Ruth Stern, Intimate Associations: The Law and Culture of American Families (2013).
4 Daniel Engster & Tamara Metz, *Introduction: Justice and the Family in Western Political Thought, in* Justice, Politics, and the Family 1 (Daniel Engster & Tamara Metz eds., 2014).
5 Nancy Folbre, The Invisible Heart: Economics and Family Values 50 (2001).

We expect families to support and care for their members, including children. When families need help with intrafamilial issues, one of the many places to which they turn is the justice system. "Society's problems inevitably find their way into the courts . . . ,"[6] many as family legal issues. But do a family's problems matter to anyone other than the family members? Jill Hasday summarizes the vast significance of family law:

> Family law shapes social organization, economic status, intergenerational relationships, intimacy, childhood, maturity, and everyday experience. It reflects and influences how . . . [we] think about gender, race, class, sexual orientation, and other divides and helps determine how those categories will impact people's opportunities, choices, rights, and constraints. Family law helps structure both the details of daily existence and the overarching features of society.[7]

John Eekelaar and Mavis MacLean contribute to the conversation about the importance of family law. "At its heart, family justice is about how far the community believes it should become involved in problems people encounter in their personal lives."[8] Pauline Tesler argues that the community is, in fact, "an invisible stakeholder in every divorce,"[9] as divorce "generates consequences that affect public health, community engagement, the workplace and the economy, and the raising of a healthy next generation . . . ."[10]

Families routinely request courts to undertake many tasks, including dissolving state-created marriages, determining parentage, deciding where children shall live, protecting family members from abusive behavior, determining property use and possession, creating and enforcing spousal and child support awards, terminating parental rights, sanctioning adoptions, granting name changes, and ordering withholding or withdrawal of life-sustaining medical procedures, among other tasks.[11] Pauline Tesler describes the complicated nature of family law proceedings.

> Family restructuring involves a complex multiplicity of financial and relational issues, driven by powerful emotions of traumatic dimensions that

6 Judith S. Kaye & Jonathan Lippman, *New York State Unified Court System: Family Justice Program*, 36 Fam. & Conciliation Cts. Rev. 144 (1998).
7 Jill Elaine Hasday, Family Law Reimagined 1–2 (2014).
8 John Eekelaar & Mavis MacLean, Family Justice: The Work of Family Judges in Uncertain Times 205 (2013).
9 Pauline H. Tesler, *Can This Relationship Be Saved? The Legal Profession and Families in Transition*, 55 Fam. Ct. Rev. 38, 39 (2017).
10 Pauline H. Tesler, *Can This Relationship Be Saved? The Legal Profession and Families in Transition*, 55 Fam. Ct. Rev. 38, 39 (2017); *see* Rebecca Love Kourlis, *It Is Just Good Business: The Case for Supporting Reform in Divorce Court*, 50 Fam. Ct. Rev. 549 (2012) (examining how divorce and child custody proceedings affect employee productivity and urging the business community to become involved with family court reform efforts).
11 Del. Code Ann. tit. 10, §§ 921–25, 927–29 (West 2017).

> often overwhelm parties' thinking and coping capacities as well as their physical and mental health. It often requires ongoing parenting of children after judgment, calling for nuanced recalibration of solutions as children grow up, parents relocate, and blended postdivorce families form and come apart again. Moreover, divorce and family restructuring implicate interests that go far beyond the individual spouses, affecting not only children, but also extended family and friendship networks as well as significant relationships in the community and workplace.[12]

Families are coming to courts for assistance in increasing numbers.[13] In fact, "[t]he family courts have, in effect, become an emergency room for family problems when separating or divorcing parents have nowhere else to turn for help in addressing their problems with each other and their children."[14] The problems that bring families into court "lie at the heart of what we hold most dear, our privacy, our homes, our spouses or partners, and our children."[15] Andrew Schepard, in discussing child custody in particular, also frames the issue using a medical analogy. "In the same way they go to the emergency room, parents go to the child custody [family] court when the symptoms of conflict become acute and need immediate treatment."[16] Does society have an obligation, then, like an emergency room, to dispense care to families in court?

An examination of family justice across the United States, England, Wales, and Australia demonstrates that there is a trend to reduce the significance of courts and lawyers by implementing private or government-funded resources that

12 Pauline H. Tesler, *Can This Relationship Be Saved? The Legal Profession and Families in Transition*, 55 FAM. CT. REV. 38, 39 (2017).

13 *2015 Domestic Relation Relations – Caseloads Trial Courts*, NAT'L CTR. FOR ST. CTS. (Oct. 1, 2017, 1:55 PM), http://www.ncsc.org/Sitecore/Content/Microsites/PopUp/Home/CSP/CSP_DomesticRelations. 48% of all Delaware cases are Domestic Relations cases, 47% of all Pennsylvania cases are Domestic Relations cases, 43% of all Michigan cases are Domestic Relations cases, and 42% of all New York cases are Domestic Relations cases. *Id.*

14 Kourlis et al., *IAALS' Honoring Families Initiative: Courts and Communities Helping Families in Transition Arising from Separation or Divorce*, 51 FAM. CT. REV. 351, 356 (2013); *see also* Catherine Cerulli, Ann Marie White, Nancy Chin, Neil McLaughlin, Corey Nichols-Hadeed, Elizabeth Santos, Craig J. Doran, Ronald Pawelczak, & Eric Caine, *Unlocking Family Court's Potential for Public Health Promotion*, 22 BUFF. J. GENDER, L. & SOC. POL'Y 49 (2014) (discussing a multidisciplinary partnership designed to promote health and wellness); *see also* Leonard P. Edwards, *Remarks on Receiving the William H. Rehnquist Award for Judicial Excellence at the U. S. Supreme Court*, JUV. & FAM. CT. J. 45 (Winter, 2005); *see also* the Hon. Leonard P. Edwards, *The Role of the Juvenile Court Judge Revisited*, JUV. & FAM. CT. J. 45, 33 (Winter, 2005).

15 Barbara A. Babb & Judith B. Moran, *Judicial Independence in Family* Courts, *in* JUSTICE IN JEOPARDY: REPORT OF THE AMERICAN BAR ASSOCIATION COMMISSION ON THE 21ST CENTURY JUDICIARY app. H at 13 (2003).

16 ANDREW I. SCHEPARD, CHILDREN, COURTS, AND CUSTODY: INTERDISCIPLINARY MODELS FOR DIVORCING FAMILIES 5 (2004).

displace or diminish the role of the court system.[17] Nonetheless, the study concludes that the benefits derived from these innovations may be outweighed by their limitations. The authors conclude that "despite the move to privatized forms of dispute resolution, family justice still demands a sound judicial structure."[18]

> That some involvement [by the state] can be justified can hardly be in doubt. The state surely owes duties over those with respect to whom it claims legal and political jurisdiction. It owes duties to the children who will constitute its future members; it owes duties to the vulnerable and must surely be under an obligation of some kind to endeavor to promote a just society in accordance with the values it claims to uphold.[19]

Further support for the continuing significance of courts comes from the National Center for State Courts.

> Courts exist in our system of government for several critical reasons. First, it is through courts that those seeking justice can obtain it, regardless of wealth or power. Courts exist to ensure that asymmetries of power do not dictate the outcome of disputes. Second, in our common-law system, a public record of

17 *See generally* John Eekelaar & Mavis Maclean, Family Justice: The Work of Family Judges in Uncertain Times (2013) (providing an overview of how family courts operate in England, Wales, Australia, and New Zealand); *see also* G. M. Filisko, *Model Program Brings Holistic Solutions to Divorce*, A.B.A. J., Feb. 2015, http://www.abajournal.com/magazine/article/model_program_brings_holistic_solutions_to_divorce (describing a synopsis of an innovative out-of-court center in Colorado); William J. Howe III & Jeffrey E. Hall, *Oregon's Informal Domestic Relations Trial: A New Tool to Efficiently and Fairly Manage Family Court Trials*, 55 Fam. Ct. Rev. 70 (2017); *see also* Marsha Kline Pruett & Logan Cornett, *Evaluation of the University of Denver's Center for Separating and Divorcing Families*, 55 Fam. Ct. Rev. 375 (2017) (reporting on outcomes of an out-of-court interdisciplinary divorce center operated by the University of Denver); Lynda B. Munro, Johanna S. Katz, & Meghan Sweeney, *Administrative Divorce Trends and Implications*, 50 Fam. L.Q. 427 (2016); *see also* Jane C. Murphy & Jana B. Singer, Divorced from Reality: Rethinking Family Dispute Resolution 110–19 (2015) (suggesting moving some court processes into the community and otherwise lessening the role of courts; they cite examples from other countries); Jane C. Murphy & Jana B. Singer, *Moving Family Dispute Resolution from the Court System to the Community*, 75 Md. L. Rev. 14 n.9 (2016) (stating, ". . . community-based processes will not replace family courts"); Lori W. Nelson, *LLLT—Limited License Legal Technician: What It Is, What It Isn't, and the Grey Area in Between*, 50 Fam. L.Q. 447 (2016); Andrew Schepard, Marsha Kline Pruett, & Rebecca Love Kourlis, *The Family Law Bar, The Interdisciplinary Resource Center for Separating and Divorcing Parents, and the 'Spark to Kindle the White Flame of Progress*,' 55 Fam. Ct. Rev. 84 (2017); *see generally Special Issue: Australia's Family Relationship Centres*, 51 Fam. Ct. Rev. 179–285 (2013) (including seven articles focusing on Australia's Family Relationship Centres).

18 John Eekelaar & Mavis Maclean, Family Justice: The Work of Family Judges in Uncertain Times, at i (2013).

19 John Eekelaar & Mavis Maclean, Family Justice: The Work of Family Judges in Uncertain Times 205 (2013).

> court decisions is essential for establishing and updating our legal system. When disputes are resolved in private venues, information is denied to the public and to those seeking to ensure appropriate regulation of social and economic life. And third, the judiciary plays a key role in ensuring checks and balances on the power and actions of the executive and legislative branches.[20]

Judicial authority is another important characteristic that only courts can provide. "Litigants will often respond better to guidance, encouragement, and reprimand when it emanates from the bench as opposed to from other sectors within the . . . civil justice systems."[21] Judicial oversight also helps ensure fair and equitable results, particularly where parties differ in their levels of education and understanding of the issues.[22] "[A] judicial proceeding could, in effect, protect the parties from their own ignorance of the law."[23]

Family law in particular "must continue to be an active part of the greater court. . . . Families are not well served if family law either intentionally or inattentively distances itself from the court and the greater civil discipline."[24] Catherine Ross sets forth specific reasons detailing the importance of courts to resolve family law matters.

> [F]amily matters that bring people to courts raise theoretically complex issues of vulnerability, autonomy, and paternalism. . . . [T]he controversies decided in family courts often require complex doctrinal analysis. Judges presiding over family matters must frequently consider the interaction among governing local, state, and federal law, including statutes, regulations, case law, and even constitutional issues. . . . [Family law] cases . . . turn out to be the point of contact with the justice system that frames the average citizen's experience and understanding of courts, and their respect for, or alienation from, the legal system in its entirety.[25]

Because families are asking courts to assist them in so many ways and because courts likely are here to stay, we must determine whether current court structure, function, and mission equip family courts to accomplish their tasks. If we as a

20 Richard Schauffler, *Trends: Close Up: The Rise and Fall of State Court Caseloads*, NAT'L CTR. FOR ST. CTS. (Apr. 2017), http://www.ncsc.org/~/media/Microsites/Files/Trends%202016/Close%20Up/caseloads.ashx (maintaining a newsletter published by the National Center for State Courts); *see also* Jane K. Stover, *Mirandizing Family Justice*, 39 HARV. J.L. & GENDER 189 (2016) (critiquing Family Justice Centers, or community centers designed to serve victims of domestic violence).

21 Raymond H. Brescia, *Beyond Balls and Strikes: Towards a Problem-Solving Ethic in Foreclosure Proceedings*, 59 CASE W. RES. L. REV. 305, 321 (2009).

22 Lynda B. Munro, Johanna S. Katz & Meghan Sweeney, *Administrative Divorce Trends and Implications*, 50 FAM. L.Q. 427, 442 (2016).

23 Lynda B. Munro, Johanna S. Katz & Meghan Sweeney, *Administrative Divorce Trends and Implications*, 50 FAM. L.Q. 427, 442 (2016).

24 Mark A. Juhas, *Guarding Against Family Law Exceptionalism*, ASS'N OF CERTIFIED FAM. L. SPECIALISTS J. 3, 6 n.4 (Fall 2014).

25 Catherine J. Ross, *The Failure of Fragmentation: The Promise of a System of Unified Family Courts*, 32 FAM. L.Q. 3, 4 (1998).

society truly value families and children, our obligation to them from a justice system perspective must include a commitment to assist these individuals effectively and responsibly. As Jane Spinak states, "Experience and research has [sic] led me to believe that if the state is going to intervene in families' lives via judicial proceedings, the court must add value to the intervention beyond what a social service, child welfare, or probation agency can provide."[26]

What is the precise obligation of courts to clientele in family law matters? Some have argued that in general "law is essentially an instrument: it is a human creation, designed to minimize the harms we suffer in social life."[27] First and foremost, "[t]he court is the basic institution assigned the task of resolving disputes"[28] in family law cases. Some have defined the court's "essential core functions in disputed cases"[29] as "creating and enforcing orders."[30] They believe that "[p]rotecting victims from violence, holding abusers accountable, and, ideally, setting parties on a course of rehabilitation are core functions of the legal system."[31] All the while, however, "[t]he court undertakes these core functions within the framework of the adversarial process. Court proceedings must be consistent with due process of law, as judicial orders entered . . . involve important legal rights and constitutional values."[32] Indeed, family courts are first and foremost just that—courts of law—and all citizens with legitimate family legal needs are entitled to have the court resolve their issues.

How are courts faring in their handling of family law cases, many of which are complex due to the intimate dynamics of families' lives? If and as we identify problems with existing family courts, can we suggest an ideal model to enable the court to perform better? These are the issues we tackle in this first chapter. We begin by defining a family court and providing historical background about the development of this court. We identify characteristics of family court users. We focus on how family courts are performing and identify problems which compel the need for family justice system reform. We begin our discussion of family justice system reform by proposing what we believe is the ideal court structure for resolving family law cases—the unified family court.

26 Jane M. Spinak, *Reforming Family Court: Getting It Right between Rhetoric and Reality*, 31 Wash. U. J.L. & Pol'y 11, 17 (2009).
27 Robin West, Caring for Justice 94 (1997) (footnotes omitted).
28 Kourlis et al., *IAALS' Honoring Families Initiative: Courts and Communities Helping Families in Transition Arising from Separation or Divorce*, 51 Fam. Ct. Rev. 351, 353 (2013).
29 Kourlis et al., *IAALS' Honoring Families Initiative: Courts and Communities Helping Families in Transition Arising from Separation or Divorce*, 51 Fam. Ct. Rev. 351, 353 (2013).
30 Kourlis et al., *IAALS' Honoring Families Initiative: Courts and Communities Helping Families in Transition Arising from Separation or Divorce*, 51 Fam. Ct. Rev. 351, 353 (2013).
31 Kourlis et al., *IAALS' Honoring Families Initiative: Courts and Communities Helping Families in Transition Arising from Separation or Divorce*, 51 Fam. Ct. Rev. 351, 354 (2013).
32 Kourlis et al., *IAALS' Honoring Families Initiative: Courts and Communities Helping Families in Transition Arising from Separation or Divorce*, 51 Fam. Ct. Rev. 351, 353 (2013).

What is a family court?

The historical development

"'Family court' is a term with no agreed meaning."[33] Generally, a family court is a forum within which to adjudicate the full range of legal issues involving family members.[34] "Many courts call themselves 'family courts' without fully considering the implications of that term, while others consolidate their treatment of family legal matters without specifically calling themselves 'family courts.'"[35] Family courts differ in their subject-matter jurisdiction (or the types of cases the court is empowered to decide), structure, court processes, and resources.

The family court concept evolved about the same time as Chicago inaugurated the first juvenile court in 1899, as society recognized the need for a special approach to the legal problems facing families and children.[36] In 1914, Cincinnati, Ohio, created the first court with jurisdiction over cases involving families and children, and thereafter these courts began to appear in selected cities, including Des Moines, Iowa; St. Louis, Missouri; Omaha, Nebraska; Portland, Oregon; Gulfport, Mississippi; and Baton Rouge, Louisiana, among others.[37]

The Standard Family Court Act ("the Act") of 1959 assisted states interested to create family courts. The purpose of the Act was as follows:

> [t]o protect and safeguard family life in general, and family units in particular, by affording to family members all possible help in resolving their justiciable problems and conflicts arising from their inter-personal relationships, in a single court with one specially-qualified staff, under one

33 Linda Szymanski, Theresa Homisak, & E. Hunter Hurst, III, Policy Alternatives and Current Court Practice in the Special Problem Areas of Jurisdiction over the Family 6 (1993); *accord* Robert W. Page, *Family Courts: An Effective Judicial Approach in the Resolution of Family Disputes,* 44 Juv. & Fam. Ct. J. 7 (1993); *see* Barbara A. Babb, *Fashioning an Interdisciplinary Framework for Court Reform in Family Law: A Blueprint to Construct a Unified Family Court,* 71 S. Cal. L. Rev. 469, 478–81 (1998) (describing the history of family courts).

34 Linda Szymanski, Theresa Homisak, & E. Hunter Hurst, III, Policy Alternatives and Current Court Practice in the Special Problem Areas of Jurisdiction over the Family 6 (1993); *see, e.g.*, Del. Code Ann. tit. 10, §§ 921–25, 927–29 (West 2017).

35 Barbara A. Babb, *Where We Stand: An Analysis of America's Family Law Adjudicatory Systems and the Mandate to Establish Unified Family Courts,* 32 Fam. L. Q. 31, 35 (1998) (quoting William C. Gordon, *Establishing a Family Court System,* 28 Juv. Just. 9 (1977)); *see also* Robert E. Shepherd, Jr., *The Unified Family Court: An Idea Whose Time Has Finally Come,* 8 Crim. Just. 37, 37–38 (1993).

36 Herma Hill Kay, *A Family Court: The California Proposal,* 56 Cal. L. Rev. 1205 (1968); *see* H. Ted Rubin & Victor E. Flango, Court Coordination of Family Cases 63 (1992).

37 Barbara A. Babb, *Where We Stand: An Analysis of America's Family Law Adjudicatory Systems and the Mandate to Establish Unified Family Courts,* 32 Fam. L.Q. 31, 36 (1998); *see* H. Ted Rubin & Victor E. Flango, Court Coordination of Family Cases 63 (1992).

> leadership, with a common philosophy and purpose, working as a unit, with one set of family records all in one place, under the direction of one or more specially-qualified judges.[38]

The Act permitted the family court to deviate from the traditional adversary process in order to resolve family conflicts less acrimoniously and allowed for the integration of child and family legal proceedings to promote efficiency.[39] The Act presumed that cases proceeded before judges with expertise in child and family legal matters and that the same judge determined a single family's case in order to provide continuity.[40] The Act also acknowledged the need for social services and for a case management system that contained a family's entire court records.[41]

Several states created statewide family courts after the Act's publication. Rhode Island's family court began in 1961, followed by New York in 1962 and Hawaii in 1965.[42] Delaware, South Carolina, New Jersey, and Vermont established statewide family courts over the following decades.[43] At the same time, other states created family courts in certain areas of the state, rather than a statewide family court.[44] In addition, some states expanded their juvenile courts and transformed them into family courts.[45]

38 Committee on the Standard Family Court Act of the National Probation and Parole Association, *Standard Family Court Act—Text and Commentary*, 5 NAT'L PROB. & PAROLE ASS'N J. 99, 104 (1959).

39 Barbara A. Babb, *Where We Stand: An Analysis of America's Family Law Adjudicatory Systems and the Mandate to Establish Unified Family Courts*, 32 FAM. L. Q. 31, 36 (1998); *see* H. TED RUBIN & VICTOR E. FLANGO, COURT COORDINATION OF FAMILY CASES 64–65 (1992).

40 Barbara A. Babb, *Where We Stand: An Analysis of America's Family Law Adjudicatory Systems and the Mandate to Establish Unified Family Courts*, 32 FAM. L. Q. 31, 36 (1998).

41 Barbara A. Babb, *Where We Stand: An Analysis of America's Family Law Adjudicatory Systems and the Mandate to Establish Unified Family Courts*, 32 FAM. L. Q. 31, 37 (1998); *see* Roscoe Pound, *The Place of the Family Court in the Judicial System*, 5 NAT'L PROB. & PAROLE ASS'N J. 161, 164 (1959).

42 Barbara A. Babb, *Where We Stand: An Analysis of America's Family Law Adjudicatory Systems and the Mandate to Establish Unified Family Courts*, 32 FAM. L. Q. 31, 37 (1998); *see* H. TED RUBIN & VICTOR E. FLANGO, COURT COORDINATION OF FAMILY CASES 63–64 (1992).

43 Barbara A. Babb, *Where We Stand: An Analysis of America's Family Law Adjudicatory Systems and the Mandate to Establish Unified Family Courts*, 32 FAM. L. Q. 31, 37 (1998); *see* H. TED RUBIN & VICTOR E. FLANGO, COURT COORDINATION OF FAMILY CASES 64 (1992).

44 Barbara A. Babb, *Where We Stand: An Analysis of America's Family Law Adjudicatory Systems and the Mandate to Establish Unified Family Courts*, 32 FAM. L. Q. 31, 37 (1998); *see* H. TED RUBIN & VICTOR E. FLANGO, COURT COORDINATION OF FAMILY CASES 64 (1992).

45 Barbara A. Babb, *Where We Stand: An Analysis of America's Family Law Adjudicatory Systems and the Mandate to Establish Unified Family Courts*, 32 FAM. L. Q. 31, 37 (1998); Robert E. Shepherd, Jr., *The Unified Family Court: An Idea Whose Time Has Finally Come*, 8 CRIM. JUST. 37 (1993).

"As early as 1959, then, with the publication of the Standard Family Court Act, policymakers offered a valuable court reform proposal structured to allow one court the opportunity to consider and resolve all of a family's related legal problems."[46] Have court systems achieved these laudable goals? One author of this book conducted a comprehensive survey of court structure and function several times over the last few decades.[47]

Current family court structure

The most recent survey by one of this book's authors reveals that in sixteen jurisdictions within the United States, there is statewide a separate court or division of a court dedicated solely to the resolution of family legal issues.[48] In eighteen United States jurisdictions, this type of separate court or division exists only in certain areas of a state.[49] Two United States jurisdictions currently operate a pilot program in order

46 Barbara A. Babb, *Where We Stand: An Analysis of America's Family Law Adjudicatory Systems and the Mandate to Establish Unified Family Courts*, 32 FAM. L. Q. 31, 37 (1998).

47 *See generally* Barbara A. Babb, *Fashioning an Interdisciplinary Framework for Court Reform in Family Law: A Blueprint to Construct a Unified Family Court*, 71 S. CAL. L. REV. 469 (1998); *see generally* Barbara A. Babb, *Where We Stand: Another Look at America's Family Law Adjudicatory Systems*, 35 FAM. L. Q. 627 (2002); *see generally* Barbara A. Babb, *Reevaluating Where We Stand: A Comprehensive Survey of America's Family Justice Systems*, 46 FAM. CT. REV. 230 (2008).

48 N.J. CONST. art. VI, § 3; CONN. GEN. STAT. §§ 46b-1, 46b-2 (2006); DEL. CODE ANN. tit. 10, §§ 901–902 (2006); D.C. CODE ANN. § 11–1101 (2006); HAW. REV. STAT. § 571–3 (2006); ME. REV. STAT. ANN. tit. 4, § 1 (2006); N.H. REV. STAT. ANN. 490-F:3 (2017); MASS. GEN. LAWS ch. 211B, § 1 (2006); MICH. COMP. LAWS ANN. § 600.1001 (2006); N.J. STAT. ANN. §§ 2B:3-1–2B:5-3 (2006); N.Y. FAM. CT. ACT § 113 (2006); R.I. GEN. LAWS § 8-10-3 (2006); S.C. CODE ANN. § 14-2-10 (2005); VT. STAT. ANN. tit. 4, § 451 (2006); WASH. REV. CODE ANN. § 26.12.010 (2006); W. VA. CODE § 51-2A-1 (2006); *In re* Report of the Comm'n on Family Courts, 588 So. 2d 586 (Fla. 1991) ("Family Courts I"); *In re* Report of the Comm'n on Family Courts, 633 So. 2d 14, 16 (Fla. 1994) ("Family Courts II"); *In re* Report of the Comm'n on Family Courts, 646 So. 2d 178, 179 (Fla. 1994) ("Family Courts III"); *In re* Report of the Family Court Steering Comm., 794 So. 2d 518 (Fla. 2001) ("Family Courts IV"); Telephone Interview with Debra Kulak, Reg'l Manager, Court Services Div., Family Div., in Wethersfield, Conn. (Jan. 23, 2006); Telephone Interview with Kirsten Skorpen, Family Div. Res. Coordinator, in Augusta, Me. (Jan. 3, 2006); Telephone Interview with Roland Fancher, Family Div. Adm'r, in Kalamazoo County, Mich. (Jan. 10, 2006); Telephone Interview with Alison Chambers, Dir., Family Court Services, Admin. Office of the Courts, in Charleston, W. Va. (Aug. 18, 2005).

49 ALA. CODE § 12-17-24.1 (2017); KAN. STAT. ANN. § 20–438 (2017); LA. R.S. 13:1401 (West 2014); MINN. STAT. ANN. § § 260.019, 260.021, 518.002–518.61 (West 2011); MO. REV. STAT. § 487.010 (2017); NEV. REV. STAT. § 3.0105 (West 2015); OHIO REV. CODE ANN. § 2301.03 (2017); OR. REV. STAT. § 3.405 (2017); MD. RULE 16-307 (2017); 1993 MD. Laws 198; Survey Response, Phillip Knox, Gen. Jurisdiction Court Adm'r, and Cheri Clark, Family Court Adm'r, Superior Court of Ariz., Maricopa Cnty., Phx., Ariz. (Nov. 21, 2011; Nov. 2, 2015); Survey Response, Julia Weber, Supervising Attorney, Ctr. for Families, Children & the Courts, Admin. Office of the Courts, S.F., Cal. (Jan. 2012; June 23, 2015); Survey Response, William DeLisio, Family Law Program Manager, Denver, Colo. (Aug. 2, 2011; June 2, 2015); Survey Response, Christopher Hansard, Assistant Dir. Of Research and Regulatory, Atlanta, Ga. (July 13, 2015); Survey Response,

to determine how to resolve family law matters more effectively.[50] Fifteen jurisdictions within the United States do not have a family court by any definition, as these courts hear family law cases in the mix with other civil and even criminal matters.[51] Clearly, there is room for reform in order to accomplish the exemplary goals of the Standard Family Court Act of 1959.

Dawn Marie Rubio, Admin. Dir., Court Servs. Div., Springfield, Ill. (Sept. 25, 2012); Todd Schroeder, Assistant Dir., Court Services Div., Springfield, Ill. (Oct. 5, 2015); Survey Response, Kristin Knight, Manager, Family Services, Frankfort, Ky. (Aug. 31, 2015); Survey Response, Tracy A. Buccino, Staff Attorney, General Counsel's Office, New Orleans, La. (June 30, 2015); Survey Response, Connie Kratovil-Lavelle, Deputy Exec. Dir., Dep't of Family Admin., Admin. Office of the Courts, Annapolis, Md. (Oct. 29, 2015); Survey Response, Jessie S. Carlson, Court Servs. and Programs Unit Manager, and Craig Hagensick, Research Analyst, Court Servs. Div., Minn. State Court Adm'r's Office, St. Paul, Minn. (Oct. 21, 2011); Survey Response, Richard Morrisey, Court Programs Manager, Court Bus. Servs. Div., Office of State Courts Adm'r, Jefferson City, Mo. (Sept. 15, 2011; June 2, 2015); Survey Response, Robin Sweet, Senior Court Research Analyst, and Hans Jessup, Research Analyst, Admin. Office of the Courts, Carson City, Nev. (May 23, 2011; June 3, 2015); Survey Response, Hilari B. Lipton, Child Welfare/Juvenile Justice Attorney, Santa Fe, N.M. (Jul. 20, 2015); Survey Response, Stephanie Nesbitt, Court Management Specialist, Raleigh, N.C. (Aug. 6, 2015); Survey Response, Steve Hanson, Manager – Children, Families, and the Courts Programs, Columbus, Ohio (Aug. 22, 2011); Survey Response, Stephanie Graubner Nelson, Manager, Children, Families, and the Courts Programs, Columbus, Ohio (Aug. 27, 2015); Survey Response, Shawn J. Adkison, Okla. CIP, Okla. City, Okla. (Nov. 20, 2012); Survey Response, Felice Hamilton, CIP Coordinator, Okla. City, Okla. (Oct. 27, 2015); Survey Response, Rebecca Orf, Or. Judicial Counsel, Staff Counsel, Salem, Or. (July 3, 2012); Survey Response, Leola McKenzie, Dir., Juvenile & Family Court Program, Salem, Or. (Sept. 21, 2015); Survey Response, Marcia Vandercook, Circuit Court Legal Advisor, Wis. Dir. of State Courts' Office, Madison, Wis. (Oct. 4, 2011; July 1, 2015).

50 Survey Response, Mike Commons, Manager of Family Court Project and Manager of Alternative Dispute Resolution, Indianapolis, Ind. (Sep. 4, 2015); Survey Response, Janet Skreen, Court Assoc. Coordinator, Admin. Office of the Courts, Olympia, Wash. (May 25, 2011; June 22, 2015).

51 Alaska Stat. §§ 22.10.025, 22.15.030 (2015); Iowa Code §§ 602.1102; 602.6101 (2015); Neb. Rev. Stat. §§ 43-246.01, 42-348 (West 2015); Tenn. Code Ann. §§ 16-10-101, 16-10-108, 37-1-103, 37-1-104, 37-1-203, 37-1-205 (2015); Utah Code Ann. §§ 78A-6-103 (West 2015); Survey Response, Stacey Marz, Dir., Family Law Self-Help Ctr., Anchorage, Alaska (Jun. 8, 2011; June 23, 2015); Survey Response, Donna L. Gay, Staff Attorney, Admin. Office of the Courts, Little Rock, Ark. (Sept. 7, 2011; Sept. 8, 2015); Survey Response, Viki Howard, Children and Families in the Courts Coordinator, Boise, Idaho (Dec. 21, 2011); Survey Response, Cori Erickson – Manager, Children and Families Court Servs., Boise, Idaho (Jul. 6, 2015); Survey Response, John Goerdt, Deputy State Court Adm'r, Des Moines, Iowa (Oct. 3, 2011; June 22, 2015); Telephone Interview with Kevin Lackey, Admin. Office of the Courts, in Jackson, Miss. (Jan. 3, 2006); Survey Response, Christine Wethern, Mont. Supreme Court Staff Attorney, Helena, Mont. (May 24, 2011; Oct. 5, 2015); Survey Response, Catherine M. Brooks, Professor of Law, Creighton University, Omaha, Neb. (Nov. 18, 2015); Survey Response, Cathy Ferderer, Family Law Mediation Program Dir., Office of State Court Adm'r, Bismarck, N. D. (Nov. 14, 2011; July 1, 2015); Survey Response, Kim Nieves, Dir. of Research & Statistics, Phila., Pa. (Oct. 8, 2015); Survey Response, Jill Gusso, Dir. of Court Info. and Publ'ns, S.D. Unified Judicial Sys., Pierre, S.D. (Nov. 3, 2011; Oct. 6, 2015); Survey

A cursory examination of how a few other countries handle family law matters is instructive.[52] In Canada, the provincial and territorial superior courts hear family law cases, and many of these courts have special family divisions or specialized family courts to adjudicate certain family law matters.[53] Several Canadian provinces now operate unified family courts, described later in this chapter, which allow a single court to handle all aspects of a family's legal problems.[54] The Family Court of Australia, established by Parliament in 1975, is a superior court of record that handles complex family legal disputes and exists in all Australian states and territories except Western Australia.[55] The Family Court of New Zealand, although a division of the District Courts, is designed to assist with many family legal issues.[56] Fifty-eight family courts exist throughout New Zealand.[57] In England and Wales, a single unified family court, established by statute in 2014, handles the full range of family cases, although the Family Division of the High Court of Justice hears certain cases reserved for it.[58]

Response, Leslie Barrett Kinkead, Court Improvement Program Coordinator, Nashville, Tenn. (Nov. 19, 2015); Survey Response, Judy Speer, Assistant General Counsel, Tex. Office of Court Admin., Austin, Tex. & Maria Elena Ramon, General Counsel, Tex. Office of Court Admin. (June 24, 2015); Survey Response, Dawn Rubio, Juvenile Court Adm'r, Salt Lake City, Utah (Jul. 23, 2015); Telephone Interviews with Lelia Hopper, Dir. of Court Improvement Program, & Linda R. Scott, Staff Attorney, Court Improvement Program, Va. Supreme Court, in Richmond, Va. (Jan. 25, 2006); Survey Response, Kathy Carlson, on Behalf of Joann Odendahl, State Court Adm'r, Cheyenne, Wyo. (Sept. 8, 2011); Eydie Trautwein, Children's Justice Project Coordinator/Staff Attorney, Cheyenne, Wyo. (July 15, 2015).

52 *See generally* JOHN EEKELAAR & MAVIS MACLEAN, FAMILY JUSTICE: THE WORK OF FAMILY JUDGES IN UNCERTAIN TIMES (2013) (overviewing how family courts operate in England, Wales, Australia, and New Zealand).

53 CANADA: DEPARTMENT OF JUSTICE, http://www.justice.gc.ca/eng/csj-sjc/ccs-ajc/02.html (last visited Oct. 1, 2017).

54 Barbara A. Babb, *An Analysis of Unified Family Courts in Maryland and California: Their Relevance for Ontario's Family Justice System*, 24 CAN. FAM. L.Q. 25 (2005); CANADA: DEPARTMENT OF JUSTICE, http://www.justice.gc.ca/eng/csj-sjc/ccs-ajc/02.html (last visited Oct. 1, 2017); *see also* ACTION COMM. ON ACCESS TO JUSTICE IN CIVIL AND FAM. MATTERS, ACCESS TO CIVIL AND FAMILY JUSTICE: A ROADMAP FOR CHANGE (Oct. 2013) (recommending restructuring of jurisdictions across Canada to adopt the unified family court model).

55 Alastair Nicholson, *Setting the Scene: Australian Family Law and the Family Court—A Perspective from the Bench*, 40 FAM. CT. REV. 279 (2002); FAMILY COURT OF AUSTRALIA, http://www.familycourt.gov.au/wps/wcm/connect/fcoaweb/about/ (last visited Oct. 1, 2017); *see also* Alastair Nicholson & Margaret Harrison, *Specialist but Not Unified: The Family Court of Australia*, 37 FAM. L.Q. 441 (2003).

56 *Family Court of New Zealand,* WIKIPEDIA, https://en.wikipedia.org/wiki/Family_Court_of_New_Zealand (last visited Oct. 1, 2017).

57 *Family Court of New Zealand,* WIKIPEDIA, https://en.wikipedia.org/wiki/Family_Court_of_New_Zealand (last visited Oct. 1, 2017).

58 Email from the Honourable Justice Michael Keehan, High Court Justice, to Judith Moran (Aug. 31, 2017, 10:37 EST) (on file with author). The Families and Children Act 2014, allowing the court to now order a child to live with one or both parents or spend time with a parent or someone else named in the order. 12:25, 2 October 2017, Family law in UK (England and Wales): overview, Practical Law Country Q&A 1-590-4465.

Who is using family courts?

Regardless of the particular court structure, family courts share many common attributes. Increasing numbers of families are seeking a court's assistance. An examination of data from a few states demonstrates the continued significance and impact of family law cases among state court dockets. In Maryland, for example, nearly forty-three percent of total filings in the trial court of general jurisdiction involve family law cases.[59] In New Jersey, these cases account for thirty-five percent of the state's total trial court caseload.[60] In Nevada, fifty-eight percent of the statewide trial court caseload involves family law cases.[61] In Canada, family law cases comprise one-third of civil court cases, but they account for almost half of all civil court activity.[62] "New Zealanders lodge about 60,000 applications a year in the family court, making it the second biggest jurisdiction by volume after the criminal jurisdiction."[63]

In addition to burgeoning caseloads, family courts all deal with similar issues facing families, and these problems have become increasingly complex.[64] With the legalization of same-sex marriage and the prevalence of assisted reproductive technology, for example, courts now must determine who is a parent. Family structure also has become more complicated.

> Whereas in the past just one nuclear unit consisting of a husband, wife, and children was typical, now several different types of families exist, ranging from blended, nonmarital, multigenerational, and same-sex families to immigrant families with both noncitizen and citizen members.[65]

59 MD. JUDICIARY, ANNUAL STATISTICAL ABSTRACT FISCAL YEAR 2015, TABLE CC-1.2 (2015), http://mdcourts.gov/publications/annualreport/reports/2015/fy2015statisticalabstract.pdf.

60 N.J. JUDICIARY, ANNUAL REPORT OF THE N.J. CTS. 2014–2015, 71 (2015), http://www.judiciary.state.nj.us/annual_reports/2015/2015.html.

61 SUP. CT. OF NEV. ADMIN. OFFICE OF THE CTS., ANNUAL REPORT OF THE NEVADA JUDICIARY: FISCAL YEAR 2016 APPENDIX TABLES, 1 (2016), http://nvcourts.gov/Supreme/Reports/Annual_Reports/2016_Annual_Report_of_the_Nevada_Judiciary/2016_Annual_Report_Appendix/.

62 Mary Allen, *Family Law Cases in the Civil Courts, 2012/2013*, CANADIAN CENTRE FOR JUSTICE STATISTICS (2014) http://www.statcan.gc.ca/pub/85-002-x/2014001/article/13005-eng.htm.

63 4 DIST. CT. OF N.Z. ANN. REPORT 23 (2016) http://www.districtcourts.govt.nz/assets/Uploads/DCAnnualReport-2016.pdf.

64 *See, e.g.*, Barbara A. Babb, *An Interdisciplinary Approach to Family Law Jurisprudence: Application of an Ecological and Therapeutic Perspective*, 72 IND. L.J. 775, 777–83 (1997); Steven A. Young, *Retroactive Recognition of Same-Sex Marriage for the Purposes of the Confidential Marital Communications Privilege*, 58 WM. & MARY L. REV. 319 (2016); Sonia Bychkov Green, *Interstate Intercourse: How Modern Assisted Reproductive Technologies Challenge the Traditional Realm of Conflicts of Law*, 24 WIS. J.L. GENDER & SOC'Y 25 (2009); Courtney G. Joslin, *Marriage Equality and Its Relationship to Family Law*, 129 Harv. L. REV. F. 197 (2016).

65 Jessica Dixon Weaver, *Overstepping Ethical Boundaries? Limitations on State Efforts to Provide Access to Justice in Family Courts*, 82 FORDHAM L. REV. 2705, 2712 (2014)

The advent of shared parenting has caused difficulties for courts when deciding child custody issues, after which the relationship between the parties continues in some manner, unlike other civil cases. Andrew Schepard and Peter Salem present an excellent summary of the complicated and diverse family law issues courts must address:

> Concurrently, social, political, and intellectual developments of the last quarter century have transformed and complicated family law. A listing of just some of the recent developments makes the point: covenant marriage; no-fault divorce; making inchoate property (stock options, pensions, intellectual property rights, partnership agreements) divisible at divorce; recognition of marital and premarital contracts; financial and parenting rights for cohabitants; statutory formulas for child support; joint custody and parenting plans; third-party and grandparent visitation rights; same-sex marriage and recognition of alternative family forms; greater emphasis on domestic violence and child abuse and neglect; surrogate parenting; an effort to reduce time in foster care and increase the speed of adoption; and international treaties seeking to reduce child abduction and recognize the rights of children.[66]

Further, families appear in court who "regularly face the crises and challenges surrounding unemployment, violent crime, drug and alcohol abuse, spousal and child abuse, and the stress created by competing time demands,"[67] often compounding a family's legal issues. Military families present special concerns for family court judges.[68] Immigration issues complicate the work of many family courts.[69] Growing numbers of self-represented litigants, who may represent the majority of court users, cause additional problems for courts, particularly regarding judges' struggles to adhere to the proper role of the court in the fact-finding process.[70]

(footnote omitted); *see also* Jane C. Murphy & Jana B. Singer, Divorced from Reality: Rethinking Family Dispute Resolution 60–71 (2015) (discussing changing demographics and their impact on family courts).

66 Andrew Schepard & Peter Salem, *Foreword to the Special Issue on the Family Law Education Reform Project*, 44 Fam. Ct. Rev. 513, 517 (2006).

67 Barbara A. Babb, *An Interdisciplinary Approach to Family Law Jurisprudence: Application of an Ecological and Therapeutic Perspective*, 72 Ind. L.J. 775, 779 (1997); *see* Anthony N. Maluccio, Barbara A. Pine & Elizabeth M. Tracy, Social Work Practice With Families and Children 319 (Columbia Univ. Press 2002).

68 *See* Shawn C. Marsh & Carlene Gonzalez, *A Need for Training: Preparing Juvenile and Family Court Judges on Military-Related Issues*, 65 Juvenile and Fam. Ct. J. 13 (2014) (arguing for specific training on issues related to military individuals and their families); Evan R. Seamone, *Educating Family Court Judges on the Front Lines of Combat Readjustment: Toward the Formulation and Delivery of a Core Curriculum on Military Family Issues*, 52 Fam. Ct. Rev. 458 (2014).

69 *See generally Special Issue: Immigration and the Family Court*, 50 Fam, Ct. Rev. 570–678 (highlighting nine articles on various immigration issues families and children face in family court).

70 Leslie Feitz, *Pro Se Litigants in Domestic Relations Cases*, 21 J. Am. Acad. Matrimonial L. 193 (2008) (concluding that the American judicial system's integrity requires expansion beyond traditional legal services in addressing self-represented litigants); Jona Goldschmidt, *The Pro Se Litigant's Struggle for Access to Justice: Meeting the*

Due to the important role of the family court in people's lives, it demands our serious attention. How are family courts faring in their functioning?

How are family courts performing?

Many studies have documented problems with existing family courts, so that the family justice system often may not dispense justice for children and families. According to a study by the American Bar Association,

> [i]n virtually all cases, in virtually all communities, the myriad courts and social service agencies do not communicate adequately with each other, resulting in unnecessary delay, duplication and contradictory rulings and recommendations. Moreover, the same family may have to appear in a family court, a juvenile court and a probate court, all of which are located in different parts of the community. This system wastes money and does not serve children well.[71]

Challenge of Bench and Bar Resistance, 40 FAM. CT. REV. 36 (2002) (highlighting the balance between the appearance of judicial impartiality and the *pro se* litigant's limited experience in, and access to, judicial proceedings); John M. Greacen, *Self-Represented Litigants, the Courts, and the Legal Profession: Myths and Realities*, 52 FAM. CT. REV. 662 (2014) (arguing that appropriate accommodations such as limited-scope representation benefits both self-represented litigants and members of the private bar); Bonnie Hough, *Self-Represented Litigants in Family Law: The Response of California's Courts*, 1 CAL. L. REV. CIR. 15, 16 (2010) (footnotes omitted) ("This is not simply a California issue. Utah, for example, reports that 49 percent of petitioners and 81 percent of respondents in divorce cases are self-represented. In New Hampshire's superior court domestic relations matters, almost seventy percent of cases have one self-represented party. Indeed, national data indicates that 60 to 90 percent of family law cases nationally involve at least one self-represented litigant, while 5 percent or fewer of cases in general civil dockets include a self-represented litigant."); Judith L. Kreeger, *To Bundle or Unbundle? That is the Question*, 40 FAM. CT. REV. 87 (2002) (examining, among others, the Maryland Legal Assistance Network's programs to implement limited-representation attorney programs for *pro se* litigants); Julianne Prisco, *Insuring That Good Deeds Go Unpunished: Instituting State-Provided Malpractice Protection for Pro Bono Family Lawyers*, 52 FAM. CT. REV. 725 (2014) (proposing that "all states should administer programs that allocate a legal expense fund to provide free legal malpractice coverage to family lawyers who volunteer in any capacity for no compensation."); Andrew Schepard & Peter Salem, *Foreword to the Special Issue on the Family Law Education Reform Project*, 44 FAM. CT. REV. 513, 516 (2006); Randall T. Shepard, *The Self-Represented Litigant: Implications for the Bench and Bar*, 48 FAM. CT. REV. 607 (2010) (concluding that self-represented litigants are increasingly at issue and providing "that the challenge that guides the legal profession is how we provide equal access to justice for all."); *see also* Deborah J. Chase, *Pro Se Justice and Unified Family Courts*, 37 FAM. L.Q. 403 (2003); *see generally* Connie J. A. Beck et al., *Divorce Mediation with and Without Legal Representation: A Focus on Intimate Partner Violence and Abuse*, 48 FAM. CT. REV. 631 (2010) (examining states' approaches to mediating issues of power and adequate representation for *pro se* litigants engaged in domestic violence and abuse cases).

71 *See* A.B.A PRESIDENTIAL WORKING GRP. ON THE UNMET LEGAL NEEDS OF CHILDREN & THEIR FAMILIES, AMERICA'S CHILDREN AT RISK: A NATIONAL AGENDA FOR LEGAL ACTION

Catherine Ross, Past Co-Chair and Past President of the American Bar Association's Steering Committee on the Unmet Legal Needs of Children, also has characterized the failings of the family justice system.

> Despite the prevalence of cases involving families, and the dramatic significance of the outcome of such cases to litigants' lives, the courts that handle these cases are usually understaffed, by both judges and support staff, underfunded, fragmented, disorganized, and at or near the bottom of the judicial status hierarchy. Such courts are frequently viewed as the "despised, entry-level 'kiddie court'" from which many judges wish to escape.[72]

Another decades-old study has enumerated problems that still exist in many court systems regarding their handling of family law matters:

1 the resolution process is often time consuming, expensive, and cumbersome, with some aspects of the dispute being adjudicated more than once;
2 proper attention is not being given to child-related issues, which are being allowed to fester as part of other aspects of a family-law dispute;
3 there is inadequate systemic resort to non-judicial resolution techniques (ADR) that might provide better, quicker, cheaper, and less acrimonious solutions to many of these kinds of cases;
4 there is inadequate coordination and consolidation of litigation involving the same family—a case, or several cases, involving the same family may be dealt with by different judges or masters, or even by different courts—thus inhibiting a rational, coordinated, stable approach to both the litigation and the problems that spawned it;
5 in some instances, judges sitting on family-law cases display either a lack of interest, a lack of temperament, or a lack of understanding with respect to these cases; and
6 the courts are not giving proper attention to the special needs of poor people, who often cannot afford representation by counsel and need, or desire, to proceed *pro se.*[73]

54 (1993); *see also* Paul A. Williams, *A Unified Family Court for Missouri,* 63 UMKC L. Rev. 383, 384 (1994) (citation omitted) (quoting Ann L. Milne, *Family Law from a Family System Perspective – The Binary Equation,* 21 Pac. L.J. 933, 934 (1990) (detailing Missouri's recent legislative efforts to create a unified family court)).

72 Catherine J. Ross, *The Failure of Fragmentation: The Promise of a System of Unified Family Courts,* 32 Fam. L.Q. 3, 5 (1998).

73 Robert C. Murphy, Report of the Family Division Review Committee 6–7 (1993) (reporting results of a legislatively mandated study summarizing two in-depth reports about Maryland's family law adjudicatory system); *see* Steven Baron, *The Scope of Family Court Intervention,* 4 J. Ctr. for Fam. Child. & Cts. 115, 124–26 (2003); *see* Deborah Chase & Peggy Fulton Hora, *The Best Seat in the House: The Court Assignment and Judicial Satisfaction,* 47 Fam. Ct. Rev. 209, 213 (2009); *see Failure to Protect: The Crisis in America's Family Courts,* Ctr. on Media, Crime, and Just. John Jay C. (May 6, 2010), https://thecrimereport.org/2010/05/06/failure-to-protect-the-crisis-in-america e28099s-family-courts/; *see generally* Univ. of Denver Inst. for the Advancement of the

A more recent report has documented very extensively some failings related to the existing family justice system:

- The harshness of adversarial justice harms people whose emotions are already raw because of impending family dissolution and exacerbates contentiousness.
- A "win-lose" mentality may breed failure to effectively deal with differences.
- Children can feel like and are often used as pawns in the battle between parents.
- Family resources may be depleted because of endless litigation rather than spent on other needs.
- Lawyers themselves can experience burnout or be threatened or even physically harmed by hostile litigants.
- Matters that are primarily psycho-social are at times decided by judges who sometimes are ill-equipped or untrained to make the best decisions.
- Well-founded fears of escalating domestic violence may go unaddressed, or worse, trigger a punitive response to the victim.
- There may be a proliferation of inconsistent orders, making justice inefficient, haphazard, and potentially damaging.
- The judicial system is swamped with family law cases.
- The burdens of litigation influence the work lives of the litigants, affecting their job performance.
- Legal education is not preparing students for the challenges of dealing with fragile families, and an adversarial ethic often exacerbates this problem.
- Effective alternative dispute resolution interventions are being used in some jurisdictions, but not everywhere, and implementation is very inconsistent.
- The child's voice is often lost, with resultant pain and resentment that may last a lifetime.
- Unchecked hostility between parents is harmful to children, while adversarial processes cause further deterioration and acrimony.
- Insufficient coordination among varied professionals who work with fragile families means lost opportunities and may lead to conflicting orders.
- The politics of judicial appointments can lead to family court judges who do not have the interest or judicial temperament to preside over family law cases.[74]

As the various studies conclude, multiple problems abound in the prevailing approach to family law decision-making and family court functioning. These deficiencies deprive the court of its power to resolve effectively, efficiently, and responsibly all of a family's legal matters. Families deserve better from the justice system.

American Legal Sys., Cases Without Counsel Research on Experiences of Self-Representation in U.S. Family Court (2016).

74 Barbara A. Babb & Gloria Danziger, *Families Matter: Recommendations to Improve Outcomes for Children and Families in Court*, CFCC (Univ. of Balt. Sch of L. Sayra and Neil Meyerhoff Ctr. for Fam. Child. and the Cts., Baltimore, Md.), June 2014 at 9–11 (footnotes omitted); *see also* Jane C. Murphy & Jana B. Singer, Divorced from Reality: Rethinking Family Dispute Resolution 26–34 (2015) (critiquing the adversary system relative to family law cases).

The ideal: A unified family court

How can we restructure or reimagine the family justice system so that it better serves families? One solution, about which we have written and have advocated for decades, is the creation of unified family courts.

> [A unified family court is] a single court system with comprehensive jurisdiction over all cases involving children and relating to the family. One specially trained and interested judge addresses the legal and accompanying emotional and social issues challenging each family. Then under the auspices of the family court judicial action, informal court processes and social service agencies and resources are coordinated to produce a comprehensive resolution tailored to the individual family's legal, personal, emotional, and social needs. The result is a one family-one judge system that is more efficient and more compassionate for families in crisis.[75]

The American Bar Association has recommended since 1994 that all jurisdictions establish unified family courts.[76] In addition, the National Council of Juvenile and Family Court Judges and the Association of Family and Conciliation Courts advocate for the creation of unified family courts.[77] Nonetheless, as indicated previously in this chapter, many states have not adopted this model.[78]

75 Paul A. Williams, *A Unified Family Court for Missouri,* 63 UMKC L. Rev. 383, 384 (1994) (citation omitted) (quoting Ann L. Milne, *Family Law from a Family System Perspective – The Binary Equation,* 21 Pac. L.J. 933, 934 (1990) (detailing Missouri's recent legislative efforts to create a unified family court)).

76 *See* A.B.A Presidential Working Grp. on the Unmet Legal Needs of Children & Their Families, America's Children at Risk: A National Agenda for Legal Action 54 (1993); *see also* Symposium, *American Bar Association Policy on Unified Family Courts,* 32 Fam. L.Q. 1 (1998); *see* Reports with Recommendations to the House of Delegates: 1994 Annual Meeting § 10C (1994).

77 *Resolution Regarding the Unified Model Court Concept Paper of the NCJFCJ Cross-Over Committee,* NCJFCJ.org, http://www.ncjfcj.org/sites/default/files/cross-over%2520concept%2520paper%2520resolution_07-22_1.pdf (last visited September 14, 2017); *see also* Katherine Lynch, *Reform of Family Justice: Children's Dispute Resolution in Hong Kong,* 17 Cardozo J. of Conflict Resol. 909, 933 (2016) (recommending the adoption of a unified family court for Hong Kong).

78 Alaska Stat. §§ 22.10.025, 22.15.030 (2015); Iowa Code §§ 602.1102; 602.6101 (2015); Neb. Rev. Stat. §§ 43–246.01, 42–348 (West 2015); Tenn. Code Ann. §§ 16-10-101, 16-10-108, 37-1-103, 37-1-104, 37-1-203, 37-1-205 (2015); Utah Code Ann. §§ 78A-6-103 (West 2015); Survey Response, Stacey Marz, Dir., Family Law Self-Help Ctr., Anchorage, Alaska (Jun. 8, 2011; June 23, 2015); Survey Response, Donna L. Gay, Staff Attorney, Admin. Office of the Courts, Little Rock, Ark. (Sept. 7, 2011; Sept. 8, 2015); Survey Response, Viki Howard, Children and Families in the Courts Coordinator, Boise, Idaho (Dec. 21, 2011); Survey Response, Cori Erickson – Manager, Children and Families Court Servs., Boise, Idaho (Jul. 6, 2015); Survey Response, John Goerdt, Deputy State Court Adm'r, Des Moines, Iowa (Oct. 3, 2011; June 22, 2015); Telephone Interview with Kevin Lackey, Admin. Office of the Courts, in Jackson, Miss. (Jan. 3, 2006); Survey Response, Christine Wethern, Mont. Supreme Court Staff Attorney, Helena, Mont. (May 24, 2011; Oct. 5, 2015);

While some have criticized unified family courts,[79]

> [n]o state that has unified its family court system has ever gone back to a more fragmented system. Conversations with judges, lawyers and mental health professionals in unified family court states … indicate that while their systems are not perfect, they are far better than what existed before.[80]

It is critical to focus on court structure because family law matters lend themselves to and even require adjudication within a specialized court. "While family law encompasses diverse legal issues, the effect of family law problems on the intimate aspects and the stability of people's lives represents a unifying theme that supports considering this body of law as a specialty area."[81] Further justification for unifying family law matters within one tribunal derives from the fact that "[t]he legal label placed on a family is often arbitrary, and the problems that families present to the court are interrelated. The courts must treat families holistically, addressing both their legal disputes and the problems that underlie them."[82] The need to address

Survey Response, Catherine M. Brooks, Professor of Law, Creighton University, Omaha, Neb. (Nov. 18, 2015); Survey Response, Cathy Ferderer, Family Law Mediation Program Dir., Office of State Court Adm'r, Bismarck, N.D. (Nov. 14, 2011; July 1, 2015); Survey Response, Kim Nieves, Dir. of Research & Statistics, Phila., Pa. (Oct. 8, 2015); Survey Response, Jill Gusso, Dir. of Court Info. and Publ'ns, S.D. Unified Judicial Sys., Pierre, S.D. (Nov. 3, 2011; Oct. 6, 2015); Survey Response, Leslie Barrett Kinkead, Court Improvement Program Coordinator, Nashville, Tenn. (Nov. 19, 2015); Survey Response, Judy Speer, Assistant General Counsel, Tex. Office of Court Admin., Austin, Tex. & Maria Elena Ramon, General Counsel, Tex. Office of Court Admin. (June 24, 2015); Survey Response, Dawn Rubio, Juvenile Court Adm'r, Salt Lake City, Utah (Jul. 23, 2015); Telephone Interviews with Lelia Hopper, Dir. of Court Improvement Program, & Linda R. Scott, Staff Attorney, Court Improvement Program, Va. Supreme Court, in Richmond, Va. (Jan. 25, 2006); Survey Response, Kathy Carlson, on behalf of Joann Odendahl, State Court Adm'r, Cheyenne, Wyo. (Sept. 8, 2011); Eydie Trautwein, Children's Justice Project Coordinator/Staff Attorney, Cheyenne, Wyo. (July 15, 2015); *See also* Barbara A. Babb, *Reevaluating Where We Stand: A Comprehensive Study of America's Family Justice Systems*, 46 FAM. CT. REV. 230 (2008); *see supra* notes 11–16 and accompanying text.

79 Anne H. Geraghty & Wallace J. Mlyniec, *Unified Family Courts: Tempering Enthusiasm with Caution*, 40 FAM. CT. REV. 435 (2002).

80 Andrew Schepard, *Editorial Notes: April 2008—Special Issue on Unified Family Courts: 'The White Flame of Progress,'* 46 FAM. CT. REV. 217, 220 (2008) (citing Andrew Schepard, *Law and Children: Introduction to the Unified Family Courts*, N.Y. L.J., Apr. 16, 1997, at 3).

81 Barbara A. Babb, *Fashioning an Interdisciplinary Framework for Court Reform in Family Law: A Blueprint to Construct a Unified Family Court*, 71 S. CAL. L. REV. 469, 514 (1998) (footnote omitted).

82 ANDREW I. SCHEPARD, CHILDREN, COURTS, AND CUSTODY: INTERDISCIPLINARY MODELS FOR DIVORCING FAMILIES 178 (2004). *See* Stephanie Domitrovich, *Utilizing an Effective Economic Approach to Family Court: A Proposal for a Statutory Unified Family Court in Pennsylvania*, 37 DUQ. L. REV. 1 (1998) (advocating for the creation of a unified family court in Pennsylvania as the most efficient forum for resolving family law matters); *see also* Linda D. Elrod, *Reforming the System to Protect Children in High Conflict*

relevant nonlegal issues is particularly acute in family law cases, as "legal problems within the family often persist beyond the resolution of a case. Most family relationships continue long after the case is over."[83] The court process involves restructuring family relationships, and it attempts to change future behavior, "but in family cases there is often no finality."[84] Thus, in addition to resolving any current disputes, family courts need to be forward-focused in their determinations.

When faced with difficulties similar to those that plague many family law decision-making tribunals, criminal justice systems in many states have responded by creating specialized problem-solving courts. "Problem-solving courts are part of the formal criminal justice system. They seek not to divert cases out of the system but rather to reengineer the system itself."[85] Beginning with the first drug treatment court established in Miami, Florida, in 1989, there are now more than 3,052 problem-solving courts in the United States, as well as increasing numbers internationally.[86] In addition to adult drug treatment courts, the most well-developed type of problem-solving court, many variations of problem-solving courts exist, including juvenile drug courts, family treatment courts, community courts, domestic violence courts, mental health courts, reentry courts, driving while intoxicated courts, homeless courts, youth courts, prostitution courts, tribal wellness courts, and veterans courts, among others.[87] Michael King refers to these courts as solution-focused courts,[88] an approach that "relies less on the court's ability to solve a problem than on an

Custody Cases, 28 WM. MITCHELL L. REV. 495, 517 (2001) (advocating for unified family courts as the best system to resolve high-conflict custody cases).

83 Jessica Dixon Weaver, *Overstepping Ethical Boundaries? Limitations on State Efforts to Provide Access to Justice in Family Courts*, 82 FORDHAM L. REV. 2705, 2714 (2014).

84 Nicholas Bala, Rachel Birnbaum, & Justice Donna Martinson, *One Judge for One Family: Differentiated Case Management for Families in Continuing Conflict*, 26 CAN. J. FAM. L. 395, 401 (2010); *see also* Richard Boldt & Jana Singer, *Juristocracy in the Trenches: Problem-Solving Judges and Therapeutic Jurisprudence in Drug Treatment Courts and Unified Family Courts*, 65 MD. L. REV. 82, 93 (2006) (discussing the role of judges in these courts).

85 GREG BERMAN & JOHN FEINBLATT, GOOD COURTS: THE CASE FOR PROBLEM SOLVING JUSTICE 42 (2005); *see* National Conference of State Court Administrators, Resolution 4, Conference of Chief Justices, Resolution 22, *In Support of Problem-Solving Courts*, Conference of Chief Justices, *at* http://cosca.ncsc.dni.us/resolutionproblemsolvingcts.html (resolving to spearhead the problem-solving model for judicial decision-making).

86 Suzanne M. Strong, et al., *Census of Problem-Solving Courts, 2012*, U.S. DEPARTMENT OF JUSTICE (Oct. 12, 2016) https://www.bjs.gov/content/pub/pdf/cpsc12.pdf; *see also* Jenni Ward, *Are Problem-Solving Courts the Way Forward for Justice?* 3–4 (Howard League for Penal Reform, Working Paper No. 2, 2014), https://howardleague.org/wp-content/uploads/2016/04/HLWP_2_2014.pdf (describing the growth in problem-solving courts through common law countries, such as the more than one hundred Specialist Domestic Violence Courts in England and Wales).

87 GREG BERMAN & JOHN FEINBLATT, GOOD COURTS: THE CASE FOR PROBLEM SOLVING JUSTICE 8 (2005); Suzanne M. Strong, et al., *Census of Problem-Solving Courts, 2012*, U.S. DEPARTMENT OF JUSTICE (Oct. 12, 2016) https://www.bjs.gov/content/pub/pdf/cpsc12.pdf.

88 Michael King, *Should Problem-Solving Courts be Solution-Focused?*, MONASH UNIV. RES. PAPER (2011) (Austrl.).

individual's self-efficacy and own ability to initiate positive behavioral change."[89] Regardless of court type, these specialized courts all work "to ensure not just that the punishment fits the crime … but that the process fits the problem. These innovative courts encourage judges and attorneys to think of themselves as problem solvers rather than as simply case processors."[90]

Families and children also deserve this problem-solving approach by courts to resolve their family legal issues, where the process fits the problems. We believe that the most appropriate forum within which this can occur is the unified family court, the blueprint for which one of us has described and has championed since 1998.[91] The essential elements of the ideal unified family court consist of the following: (a) a specialized court structure that is either a separate court, or a division or department of an existing court, and that is established at the same level and receives the same resources and support as a generalist court; (b) comprehensive subject-matter jurisdiction over the full range of family law cases, including juvenile delinquency and child welfare; (c) a case management and case processing system that includes early and hands-on contact with each family law case; (d) a judicial assignment system that results in the family appearing before one judge for the completion of one case or before one case management team for subsequent court appearances; (e) an array of court-supplied or court-connected social services to meet litigants' nonlegal needs that contribute to the exacerbation of family law problems; and (f) a user-friendly court that is accessible to all family law litigants, including the large volume of self-represented litigants.[92] A brief discussion of the importance of each of these characteristics follows.

89 Barbara A. Babb & David B. Wexler, *Therapeutic Jurisprudence, in* Springer Encyclopedia of Criminology and Criminal Justice 2 (Gerben Bruinsma & David Weisburd eds., 2014); Michael King, *Should Problem-Solving Courts Be Solution-Focused?,* Monash Univ. Res. Paper (2011) (Austrl.).

90 Greg Berman & John Feinblatt, Good Courts: The Case for Problem Solving Justice 5 (2005).

91 Barbara A. Babb, *Fashioning an Interdisciplinary Framework for Court Reform in Family Law: A Blueprint to Construct a Unified Family Court,* 71 S. Cal. L. Rev. 469 (1998). *See also* Barbara A. Babb, *Unified Family Courts: An Interdisciplinary Framework and a Problem-Solving Approach, in* Problem Solving Courts: Social Science and Legal Perspectives 65, 81 (Richard L. Wiener & Eve M. Brank eds., 2013); Barbara A. Babb, *An Analysis of Unified Family Courts in Maryland and California: Their Relevance for Ontario's Family Justice System,* 24 Can. Fam. L.Q. 25 (2005); Barbara A. Babb, *An Interdisciplinary Approach to Family Law Jurisprudence: Application of an Ecological and Therapeutic Perspective,* 72 Ind. L.J. 775, 788 (1997); Barbara A. Babb, *Reevaluating Where We Stand: A Comprehensive Survey of America's Family Justice Systems,* 46 Fam. L. Q. 230 (2008); Barbara A. Babb, *Where We Stand: An Analysis of America's Family Law Adjudicatory Systems and the Mandate to Establish Unified Family Courts,* 32 Fam. L.Q. 31 (1998); Barbara A. Babb, *Where We Stand Redux: Another Look at America's Family Law Adjudicatory Systems,* 35 Fam. L.Q. 627 (2002).

92 Barbara A. Babb, *Fashioning an Interdisciplinary Framework for Court Reform in Family Law: A Blueprint to Construct a Unified Family Court,* 71 S. Cal. L. Rev. 469 (1998). *See also* Barbara A. Babb, *Unified Family Courts: An Interdisciplinary Framework and a Problem-Solving Approach, in* Problem Solving Courts: Social Science and Legal Perspectives 65, 81 (Richard L. Wiener & Eve M. Brank eds., 2013);

Separate court structure

The diversity of a family's legal problems, along with their interrelated nature, the intimacy of the participants, and the effects of these problems on the stability of people's lives, requires that specialized courts hear and address family law issues.[93] As Lindsay Arthur long ago has noted,

> a single court could examine the entire relationship between parent and parent, parent and child, child and child, family and in-laws, and family and the public. And, having explored the whole complex of relationships, a single court could provide consistent and continuing consideration of each aspect of the problem.[94]

In addition, having a single court address the family's legal needs can "reduce the opportunities for inconsistent handling and errors based upon inaccurate or incomplete information."[95]

This single court structure can consist of either a separate specialized court or a division or department of an existing court, known, for example, as a family division or family department.[96] Available financial resources largely determine whether to house the specialized family court in a separate structure or whether to create the court as an autonomous division of the existing trial court.[97]

> Given the numbers of family law cases our nation's justice systems are handling, along with the importance of family legal matters in people's lives and their effects on society, it is imperative that any family court, regardless of its

Barbara A. Babb, *An Analysis of Unified Family Courts in Maryland and California: Their Relevance for Ontario's Family Justice System*, 24 CAN. FAM. L.Q. 25 (2005); Barbara A. Babb, *An Interdisciplinary Approach to Family Law Jurisprudence: Application of an Ecological and Therapeutic Perspective*, 72 IND. L.J. 775, 788 (1997); Barbara A. Babb, *Reevaluating Where We Stand: A Comprehensive Survey of America's Family Justice Systems*, 46 FAM. L.Q. 230 (2008); Barbara A. Babb, *Where We Stand: An Analysis of America's Family Law Adjudicatory Systems and the Mandate to Establish Unified Family Courts*, 32 FAM. L.Q. 31 (1998); Barbara A. Babb, *Where We Stand Redux: Another Look at America's Family Law Adjudicatory Systems*, 35 FAM. L.Q. 627 (2002).

93 Barbara A. Babb, *Fashioning an Interdisciplinary Framework for Court Reform in Family Law: A Blueprint to Construct a Unified Family Court*, 71 S. CAL. L. REV. 469, 514 (1998).

94 Lindsay G. Arthur, *A Family Court—Why Not?*, 51 MINN. L. REV. 226 (1966) (citation omitted) (advocating, in an early article, consolidation of family law litigation and court treatment of the entire family problem).

95 CAROL R. FLANGO, VICTOR E. FLANGO, & H. TED RUBIN, HOW ARE COURTS COORDINATING FAMILY CASES? 19 (1999).

96 Barbara A. Babb, *Reevaluating Where We Stand: A Comprehensive Study of America's Family Justice Systems*, 46 FAM. CT. REV. 230 (2008).

97 Barbara A. Babb, *Fashioning an Interdisciplinary Framework for Court Reform in Family Law: A Blueprint to Construct a Unified Family Court*, 71 S. CAL. L. REV. 469, 516–17 (1998).

> structure, be established at the same level and receive the same resources and support as a trial court of general jurisdiction.[98]

The importance of family courts demands that their status be equivalent to trial courts of general jurisdiction.

Comprehensive subject-matter jurisdiction

A unified family court must have the power to address and to resolve all of a family's legal and related nonlegal problems. To accomplish this, the court needs comprehensive subject-matter jurisdiction, conferred by statute or court rule, over the full range of family law issues.[99] A court without this ability to determine related legal matters is less than fully effective, the likely result of which is that the family may need to appear in more than one forum in order to have all of its issues decided.

> Subject matter jurisdiction should include dissolution and related matters, such as distribution of marital property, separation, and annulment; child custody, visitation, modification, and interstate custody cases; child support establishment, modification, enforcement, and uniform interstate family support cases; determination of paternity; child abuse and neglect; termination of parental rights; domestic violence proceedings; adoption; juvenile delinquency proceedings; adult and juvenile guardianship and conservatorship; mental health matters, including civil commitment and confinement; legal-medical issues, including right to die, abortion, and living wills; emancipation; and name change.[100]

98 Barbara A. Babb, *Unified Family Courts: An Interdisciplinary Framework and a Problem-Solving Approach, in* PROBLEM SOLVING COURTS: SOCIAL SCIENCE AND LEGAL PERSPECTIVES 65, 75 (Richard L. Wiener & Eve M. Brank eds., 2013); Barbara A. Babb, *Fashioning an Interdisciplinary Framework for Court Reform in Family Law: A Blueprint to Construct a Unified Family Court,* 71 S. CAL. L. REV. 469, 516 (1998); Barbara A. Babb, *Reevaluating Where We Stand: A Comprehensive Study of America's Family Justice Systems,* 46 FAM. CT. REV. 230, 232 (2008).

99 Family law matters are defined to include divorce, annulment, and property distribution; child custody and visitation; alimony and child support; paternity, adoption, and termination of parental rights; juvenile cases (juvenile delinquency, child abuse, and child neglect); domestic violence, criminal non-support; name change; guardianship of minors and disabled persons; and withholding or withdrawal of life-sustaining medical procedures, involuntary admissions, and emergency evaluations. *See, e.g.*, DEL. CODE ANN. tit. 10, §§ 921–25, 927–28 (2017).

100 Barbara A. Babb, *Unified Family Courts: An Interdisciplinary Framework and a Problem-Solving Approach, in* PROBLEM SOLVING COURTS: SOCIAL SCIENCE AND LEGAL PERSPECTIVES 65, 76 (Richard L. Wiener & Eve M. Brank eds., 2013); Barbara A. Babb, *Fashioning an Interdisciplinary Framework for Court Reform in Family Law: A Blueprint to Construct a Unified Family Court*, 71 S. CAL. L. REV. 469, 518 (1998); *see, e.g.*, Md. Rule 16–307 (West 2017); *see also* Mark Hardin, *Child Protection Cases in a Unified Family Court*, 32 FAM. L.Q. 147 (1998) (discussing the advantages and disadvantages of including child protection cases in a unified family court); *see also* Gloria Danziger, *Delinquency Jurisdiction in a Unified Family Court: Balancing Intervention, Prevention, and Adjudication*, 37 FAM. L.Q. 381 (2003).

Recognition of the need for comprehensive subject-matter jurisdiction comports with family systems theory, "a view of families now widely accepted in the social sciences which postulates that the family is a living system and that individuals' problems are best understood through the lens of intrafamily interactions."[101] The court needs the power to address all of the related problems affecting the family in order to accommodate all of the intrafamily dynamics.

There is a difference of opinion among experts about whether criminal jurisdiction over intrafamilial violence is appropriate for a unified family court.[102] As a consequence, some jurisdictions have created integrated domestic violence courts to hear both civil and criminal issues involving family violence, with the aim of protecting victims and promoting offender accountability.[103]

101 *Developments in the Law: VI. Unified Family Courts and the Child Protection Dilemma*, 116 Harv. L. Rev. 2099, 2105 (2003); *see also* Susan L. Brooks, *A Family Systems Paradigm for Legal Decision Making Affecting Child Custody*, 6 Cornell J.L. & Pub. Pol'y 1 (1996).

102 Sanford N. Katz & Jeffrey A. Kuhn, Recommendations for a Model Family Court 8 (1991) (discussing the arguments for and against including criminal jurisdiction over intrafamilial matters as part of the family court: "While proponents for inclusion of this jurisdiction in family court argued that such a system promotes coordinated delivery of services to the family and discouraging multiple interviewing of victims, as well as fragmented delivery, those arguing against such jurisdiction cited possible due process violations and community pressure for a more punitive stance toward offenders as rendering such jurisdiction inappropriate for the family court."). *See also* Linda Szymanski, Theresa Homisak, & E. Hunter Hurst, III, Policy Alternatives and Current Court Practice in the Special Problem Areas of Jurisdiction over the Family 8–9 (1993). The authors suggest additional arguments against including criminal jurisdiction in family court: "Inclusion of criminal jurisdiction within the family court can present a host of problems . . . . First, there is a philosophical divergence between juvenile court and criminal court. Juvenile court's intervention is justified on the basis of protecting the child and is not intended as punishment but as remediation. Criminal proceedings require the availability of jury trial with the increased administrative burden on the restructured court system, unless the criminal jurisdiction is limited to misdemeanors." *Id.* (citation omitted). *See also* Martin Guggenheim, *Constitutional and Due Process Concerns: Juvenile and Family Courts of the Future, in* Families in Court: Recommendations from a National Symposium 179, 181 (Meredith Hofford ed., 1989) (addressing constitutional due process considerations for case management of family violence matters); *see also* Joan S. Meier & Sean Dickson, *Mapping Gender: Shedding Empirical Light on Family Courts' Treatment of Cases Involving Abuse and Alienation*, 35 L. & Inequality 311, 332 (2017) (documenting empirical evidence that family courts are biased against women reporting abuse); *but see* Carolyn D. Schwarz, *Unified Family Courts: A Saving Grace for Victims of Domestic Violence Living in Nations with Fragmented Court Systems*, 42 Fam. Ct. Rev. 304 (2004) (arguing for the establishment of unified family courts, as they serve needs of domestic violence victims better than fragmented courts).

103 Danielle Malangone, *Integrating Procedural Justice in Domestic Violence Cases*, Ctr. for Court Innovation, http://www.courtinnovation.org/sites/default/files/documents/DVFactSheet_November2016_IntegratingPJinDVCases.pdf; Judith S. Kaye, *Delivering Justice Today: A Problem-Solving Approach*, 22 Yale L. & Pol'y Rev. 125, 143 (2004); *see also* Billie Lee Dunford Jackson, Lorettea Frederick, Barbara Hart, & Meredith Hofford, *Unified Family Courts: How Will They Serve Victims of Domestic Violence?*, 32 Fam. L.Q. 131

Specialized case management and judicial assignment system

Family legal problems must receive prompt attention by the courts, as delay affords parties' problems the potential to escalate and to cause harm. Operating an effective unified family court thus requires a high level of administrative coordination.[104] "Case management and case processing, or the method by which cases proceed from initial filing through resolution, should proceed without undue delay and with active, hands-on participation from court personnel as early as possible."[105] The aim is to conduct a form of triage, "a word used in the medical field for prioritizing patients on the basis of the severity of their condition, a method of rationing treatment, when resources are insufficient for all to be treated immediately."[106] The triage method needs to occur early in the court process to determine which cases need immediate attention, including the allocation of scarce judicial resources, and how to meet most effectively the legal and nonlegal needs of the family.[107] There are various options concerning who should conduct the case management.

> A judge, a professional court administrator, a trained intake worker, or a team of these personnel can evaluate each case filing or intake and can determine whether the parties require immediate attention. The initial evaluation process also can result in referral of the parties to appropriate [social] services, as well as scheduling an early status conference. At this conference, the parties, their attorneys, and the judge can frame the issues in the case, discuss settlement possibilities, and consider alternatives to an adversarial trial or hearing.[108]

(1998) (cautioning that a unified family court must not lose its mandate to protect battered women and their children).

104 Barbara A. Babb, *Unified Family Courts: An Interdisciplinary Framework and a Problem-Solving Approach, in* Problem Solving Courts: Social Science and Legal Perspectives 65, 79 (Richard L. Wiener & Eve M. Brank eds., 2013); Barbara A. Babb, *Fashioning an Interdisciplinary Framework for Court Reform in Family Law: A Blueprint to Construct a Unified Family Court*, 71 S. Cal. L. Rev. 469, 521–22 (1998).

105 Barbara A. Babb, *Fashioning an Interdisciplinary Framework for Court Reform in Family Law: A Blueprint to Construct a Unified Family Court*, 71 S. Cal. L. Rev. 469, 519–20 (1998).

106 Victor E. Flango & Thomas M. Clarke, Reimagining Courts: A Design for the Twenty-First Century 36 (2015) (footnote omitted).

107 *See* Nicholas Bala, Rachel Birnbaum, & Justice Donna Martinson, *One Judge for One Family: Differentiated Case Management for Families in Continuing Conflict*, 26 Can. J. Fam. L. 395 (2010) (advocating for unified family courts as the best system for case management); *see* Peter Salem, Debra Kulak, & Robin M. Deutsch, *Triaging Family Court Services: The Connecticut Judicial Branch's Family Civil Intake Screen*, 27 Pace L. Rev. 741 (2007); *see* Peter Salem, *The Emergence of Triage in Family Court Services: The Beginning of the End for Mandatory Mediation?* 47 Fam. Ct. Rev. 371 (2009); *see also* Andrew I. Schepard, Children, Courts, and Custody: Interdisciplinary Models for Divorcing Families, 113–24 (2004) (discussing differentiated case management, or a particular case management process used in many jurisdictions).

108 Barbara A. Babb, *Fashioning an Interdisciplinary Framework for Court Reform in Family Law: A Blueprint to Construct a Unified Family Court*, 71 S. Cal. L. Rev. 469, 520 (1998) (footnotes omitted).

Some believe, however, that effective case management involves "using judge time for the 'highest and best' purpose—conducting trials—and shedding administrative duties to court administrators or other quasi-judicial personnel when possible."[109] Regardless of the personnel designated to conduct the case management, it is an ongoing process, continues throughout the life of the case, and requires constant monitoring.[110]

The method of judicial assignment is another important consideration related to case management and case processing. The one judge-one case method of judicial assignment means that the same judge oversees and hears a case from start to finish.[111] This approach allows a judge to become knowledgeable about the family's situation and facilitates the design of a more effective resolution to the family's problems. The one judge-one family judicial assignment system places the family before the same judge every time the parties come to court for the resolution of family legal issues.[112] This method also permits judges to know each family's circumstances, but it can compromise judges' ability to remain impartial "if the judges do not guard against becoming so familiar that they are no longer unbiased."[113] On the other hand, "[a]lthough a judge must exhibit the qualities of dispassion and disengagement, he or she need not be ignorant in order to be impartial, nor remote in order to be dispassionate."[114] "A corollary is that family members … feel better understood and more wisely handled by 'their judge.'"[115] In addition, family members are more likely to obey court orders, knowing they need to appear before the same judge.[116]

109 Victor E. Flango & Thomas M. Clarke, Reimagining Courts: A Design for the Twenty-First Century 61 (2015).

110 Barbara A. Babb, *Fashioning an Interdisciplinary Framework for Court Reform in Family Law: A Blueprint to Construct a Unified Family Court*, 71 S. Cal. L. Rev. 469, 520–21 (1998) (footnotes omitted).

111 Robert F. Peckham, *A Judicial Response to the Cost of Litigation: Case Management, Two-Stage Discovery Planning and Alternative Dispute Resolutions*, 37 Rutgers L. Rev. 253, 257 (1985); *see also* Barbara A. Babb, *Reevaluating Where We Stand: A Comprehensive Study of America's Family Justice Systems*, 46 Fam. Ct. Rev. 230, 253 app. D (2008).

112 Barbara A. Babb, *Reevaluating Where We Stand: A Comprehensive Study of America's Family Justice Systems*, 46 Fam. Ct. Rev. 230, 253 app. D n.3 (2008); *see* Corey Shdaimah & Alicia Summers, *Baltimore City's Model Court: Professional Stakeholders' Experience with Baltimore City's One Family, One Judge Docketing*, 51 Fam. Ct. Rev. 286 (2013) (finding positive perceptions of the one family, one judge model).

113 Barbara A. Babb, *Unified Family Courts: An Interdisciplinary Framework and a Problem-Solving Approach, in* Problem Solving Courts: Social Science and Legal Perspectives 65, 78 (Richard L. Wiener & Eve M. Brank eds., 2013); Ann H. Geraghty & Wallace J. Mylniec, *Unified Family Courts: Tempering Enthusiasm with Caution*, 40 Fam. Ct. Rev. 435, 438–40 (2002).

114 Robert F. Peckham, *A Judicial Response to the Cost of Litigation Management, Two-Stage Discovery Planning and Alternative Dispute Resolution*, 37 Rutgers L. Rev. 253, 262 (1985).

115 Carol R. Flango, Victor E. Flango, & H. Ted Rubin, How Are Courts Coordinating Family Cases? 24 (1999).

116 Carol R. Flango, Victor E. Flango, & H. Ted Rubin, How Are Courts Coordinating Family Cases? 24 (1999).

A type of case management referred to as the one family-one team approach ensures that the same team of court administrative personnel, which may include quasi-judicial officers,[117] reviews a family's case every time a family member files a matter with the court and during the entire court process.[118] This technique promotes consistency in case processing due to the team's knowledge about the family, but it avoids the potential for "judicial overfamiliarity"[119] that is the likely result of employing the one judge-one family judicial assignment system. "Teams composed of professional court staff can proactively manage each case by providing intake, screening, assessment, calendar coordination, and case monitoring services to the parties and to the judges."[120] Further, this type of case management promotes the family-friendly nature of the court.[121]

Whatever the judicial assignment method, the intent of the case management scheme is "to improve consistency for the family, to eliminate the problems associated with different judges evaluating discrete aspects of a case, and to increase the judge's ability to make informed decisions regarding proper outcome goals and services for the family."[122] A type of automated case processing system that provides the court with relevant information about each family is a necessary component. The system needs to inform court personnel about pending and prior court actions and outcomes.[123]

117 Carol R. Flango, Victor E. Flango, & H. Ted Rubin, How Are Courts Coordinating Family Cases? 27 (1999).

118 Barbara A. Babb, *Unified Family Courts: An Interdisciplinary Framework and a Problem-Solving Approach, in* Problem Solving Courts: Social Science and Legal Perspectives 65, 78 (Richard L. Wiener & Eve M. Brank eds., 2013); *see also* Barbara A. Babb, *Reevaluating Where We Stand: A Comprehensive Study of America's Family Justice Systems*, 46 Fam. Ct. Rev. 230, 231 (2008).

119 Barbara A. Babb, *Unified Family Courts: An Interdisciplinary Framework and a Problem-Solving Approach, in* Problem Solving Courts: Social Science and Legal Perspectives 65, 78 (Richard L. Wiener & Eve M. Brank eds., 2013).

120 Carol R. Flango, Victor E. Flango, & H. Ted Rubin, How Are Courts Coordinating Family Cases? 30 (1999).

121 Carol R. Flango, Victor E. Flango, & H. Ted Rubin, How Are Courts Coordinating Family Cases? 27 (1999).

122 *Developments in the Law: VI. Unified Family Courts and the Child Protection Dilemma*, 116 Harv. L. Rev. 2099, 2108 (2003) (footnote omitted); *see also* John M. Greacen & Pamela A. Gagel, Univ. of Denver. Inst. for the Advancement of the American Legal Sys., Family Law in Focus: A Retrospective Study of Colorado's Early Experiments with Proactive Case Processing, 1 (2013) (finding that "proactive case management in family law cases provides substantial benefits for the litigants, including: Faster resolution of their cases (by an average of more than two months per case); Court assistance . . . to more cases reaching an agreement between the parties; and Reduction in the number of cases dismissed by the court for failure of the filing party to take the steps needed to get the case resolved[.]").

123 Carol R. Flango, Victor E. Flango, & H. Ted Rubin, How Are Courts Coordinating Family Cases? 50, 50–56 (1999) (describing various automated case processing systems used by some courts).

An array of services

In light of the complex issues that drive families into the court system, legal remedies often are ineffective without providing additional services.

> A model unified family court . . . must have available an array of social services that it can offer families to assist court professionals' understanding of the context of a family's legal problems and to address effectively social and psychological issues related to the family's functioning.[124]

"The accelerated and coordinated provision of social services is . . . unified under the authority of the family court, as is coordination of collateral and ancillary matters . . . for family members not directly before the court."[125] While "family courts are not meant to act as social service departments armed with the power of coercion,"[126] this informed understanding about a family's circumstances can permit a judge to craft creative solutions to the family's problems, leading to more responsible decision-making and more effective problem-solving for the family.[127] Further, courts often assume this expanded role of coordinating services because the necessity to do this is now more apparent and because state and federal law often requires courts to provide this monitoring.[128]

The particular services can vary depending upon the needs of the clients and the community, which the court can determine based upon a needs assessment.[129] All

124 Barbara A. Babb, *Fashioning an Interdisciplinary Framework for Court Reform in Family Law: A Blueprint to Construct a Unified Family Court*, 71 S. Cal. L. Rev. 469, 523 (1998).

125 Stephen Cribari, *Therapeutic Power and Judicial Authority*, Unified Fam. Chron., Spring 1999, at 1.

126 Edward P. Mulvey, *Family Courts: The Issue of Reasonable Goals*, 6 L. & Hum. Behav. 49, 56 (1982).

127 *See* Bill Eddy, The Future of Family Court: Structure, Skills and Less Stress 1 (2012) (arguing that the majority of individuals involved in highly contested child custody cases "include one or both parents with a mental health problem presenting as a legal problem," that courts must offer litigants training in conflict resolution skills, and that judges must receive training about mental health problems in order to communicate more effectively with litigants).

128 Carol R. Flango, Victor E. Flango, & H. Ted Rubin, How Are Courts Coordinating Family Cases? 58 (1999).

129 Under Md. Rule 16–307(a)(3) (West 2017), the following services must be available through the family division: "mediation in custody and visitation matters, custody investigations, trained personnel to respond to emergencies, mental health evaluations and evaluations for alcohol and drug abuse, information services, including procedural assistance to *pro se* litigants, information regarding lawyer referral services, parenting seminars, and any additional family support services for which funding is provided." The Family Division of the Circuit Court for Baltimore City has offered the following programs: Substance abuse services, supervised visitation program, medical services office, neutral drop-off, family mediation service, Domestic Violence Ex Parte Project, Protective Order Advocacy and Representation Project, Assisted Pro Se Litigation Project, parenting seminars, Children's Group, and the Volunteer Attorney Settlement Panel. Barbara A. Babb & Judith D. Moran, *Substance Abuse, Families, and Unified*

family courts, however, must provide alternative dispute resolution procedures, such as negotiation, mediation, neutral case evaluation, and other informal processes, in order to allow families the option to step away from the traditional adversarial system to try to resolve some of their problems. "The services . . . can be divided into two loose, sometimes overlapping categories: services directly related to the court case itself and services designed to treat the problems underlying the family's . . . courtroom appearances. All of these services aim at remediation and prevention, expecting that a coordinated response to a family's social, legal, and other needs will reduce the likelihood of future court visits."[130] Susan Brooks and Dorothy Rogers have argued that "[t]he key to effectiveness . . . . is offering services in a preventive and non-coercive fashion."[131] Thus, "[t]he earlier the court incorporates these alternatives into family law proceedings, the more successful the court becomes at circumventing the adversary process and locating services to assist families."[132]

The court can supply the services, or it can connect families to existing services within the community, thereby forging a court-community connection.[133] "[C]ourts are most successful in a supportive environment where the community and all of its agencies are working together to strengthen families."[134] It is likely that the parties may accept court-connected services more easily, as they may view these services as unbiased due to their court affiliation.[135] Further, "[w]hen services are provided in court, the law provides minimum guarantees of fairness and accountability that do not exist in the same way when those services are provided in community or private settings."[136] In addition,

Family Courts: The Creation of a Caring Justice System, 3 J. HEALTH POL'Y & L. 1 (1999); *see also* Peter Salem, *The Challenges of Family Court Service Reform*, 52 FAM. CT. REV. 670 (2014) (arguing that services should be based upon needs and resources).

130 *Developments in the Law: VI. Unified Family Courts and the Child Protection Dilemma,* 116 HARV. L. REV. 2099, 2112 (2003) (footnotes omitted).

131 Susan L. Brooks & Dorothy E. Roberts, *Social Justice and Family Court Reform*, 40 FAM. CT. REV. 453, 455 (2002).

132 Barbara A. Babb, *Fashioning an Interdisciplinary Framework for Court Reform in Family Law: A Blueprint to Construct a Unified Family Court,* 71 S. CAL. L. REV. 469, 522 (1998) (footnotes omitted).

133 Md. Rule 16–307(b)(3) (West 2017) (every jurisdiction must possess a Family Services Coordinator and follow specific designated tasks); A.B.A. PRESIDENTIAL WORKING GRP. ON THE UNMET LEGAL NEEDS OF CHILDREN & THEIR FAMILIES, AMERICA'S CHILDREN AT RISK: A NATIONAL AGENDA FOR LEGAL ACTION 54 (1993).

134 CAROL R. FLANGO, VICTOR E. FLANGO, & H. TED RUBIN, HOW ARE COURTS COORDINATING FAMILY CASES? 86, 59–70 (1999) (describing models of coordination between courts and social service agencies).

135 Barbara A. Babb, *Fashioning an Interdisciplinary Framework for Court Reform in Family Law: A Blueprint to Construct a Unified Family Court,* 71 S. CAL. L. REV. 469, 522 (1998).

136 Gabrielle Davis, Nancy Ver Steegh, & Loretta Frederick, *An Appeal for Autonomy, Access, and Accountability in Family Court Reform Efforts*, 52 FAM. CT. REV. 655, 658 (2014); *see* Peter Salem, *The Challenges of Family Court Service Reform*, 52 FAM. CT. REV. 670, 674 (2014) (outlining the advantages and disadvantages of court services and community-based services).

> [r]egular family court coordinator conferences with the family and the human service agency staff foster the accountability of the family, the judge, and the intervention agencies alike. Some families need many services, and the court can help make it easier for a family to get the services it needs.[137]

The court's coordination of the services, regardless of where they are supplied, provides judges with information about the family that supports improved decision-making and utilizes resources most efficiently.[138]

In addition to alternative dispute resolution services, other services can include parent education programs, children's programs, supervised visitation, substance abuse services, counseling, domestic violence services, neutral visitation drop-off sites, and assistance for self-represented litigants, to name but a few options.[139] As a means to promote accountability, courts must seek empirical evidence regarding the effectiveness of any services provided, and they must make every effort to provide needed services to the family as early as possible in the court process.[140] Andrew Schepard's and James Bozzomo's survey of unified family courts has indicated that the unified family court model "is a positive development for families and children,"[141] due largely to the "mental-health or social-

137 Carol R. Flango, Victor E. Flango, & H. Ted Rubin, How Are Courts Coordinating Family Cases? 5 (1999).

138 Carol R. Flango, Victor E. Flango, & H. Ted Rubin, How Are Courts Coordinating Family Cases? 7 (1999).

139 Barbara A. Babb & Judith D. Moran, *Substance Abuse, Families, and Unified Family Courts: The Creation of a Caring Justice System*, 3 J. Health Pol'y & L. 1, 25–32 (1999); Barbara A. Babb, *Fashioning an Interdisciplinary Framework for Court Reform in Family Law: A Blueprint to Construct a Unified Family Court*, 71 S. Cal. L. Rev. 469, 523 n.293 (1998); Barbara A. Babb & Judith D. Moran, *Baltimore City's Child-Focused Court*, 33 Md. B.J. 42 (2000); *see* Tamara A. Fackrell, Alan J. Hawkins, & Nicole M. Kay, *How Effective Are Court-Affiliated Divorcing Parents Education Programs: A Meta-Analytic Study*, 49 Fam. Ct. Rev. 107 (2011) (reviewing all empirical studies of the effectiveness of court-affiliated parent education programs); *see* Shelley Kierstead, *Parent Education Programs in Family Courts: Balancing Autonomy and State Interventions*, 49 Fam. Ct. Rev. 140 (2011) (addressing how court-connected parent education programs can help parents with minimal state intrusion); *see* Susan L. Pollet, *A Nationwide Survey of Programs for Children of Divorcing and Separating Parents*, 47 Fam. Ct. Rev. 523 (2009) (providing an overview of programs throughout the United States for children of separating and divorcing families); *see* Peter Salem, Irwin Sandler, & Sharlene Wolchik, *Taking Stock of Parent Education in the Family Courts: Envisioning a Public Health Approach*, 51 Fam. Ct. Rev. 131 (2013) (reviewing parent education programs and evaluations efforts); *see* Amanda Sigal, Irwin Sandler, Sharlene Wolchik, & Sanford Braver, *Do Parent Education Programs Promote Healthy Postdivorce Parenting? Critical Distinctions and a Review of the Evidence*, 49 Fam. Ct. Rev. 120 (2011) (reviewing evidence to determine whether parent education programs change post-divorce parenting).

140 H. Ted Rubin & Victor Eugene Flango, Court Coordination of Family Cases 9 (1992); Barbara A. Babb & Jeffrey A. Kuhn, Performance Standards and Measures for Maryland's Family Divisions 6, 48 (2002).

141 Andrew Schepard & James W. Bozzomo, *Efficiency, Therapeutic Justice, Mediation, and Evaluation: Reflections on a Survey of Unified Family Courts*, 37 Fam. L.Q. 333, 335 (2003).

service interventions that have a positive impact on their lives."[142] Nonetheless, Schepard and Bozzomo caution that evaluating courts and court services is a difficult, complicated process and that "[i]t usually takes a long-term study over a number of years to measure the impact of interventions on the lives of families and children."[143] An assessment of court services entails "evaluating the quality of the process, the timeliness of the decision-making, accessibility, and the satisfaction of those who use court services."[144]

A user-friendly court

If court intervention is required to resolve family legal issues, it is imperative that parties have easy access to the family justice system and that the system is convenient for them to use. "The mechanisms to achieve this result range from new information technologies, such as computerized kiosks that disseminate prepared legal forms,[145] to the creation of 'a new service paradigm in the justice system.'[146]"[147] Some jurisdictions now are experimenting with a court navigation process, or a systematic guide to assist litigants with the court process.[148] The tremendous volume of self-represented litigants in family law cases[149] makes the need for a user-friendly system even more compelling.

142 Andrew Schepard & James W. Bozzomo, *Efficiency, Therapeutic Justice, Mediation, and Evaluation: Reflections on a Survey of Unified Family Courts*, 37 FAM. L.Q. 333, 336 (2003).

143 Andrew Schepard & James W. Bozzomo, *Efficiency, Therapeutic Justice, Mediation, and Evaluation: Reflections on a Survey of Unified Family Courts*, 37 FAM. L.Q. 333, 352–53 (2003) ("Causality can be established with reasonable certainty only by comparing identical groups randomly assigned to different legal arrangements. Court systems face administrative and ethical problems in allowing researchers to randomly assign parents and children to different tracks for evaluation purposes."); *see* Christopher N. Wu, *Making Families and Children a High Priority in the Courts: California's Center for Families, Children & the Courts*, 40 FAM. CT. REV. 417 (2002) (describing how the California Administrative Office of the Courts assesses the functioning of its family courts and demonstrates accountability).

144 CAROL R. FLANGO, VICTOR E. FLANGO, & H. TED RUBIN, HOW ARE COURTS COORDINATING FAMILY CASES? 6 (1999).

145 STEPHEN P. JOHNSON, JUST SOLUTIONS: SEEKING INNOVATION AND CHANGE IN THE AMERICAN JUSTICE SYSTEM 29 (1994).

146 STEPHEN P. JOHNSON, JUST SOLUTIONS: SEEKING INNOVATION AND CHANGE IN THE AMERICAN JUSTICE SYSTEM 34 (1994).

147 Barbara A. Babb, *Fashioning an Interdisciplinary Framework for Court Reform in Family Law: A Blueprint to Construct a Unified Family Court*, 71 S. CAL. L. REV. 469, 524 (1998).

148 Opinion, *Letters: Family Court Must Be in a Center City Location*, PHILA. INQUIRER, July 26, 2010, at A8; INST. FOR THE ADVANCEMENT OF THE AMERICAN LEGAL SYS., A COURT COMPASS FOR LITIGANTS (2016); Ayelet Sela, *Streamlining Justice: How Online Courts Can Resolve the Challenges of Pro Se Litigation*, 26 CORNELL J.L. & PUB. POL'Y 331, 336 (2016).

149 Bonnie Hough, *Self-Represented Litigants in Family Law: The Response of California's Courts*, 1 CAL. L. REV. CIR. 15, 16 (2010); Ayelet Sela, *Streamlining Justice: How*

Features that contribute to a user-friendly court include locating the court in a central spot, maintaining appropriate waiting rooms for children and witnesses, offering separate interview rooms for privacy, and providing appropriate courthouse security.[150] Finally, all court personnel must receive training about the importance of treating family law clientele courteously.[151]

Conclusion

Families play a critical role in society's functioning. When they experience legal problems related to the performance of their obligations, families continue to turn in increasing numbers to the justice system for help. We have documented shortcomings in the operation of many family justice systems, and we have endorsed the unified family court model as the ideal structure within which to resolve family legal matters. The unified family court is the system that has the greatest potential to enhance family law decision-making.

In addition to changing court structure, fashioning an effective family justice system requires us to rethink how we conceptualize families. "A family must be viewed as a 'natural social system,' with properties all its own."[152] The ecology of human development, a theoretical perspective from the social sciences, assists us with this task of comprehending the nature and breadth of a family's functioning, including the ability to understand more completely the family's legal problems. This approach also enables us to design a more effective family justice system. We detail the ecology of human development in Chapter 2. Once a more responsive court structure exists, court actors, including judges, lawyers, court personnel, and service providers, must utilize their power to ensure that the family justice system actually helps the people it serves by improving their lives. We also describe the theoretical foundation that undergirds this approach, known as therapeutic jurisprudence, in Chapter 2.

Given the number of people utilizing the family courts and the enormous influence courts have on families' and children's everyday lives, we must not overlook the responsibility to improve the family justice system—starting with the creation of unified family courts.

Online Courts Can Resolve the Challenges of Pro Se Litigation, 26 Cornell J.L. & Pub. Pol'y 331, 335 (2016).

150 Barbara A. Babb, *Unified Family Courts: An Interdisciplinary Framework and a Problem-Solving Approach, in* Problem Solving Courts: Social Science and Legal Perspectives 65, 81 (Richard L. Wiener & Eve M. Brank eds., 2013); *see* Sanford N. Katz & Jeffrey A. Kuhn, Recommendations for a Model Family Court 8 (1991); Laura Duncan, *Courthouse Day Care Programs Increasing*, A J., Oct. 1995, at 22–23 (describing some features of the more than 30 child care centers within American courthouses and noting that California, Massachusetts, and New York have legislatively appropriated funding to construct these centers).

151 Stephen P. Johnson, Just Solutions: Seeking Innovation and Change in the American Justice System 34 (1994).

152 Edward P. Mulvey, *Family Courts: The Issue of Reasonable Goals*, 6 L. & Hum. Behav. 49, 50 (1982) (citations omitted).

2 The unified family court's ecological and therapeutic capacities

A crucial interdisciplinary paradigm

Introduction

> We need court leaders who understand the importance of anticipating and managing change, so that the courts are prepared to confront the challenges that millions of ordinary people bring into our courthouses every single day . . . . These are people who are dealing with personal crises and [are] placing their hopes in the fairness and wisdom of judges and the legal system. And when we succeed in meeting these challenges, we send the message that our commitment as an institution is to serve the public in the best way possible and that our only agenda is to administer justice efficiently and effectively for the well-being of our citizens . . . . Court reform gives us credibility and strengthens our independence as a branch of government.[1]

Court structure alone, including the unified family court model, is not a complete solution to the many problems surrounding the family justice system. Catherine Ross attributes the "lack of a jurisprudential framework"[2] in the development of family courts as a major contributor to the family justice system's shortcomings. One of the authors of this book has advocated for decades about the application of an interdisciplinary approach to family law decision-making and to court reform in family law that provides this critical jurisprudential component and supplies added value to the court process.[3]

> A research paradigm from the social sciences, known as the ecology of human development, provides a comprehensive analytical tool . . . . To address the special needs of families who present themselves to the court system, a

1 Jonathan Lippman, *William H. Rehnquist Award for Judicial Excellence Address*, 47 FAM. CT. REV. 199, 203 (2009).

2 Catherine J. Ross, *The Failure of Fragmentation: The Promise of a System of Unified Family Courts*, 32 FAM. L.Q. 3, 6 (1998).

3 Barbara A. Babb, *An Interdisciplinary Approach to Family Law Jurisprudence: Application of an Ecological and Therapeutic Perspective*, 72 IND. L.J. 775, 788 (1997); Barbara A. Babb, *Fashioning an Interdisciplinary Framework for Court Reform in Family Law: A Blueprint to Construct a Unified Family Court*, 71 S. CAL. L. REV. 469, 507 (1998); Barbara A. Babb, *Unified Family Courts: An Interdisciplinary Framework and a Problem-Solving Approach*, *in* PROBLEM SOLVING COURTS: SOCIAL SCIENCE AND LEGAL PERSPECTIVES 65, 81 (Richard L. Wiener & Eve M. Brank eds., 2013).

> concept from mental health law, known as therapeutic jurisprudence, assists the court in understanding how it intervenes in the lives of families. Application of these two perspectives provides an interdisciplinary ecological and therapeutic framework . . . . This interdisciplinary approach helps judges and other court system professionals consider the many influences on human behavior and family life, thereby empowering the system to offer more pragmatic and effective solutions to contemporary family legal issues.[4]

We now provide a comprehensive account of these two critical underpinnings for the family court's structure and function.

The ecology of human development

Given the complex nature of family law cases, the court process must encourage a comprehensive understanding of both the legal and the nonlegal issues facing the parties. The ecology of human development, a theoretical social science research paradigm developed by Urie Bronfenbrenner, provides a valuable framework to foster a holistic approach.[5] "This social science model promotes an understanding of the interaction among individuals, institutions, and the social environment, thus helping to identify problems and to propose solutions."[6] Clare Huntington lends support to the importance of this perspective:

> [R]elationships do not exist in a vacuum. Neighborhoods matter. Raising a child in a community with safe streets, adequate playgrounds, and good schools means a parent's job is that much easier. Families matter. The relationships we grow up with as children influence our experience in school and the kinds of relationships we envision for ourselves as adults. And the workplace matters. Whether a job pays enough to support a family and whether an employer makes it possible to meet family responsibilities affect relationships at home. In all these ways, context matters.[7]

4 Barbara A. Babb, *Fashioning an Interdisciplinary Framework for Court Reform in Family Law: A Blueprint to Construct a Unified Family Court*, 71 S. CAL. L. REV. 469, 507 (1998).

5 *See* URIE BRONFENBRENNER, THE ECOLOGY OF HUMAN DEVELOPMENT (1979). *See also* MAKING HUMAN BEINGS HUMAN: BIOECOLOGICAL PERSPECTIVES ON HUMAN DEVELOPMENT (Urie Bronfenbrenner, ed., 2005).

6 Barbara A. Babb, *An Interdisciplinary Approach to Family Law Jurisprudence: Application of an Ecological and Therapeutic Perspective*, 72 IND. L.J. 775, 788 (1997).

7 CLARE HUNTINGTON, FAILURE TO FLOURISH: HOW LAW UNDERMINES FAMILY RELATIONSHIPS, at xi (2014); *see also* Shantel D. Crosby, Carl L. Algood, Brittany Sayles, & Jayne Cubbage, *An Ecological Examination of Factors that Impact Well-Being Among Developmentally Disabled Youth in the Juvenile Justice System*, 68 JUV. & FAM. CT. J. 5 (2017) (applying the ecological approach to understand youth in the juvenile justice system); *see also* Barbara Bennett Woodhouse, *Reframing the Debate about the Socialization of Children: An Environmentalist Paradigm*, U. CHI. LEGAL FORUM 85 (2004) (calling for an ecological approach to support child policy decisions); *see also* Barbara Bennett

The ecological approach encourages pursuing strategies to establish and to strengthen connections among all the competing influences on families' and children's lives, or their context, as a means to enhance their functioning. In order to account for these competing influences, Bronfenbrenner arranges and names the settings from smallest to largest. He envisions a person's life experiences "as a set of nested structures, each inside the next, like a set of Russian dolls."[8]

The "microsystem"[9] is the most immediate context and the one individuals experience daily, such as the parent-child relationship, the husband-wife relationship, and the child-teacher relationship. The "mesosystem"[10] is Bronfenbrenner's next level, describing the relationships between the microsystems, such as the degree of connection between a child's school and home setting, or between a child's home and church setting. "The central principle here is that the stronger and more complementary the links between settings, the more powerful the resulting mesosystem will be as an influence on the child's development."[11] The next system Bronfenbrenner describes is the "exosystem,"[12] or settings in which one does not participate but which, nevertheless, influence one's life, such as a parent's place of employment and its influence on the life of the child. The final system, or "macrosystem refers to consistencies . . . that exist . . . at the level of the subculture or the culture as a whole, along with any belief systems or ideology underlying such consistencies."[13]

The macrosystem ideology or social policy creates various risks and opportunities for the individual. In defining macrosystem risk and opportunity,

> macrosystem risk is any social pattern or societal event that impoverishes the ability and willingness of adults to care for children and children to learn from adults, while opportunity is the social pattern or event that encourages and supports parents and children.[14]

An example of macrosystem risk is a national economic policy that contributes to child and family poverty; an example of macrosystem opportunity is a national

Woodhouse, *Ecogenerism: An Environmentalist Approach to Protecting Endangered Children*, 12 Va. J. Soc. Pol'y & L. 409 (2005) (advocating reframing children's law by adopting an ecological paradigm); *see also* Clare Huntington, *Early Childhood Development and the Law*, 90 S. Cal. L. Rev. 755 (2017) (advocating for the incorporation of research about early childhood development into the law).

8 Urie Bronfenbrenner, The Ecology of Human Development 3 (1979).

9 Urie Bronfenbrenner, The Ecology of Human Development 7, 22 (1979).

10 Urie Bronfenbrenner, The Ecology of Human Development 7–8, 25 (1979).

11 James Garbarino & Robert H. Abrahamowitz, *The Ecology of Human Development, in* Children and Families in the Social Environment 11, 26 (James Garbarino et al. eds., 2d ed. 1992).

12 Urie Bronfenbrenner, The Ecology of Human Development 7–8, 25 (1979).

13 Urie Bronfenbrenner, The Ecology of Human Development 26 (1979).

14 James Garbarino & Robert H. Abrahamowitz, *The Ecology of Human Development, in* Children and Families in the Social Environment 11, 28 (James Garbarino et al. eds., 2d ed. 1992).

policy that values families by giving economic incentives for families with young children.[15]

Bronfenbrenner also prescribes a life-course perspective when dealing with families' and children's lives, responding to the fact that situations and their effects on individuals may change over time.[16] In addition to looking at families' and children's interactions from a holistic or ecological perspective, we also must examine their functioning over time and throughout the lives of the family members.

"The most important thing about this ecological perspective is that it reveals connections that might otherwise go unnoticed and helps us look beyond the immediate and the obvious to see where the most significant influences lie."[17] "[T]he ecological perspective . . . . offers a kind of map for steering a course of study and intervention."[18] Bronfenbrenner argues that strengthening the interconnections between and among systems enhances individual and family development.[19]

Family justice system professionals can utilize the ecological approach to help identify the breadth and scope of factors affecting families' and children's lives. These professionals' crucial role is to assist with the identification of the various systems and to use the law's power to strengthen system interconnectedness, allowing

15 Barbara A. Babb, *An Interdisciplinary Approach to Family Law Jurisprudence: Application of an Ecological and Therapeutic Perspective*, 72 IND. L.J. 775, 790 (1997); *see also* James Garbarino & Robert H. Abrahamowitz, *The Ecology of Human Development, in* CHILDREN AND FAMILIES IN THE SOCIAL ENVIRONMENT 11, 28 (James Garbarino et al. eds., 2d ed. 1992).

16 James Garbarino & Robert H. Abrahamowitz, *An Introduction, in* CHILDREN AND FAMILIES IN THE SOCIAL ENVIRONMENT 1, 9–10 (James Garbarino et al. eds., 2d ed. 1992); James Garbarino & Robert H. Abrahamowitz, *The Ecology of Human Development, in* CHILDREN AND FAMILIES IN THE SOCIAL ENVIRONMENT 11, 29–30 (James Garbarino et al. eds., 2d ed. 1992). The following illustrates the need for a life-course perspective: "Since most data are a cross-sectional snapshot of families, families are assumed to be static. A more realistic (though much more difficult) approach is to recognize and analyze the fluidity, change, and transitions as individuals live in a variety of family patterns. There are periods in the life cycle when an individual family may be one in which the father works and the mother stays home with the children. This stage is relatively short-lived when the total family life course is analyzed. There are periods, also, when women (and men) find themselves raising a family without a spouse present, but again, for many this is a transition period. None of these types or stages, however, should be viewed as the dominant or "ideal" family type. No one family type is superior to another or to be favored over others. Effective policies and services should be sensitive to the needs and stresses of certain types of families and recognize that some families are at greater risk (statistically) than others." ROBERT M. MARONEY, FAMILIES, SOCIAL SERVICES, AND SOCIAL POLICY: THE ISSUES OF SHARED RESPONSIBILITY 50 (1980); *see generally* EXAMINING LIVES IN CONTEXT: PERSPECTIVES ON THE ECOLOGY OF HUMAN DEVELOPMENT (Phyllis Moen et al. eds., 1995).

17 James Garbarino & Robert H. Abrahamowitz, *The Ecology of Human Development, in* CHILDREN AND FAMILIES IN THE SOCIAL ENVIRONMENT 11, 19 (James Garbarino et al. eds., 2d ed. 1992).

18 James Garbarino & Robert H. Abrahamowitz, *The Ecology of Human Development, in* CHILDREN AND FAMILIES IN THE SOCIAL ENVIRONMENT 11, 28 (James Garbarino et al. eds., 2d ed. 1992).

19 URIE BRONFENBRENNER, THE ECOLOGY OF HUMAN DEVELOPMENT 214 (1979).

the law to intervene more effectively in people's lives. "Courts must view neighborhoods, religious organizations, and other associations or institutions within which family members participate as having the potential to influence the family's legal matters."[20] The structure and function of the entire family justice system must aim to assist with the identification of the "family ecology"[21] for each family, helping to reveal its interdependent nature. This ecological framework directs court professionals "to look beyond the individual litigants involved in any family law matter, to holistically examine the larger social environments in which participants live, and to fashion legal remedies that strengthen a family's supportive relationships."[22]

Therapeutic jurisprudence

"Family law cases focus on some of the most intimate, emotional, and all-encompassing aspects of parties' personal lives."[23] Further, "families increasingly are appearing before the courts for assistance in making decisions and rendering judgements about every aspect of life from birth . . . through childhood . . . , adolescence . . . , adulthood . . . , and old age . . . ."[24] Based upon the law's power to reorder families' and children's lives, we owe families the duty of effective intervention regarding both legal and related nonlegal issues, as stated poignantly by Michael Town:

> How deeply into the domestic realm can or should government go when it intervenes in the lives of families and children? Conversely, what is government's duty to families and children who are in legal and social distress? These political and philosophical questions still bedevil public officials in America today. Yet when society chooses to intervene, it must be done well and there must be accountability.[25]

Clare Huntington agrees. "Rather than pretend that legal regulation of families is minimal, it is far more useful to reflect honestly and holistically on the role of law and reconsider what the law can do to help build strong, stable, positive relationships."[26] She goes on to say that

20 Barbara A. Babb, *Fashioning an Interdisciplinary Framework for Court Reform in Family Law: A Blueprint to Construct a Unified Family Court*, 71 S. Cal. L. Rev. 469, 508 (1998).
21 Mary Ann Glendon, The Transformation of Family Law: State, Law, and Family in The United States and Western Europe 308 (1989).
22 Barbara A. Babb, *An Interdisciplinary Approach to Family Law Jurisprudence: Application of an Ecological and Therapeutic Perspective*, 72 Ind. L.J. 775, 803 (1997).
23 Barbara A. Babb, *Fashioning an Interdisciplinary Framework for Court Reform in Family Law: A Blueprint to Construct a Unified Family Court*, 71 S. Cal. L. Rev. 469, 471 (1998).
24 Marsha Kline Pruett, *Mental Notes: Reform as Metaphor and Reality*, 44 Fam. Ct. Rev. 571, 571 (2006).
25 Michael A. Town, The Unified Family Court: Therapeutic Justice for Families and Children 1 (Mar. 11, 1994) (transcript available in Chicago Bar Association Building).
26 Clare Huntington, Failure to Flourish: How Law Undermines Family Relationships, at xvii (2014).

> [o]ur legal system is already deeply involved in every aspect of family life, from defining what a family is in the first place to subsidizing families through public education and deductions for dependents. The real question is not the magnitude of that involvement, but the ends it serves.[27]

Therapeutic jurisprudence assists family law professionals to identify beneficial outcomes for parties. Therapeutic jurisprudence is a concept that has emerged from mental health law and now is applied internationally to broad areas of the law.[28]

> [M]ultitudes of international scholars and practitioners are engaged in the study and practice of therapeutic jurisprudence, as evidenced by postings on and membership in the International Network on Therapeutic Jurisprudence, a therapeutic jurisprudence listserv, a Facebook page, and several international conferences to date on the subject. Many law school course offerings worldwide focus on therapeutic jurisprudence . . . . One United States law school has created a family law and family justice system center, the University of Baltimore [Sayra and Neil Meyerhoff] Center for Families, Children and the Courts, whose work is grounded in therapeutic jurisprudence.[29]

As one author of this book has promoted, it is particularly appropriate to employ therapeutic jurisprudence in family law cases, since its application requires the court to focus on outcomes that actually help families and children.[30]

What, then, is therapeutic jurisprudence? David Wexler, one of the co-founders with the late Bruce Winick of the concept in the 1980s, defines it as follows:

27 Clare Huntington, *Help Families from Day 1*, N.Y. Times, Sept. 3, 2014, at A21.

28 *See generally* Judging in a Therapeutic Key: Therapeutic Jurisprudence and the Courts (Bruce J. Winick & David B. Wexler eds., 2003); Practicing Therapeutic Jurisprudence: Law as a Helping Profession (Dennis P. Stolle, David B. Wexler, & Bruce J. Winick, eds., 2000); Law in a Therapeutic Key: Developments in Therapeutic Jurisprudence (David B. Wexler & Bruce J. Winick eds., 1997); *The Jurisprudence of Therapeutic Jurisprudence, in* Law in a Therapeutic Key: Developments in Therapeutic Jurisprudence 645 (David B. Wexler & Bruce J. Winick eds., 1997); Essays in Therapeutic Jurisprudence (David B. Wexler & Bruce J. Winick eds.,1991); Therapeutic Jurisprudence: The Law as a Therapeutic Agent (David B. Wexler & Bruce J. Winick eds., 1990); *International Network on Therapeutic Jurisprudence*, https://law2.arizona.edu/depts/upr-intj/ (last visited Oct. 5, 2017); Pauline Spencer, *To Dream the Impossible Dream? Therapeutic Jurisprudence in Mainstream Courts*, 2012 Int'l Conference on L. & Soc'y (2012).

29 Barbara A. Babb & David B. Wexler, *Therapeutic Jurisprudence, in* Springer Encyclopedia of Criminology and Criminal Justice 2 (Gerben Bruinsma & David Weisburd eds., 2014).

30 Barbara A. Babb, *An Interdisciplinary Approach to Family Law Jurisprudence: Application of an Ecological and Therapeutic Perspective*, 72 Ind. L.J. 775, 777–800 (1997); Barbara A. Babb, *Fashioning an Interdisciplinary Framework for Court Reform in Family Law: A Blueprint to Construct a Unified Family Court*, 71 S. Cal. L. Rev. 469, 509 (1998); *see also* Vicki Lens, *Against the Grain: Therapeutic Judging in a Traditional Family Court*, L. & Soc. Inquiry 1, 15 (Summer 2015) (suggesting that judges in traditional family courts can employ therapeutic jurisprudence).

"Therapeutic jurisprudence is the study of the role of law as a therapeutic agent. It looks at the law as a social force that, like it or not, may produce therapeutic [helpful] or anti-therapeutic [harmful] consequences," both intended and unintended.[31] Therapeutic jurisprudence is a perspective or framework and a field of inquiry—"a lens through which to examine the effects of substantive laws, legal rules, legal procedures, and the behavior of legal actors, including judges, lawyers, court personnel, and service providers, on the psychological and emotional well-being of justice system participants . . . ."[32] In addition to emphasizing the need to conduct empirical research about the effects of justice system outcomes on families' and children's lives, the use of therapeutic jurisprudence encourages that empirical findings from social and behavioral sciences drive reforms and practices that promote well-being.[33]

Adopting a therapeutic jurisprudence, however, does not interfere with traditional justice notions.

> [T]herapeutic consequences should not trump other considerations, such as due process, nor is the approach paternalistic or coercive, as it emphasizes the importance of self-determination and autonomy. Abiding by the notion of therapeutic jurisprudence, if all other judicial and legal issues are equal, the law ought to be restructured [or applied] to accomplish therapeutic outcomes. The difficulty arises when determining what normative values should take priority. Therapeutic jurisprudence does not answer this. It initiates the question and then sharpens and focuses the debate.[34]

Therapeutic jurisprudence simply acknowledges that the law itself acts as a "therapist or healing agent. In the same manner as iatrogenic or harmful consequences exist in medicine, law has the potential to produce psychological harm . . . ."[35] The task of therapeutic jurisprudence is to ensure the maximization of therapeutic outcomes in each case, while still abiding by the rule of law and honoring justice system values. "Adopting a therapeutic . . . approach to legal problems does not mean that judges

31 David B. Wexler, *Putting Mental Health into Mental Health Law: Therapeutic Jurisprudence, in* ESSAYS IN THERAPEUTIC JURISPRUDENCE 3, 8 (David B. Wexler & Bruce J. Winick eds., 1991).

32 Barbara A. Babb & David B. Wexler, *Therapeutic Jurisprudence, in* SPRINGER ENCYCLOPEDIA OF CRIMINOLOGY AND CRIMINAL JUSTICE 1 (Gerben Bruinsma & David Weisburd eds., 2014).

33 Barbara A. Babb & David B. Wexler, *Therapeutic Jurisprudence, in* SPRINGER ENCYCLOPEDIA OF CRIMINOLOGY AND CRIMINAL JUSTICE 1 (Gerben Bruinsma & David Weisburd eds., 2014).

34 Barbara A. Babb & David B. Wexler, *Therapeutic Jurisprudence, in* SPRINGER ENCYCLOPEDIA OF CRIMINOLOGY AND CRIMINAL JUSTICE 3 (Gerben Bruinsma & David Weisburd eds., 2014) (footnotes omitted).

35 Barbara A. Babb & David B. Wexler, *Therapeutic Jurisprudence, in* SPRINGER ENCYCLOPEDIA OF CRIMINOLOGY AND CRIMINAL JUSTICE 2 (Gerben Bruinsma & David Weisburd eds., 2014).

and lawyers function as therapists or social worker,"[36] however. "Instead, it requires that legal actors [judges, attorneys, court personnel] consciously consider the problems that may have precipitated the . . . behavior and how to effectively address those concerns."[37] To accomplish this, "therapeutic jurisprudence encourages and invites interdisciplinary collaboration with other professionals who can better understand and assist the stakeholders in the legal system."[38]

Scholars and practitioners applying therapeutic jurisprudence often have combined it with other doctrines, many of which are important considerations in the practice of family law. For example, Peggy Hora, William Schma, and Jonathan Rosenthal have connected therapeutic jurisprudence to problem-solving courts, advocating that therapeutic jurisprudence forms the framework for those courts.[39] Dennis Stolle has paired therapeutic jurisprudence with preventive law, which advocates that lawyers try to identify and to address potential legal problems early.[40] Susan Daicoff has incorporated therapeutic jurisprudence as a key component of what she describes as comprehensive law.[41] Another collaboration has occurred uniting therapeutic jurisprudence and procedural justice, or the focus on the legal proceedings and whether individuals have a "sense of feeling fairly treated, of being accorded respect, of being able to understand the proceedings, and of being heard during the legal process."[42] Procedural justice is a critical notion because "people who are satisfied with legal proceedings are more willing to comply with courts' decisions and, in turn, have greater confidence in the justice system."[43] In the family law and family justice system reform arena, one of this

36 Barbara A. Babb & David B. Wexler, *Therapeutic Jurisprudence*, *in* Springer Encyclopedia of Criminology and Criminal Justice 3 (Gerben Bruinsma & David Weisburd eds., 2014).

37 Barbara A. Babb & David B. Wexler, *Therapeutic Jurisprudence*, *in* Springer Encyclopedia of Criminology and Criminal Justice 3 (Gerben Bruinsma & David Weisburd eds., 2014).

38 Megan F. Chaney, *Postadjudicatory Juvenile Defense Attorneys: More Thoughts on Reimagining Juvenile Justice*, 42 Cap. U. L. Rev. 491, 514–15 (2014).

39 Peggy Fulton Hora et al., *Therapeutic Jurisprudence and the Drug Treatment Court Movement: Revolutionizing the Criminal Justice System's Response to Drug Abuse and Crime in America*, 74 Notre Dame L. Rev. 439 (1999); *see* Deborah Chase & Peggy Fulton Hora, *The Best Seat in the House: The Court Assignment and Judicial Satisfaction*, 47 Fam. Ct. Rev. 209 (2009).

40 Dennis P. Stolle et al., *Integrating Preventive Law and Therapeutic Jurisprudence: A Law and Psychology Based Approach to Lawyering*, 34 Cal. W. L. Rev. 15 (1997).

41 Susan Daicoff, *Law as a Healing Profession: The "Comprehensive Law Movement,"* 6 Pepp. Disp. Resol. L.J. 43 (2006).

42 Barbara A. Babb & David B. Wexler, *Therapeutic Jurisprudence*, *in* Springer Encyclopedia of Criminology and Criminal Justice 4 (Gerben Bruinsma & David Weisburd eds., 2014); Susan Goldberg, Nat'l Judicial Inst., Judging for the 21st Century: A Problem-Solving Approach (2005).

43 Barbara A. Babb & David B. Wexler, *Therapeutic Jurisprudence*, *in* Springer Encyclopedia of Criminology and Criminal Justice 5 (Gerben Bruinsma & David Weisburd eds., 2014); Susan Goldberg, Nat'l Judicial Inst., Judging for the 21st Century: A Problem-Solving Approach (2005).

book's authors has paired therapeutic jurisprudence with the ecology of human development, defined above.[44]

In the family law context, applying therapeutic jurisprudence calls upon legal actors, including judges, attorneys, and court personnel, to focus on achieving outcomes that actually help or improve the lives of families and children involved in family legal proceedings.[45] Nonetheless, the individual's own viewpoint determines what constitutes a therapeutic outcome, which is something legal actors must identify and attempt to honor.[46] In turn, "attorneys and decision-makers must contemplate legal outcomes intended to produce more effective functioning on the part of families and children."[47] For example, in family law cases, where justice system participants are likely to have ongoing interaction, "family law should seek to preserve and repair emotional relationships, preparing the former family members for the contact that will almost certainly continue after the legal proceedings end," thereby requiring a prospective orientation from the court.[48] "In the field of family law, therapeutic jurisprudence should strive to protect families from present and future harms, to reduce emotional turmoil, to promote family harmony or preservation, and to provide individualized and efficient, effective justice."[49]

Clare Huntington summarizes the law's responsibilities.

> [F]amily law should concern itself more with the *manner* of [family] transition, paving the way for smoother relationships following the legal conflict. Throughout this process, family law should balance the possibility of repair with the necessity of keeping family members safe, remaining attentive to violence in the home . . . . [D]ispute-resolution family law should work

44 Barbara A. Babb, *Unified Family Courts: An Interdisciplinary Framework and a Problem-Solving Approach, in* Problem Solving Courts: Social Science and Legal Perspectives 65, 81 (Richard L. Wiener & Eve M. Brank eds., 2013); Barbara A. Babb, *An Interdisciplinary Approach to Family Law Jurisprudence: Application of an Ecological and Therapeutic Perspective*, 72 Ind. L.J. 775 (1997); Barbara A. Babb, *Fashioning an Interdisciplinary Framework for Court Reform in Family Law: A Blueprint to Construct a Unified Family Court*, 71 S. Cal. L. Rev. 469 (1998).

45 Barbara A. Babb, *An Interdisciplinary Approach to Family Law Jurisprudence: Application of an Ecological and Therapeutic Perspective*, 72 Ind. L.J. 775, 777–80 (1997); Barbara A. Babb, *Fashioning an Interdisciplinary Framework for Court Reform in Family Law: A Blueprint to Construct a Unified Family Court*, 71 S. Cal. L. Rev. 469, 472–73 (1998).

46 Bruce J. Winick, *The Jurisprudence of Therapeutic Jurisprudence, in* Law in a Therapeutic Key: Developments in Therapeutic Jurisprudence 653 (David B. Wexler & Bruce J. Winick eds., 1997).

47 Barbara A. Babb, *Unified Family Courts: An Interdisciplinary Framework and a Problem-Solving Approach, in* Problem Solving Courts: Social Science and Legal Perspectives 65, 70 (Richard L. Wiener & Eve M. Brank eds., 2013); Bruce J. Winick, *The Jurisprudence of Therapeutic Jurisprudence, in* Law in a Therapeutic Key: Developments in Therapeutic Jurisprudence 655 (David B. Wexler & Bruce J. Winick eds., 1997).

48 Clare Huntington, Failure to Flourish: How Law Undermines Family Relationships 109 (2014).

49 Barbara A. Babb, *An Interdisciplinary Approach to Family Law Jurisprudence: Application of an Ecological and Therapeutic Perspective*, 72 Ind. L.J. 775, 800 (1997).

> toward three goals: restructuring families with an eye to the future, opening the door to repairing relationships, and keeping family members safe.[50]

At the same time, however, "[t]herapeutic considerations are but one category of important considerations, as are autonomy, integrity of the fact-finding process, community safety, and more."[51]

Adopting a therapeutic jurisprudence perspective in family law means that all professionals involved in the family justice system, including judges, attorneys, court personnel, special magistrates, mental health professionals, and mediators, among others, must understand and adhere to this orientation.[52] Research has demonstrated that judges in unified family courts who adopt this approach have greater job satisfaction, which also positively impacts court staff, attorneys, and clients.[53] "Judicial satisfaction . . . relates not only to the individual judge but to the very quality of justice delivered in the courtroom."[54] A therapeutic jurisprudence orientation, then, "has the potential to facilitate problem-solving and to positively enhance the quality of the parties' daily lives, thereby rendering a more effective outcome for individuals and families."[55]

Putting the pieces together to improve family justice

How can these concepts—a unified family court, the ecology of human development, and therapeutic jurisprudence—contribute to the improvement of both family law decision-making and the operation of the family justice system itself?

The model unified family court described in Chapter 1 equips the justice system to approach the whole of the problems that bring families into court, including legal and related nonlegal issues. As discussed, "[a] unified family court is one that coordinates the work of independent forums and agencies, each of which has some limited role to resolve family legal matters."[56] Empowering the court with

50 Clare Huntington, Failure to Flourish: How Law Undermines Family Relationships 109–10 (2014).

51 David B. Wexler & Bruce J. Winick, *Patients, Professionals, and the Path of Therapeutic Jurisprudence: A Response to Petrila, in* Law in a Therapeutic Key: Developments in Therapeutic Jurisprudence 707, 708 (David B. Wexler & Bruce J. Winick eds., 1997) (citation omitted); Bruce J. Winick, *The Jurisprudence of Therapeutic Jurisprudence, in* Law in a Therapeutic Key: Developments in Therapeutic Jurisprudence 714 (David B. Wexler & Bruce J. Winick eds., 1997).

52 *See also* Barbara A. Babb, *Unified Family Courts: An Interdisciplinary Framework and a Problem-Solving Approach, in* Problem Solving Courts: Social Science and Legal Perspectives 65, 70 (Richard L. Wiener & Eve M. Brank eds., 2013).

53 Deborah Chase & Peggy Fulton Hora, *The Best Seat in the House: The Court Assignment and Judicial Satisfaction*, 47 Fam. Ct. Rev. 209, 234 (2009).

54 Deborah Chase & Peggy Fulton Hora, *The Best Seat in the House: The Court Assignment and Judicial Satisfaction*, 47 Fam. Ct. Rev. 209, 234 (2009).

55 Barbara A. Babb, *An Interdisciplinary Approach to Family Law Jurisprudence: Application of an Ecological and Therapeutic Perspective*, 72 Ind. L.J. 775, 802 (1997).

56 Barbara A. Babb, *Unified Family Courts: An Interdisciplinary Framework and a Problem-Solving Approach, in* Problem Solving Courts: Social Science and Legal Perspectives 65, 74 (Richard L. Wiener & Eve M. Brank eds., 2013); *see* Roscoe Pound,

comprehensive subject-matter jurisdiction over all family law matters is key to enabling this holistic approach.

> This archetypic unified family court, which considers a family's problems in a comprehensive and coordinated manner, should serve as a blueprint for . . . family law court reform. Adopting this model can promote dispute resolution outcomes which enable individuals and families to address more effectively their underlying family legal issues and to improve their functioning.[57]

The ecology of human development serves as a roadmap to focus the attention of attorneys and judges on all of the systems within which families and children function in order to identify problems and to devise solutions. "Courts [and attorneys] must be guided to view schools, neighborhoods, places of employment, and other institutions within which family members participate as potential influences upon a family's legal matters."[58] Court structure and operation must permit it to account for the complex factors affecting children and families' lives.[59] A framework utilizing the ecology of human development assists all family justice system professionals to accomplish this task.

> This structured consideration of the family's ecology by all court professionals facilitates problem-solving and enables family law decision-makers to understand more completely the comprehensive nature of the family's functioning. An ecological structure to guide family law court reform leads to the design of a court system that empowers decision-makers to apply the law in a manner that more effectively resolves the family's legal issues.[60]

Therapeutic jurisprudence orients the court and all legal actors to craft resolutions to family legal and nonlegal issues that improve the well-being of the participants. Family courts function by intervening in families' and children's lives, so that "it is intrinsic to the family law decision-making process that 'intervention ought to aim to improve the participants' underlying behavior or situation.'"[61] "Resolving family legal disputes with the aim of improving the lives of families and

The Place of the Family Court in the Judicial System, 5 NAT'L PROB. & PAROLE ASS'N J. 161 (1959).

57 Barbara A. Babb, *Fashioning an Interdisciplinary Framework for Court Reform in Family Law: A Blueprint to Construct a Unified Family Court*, 71 S. CAL. L. REV. 469, 478 (1998).

58 Barbara A. Babb, *Unified Family Courts: An Interdisciplinary Framework and a Problem-Solving Approach, in* PROBLEM SOLVING COURTS: SOCIAL SCIENCE AND LEGAL PERSPECTIVES 65, 73–74 (Richard L. Wiener & Eve M. Brank eds., 2013).

59 Barbara A. Babb, *Fashioning an Interdisciplinary Framework for Court Reform in Family Law: A Blueprint to Construct a Unified Family Court*, 71 S. CAL. L. REV. 469, 508 (1998).

60 Barbara A. Babb, *Fashioning an Interdisciplinary Framework for Court Reform in Family Law: A Blueprint to Construct a Unified Family Court*, 71 S. CAL. L. REV. 469, 509 (1998).

61 Barbara A. Babb, *Fashioning an Interdisciplinary Framework for Court Reform in Family Law: A Blueprint to Construct a Unified Family Court*, 71 S. CAL. L. REV. 469, 509 (1998)

children requires structuring the court system to enhance the system's potential to maximize the therapeutic consequences of court intervention."[62] This orientation applies to judges and to court personnel, such as mental health professionals, involved in the family law decision-making process.

> Adopting therapeutic jurisprudence as the goal of a model family law adjudicatory system requires careful consideration of the therapeutic implications resulting from all aspects of the court process. Envisioning therapeutic jurisprudence as the outcome, however, encourages the discovery of creative ways to effectively resolve family conflicts.[63]

What accounts for therapeutic practices in the family justice system? One indicator is the mission statement of the family court itself. An excellent example of one such statement grounded in therapeutic jurisprudence is the mission statement intended to guide the operation of Maryland's family justice system:

> The mission of Maryland's Family Divisions is to provide a fair and efficient forum to resolve family legal matters in a problem-solving manner, with the goal of improving the lives of families and children who appear before the court. To that end, the court shall make appropriate services available for families who need them. The court also shall provide an environment that supports judges, court staff, and attorneys so that they can respond effectively to the many legal and nonlegal issues of families in the justice system.[64]

Maryland also has identified system values to guide the operation of its family courts. Many of these values promote therapeutic outcomes for families and children:

> Preserving the rule of law; [s]tabilizing families in transition; [p]roviding forums for prompt conflict resolution; [p]romoting co-parenting relationships; [f]ostering parents as primary family decision-makers; [m]aximizing the use of alternative resolution methods and programs; [p]roviding safety and protection; [p]reserving family relationships where possible; [s]upporting linkages between resource needs and available resources on behalf of parents and their children;

(quoting Barbara A. Babb, *An Interdisciplinary Approach to Family Law Jurisprudence: Application of an Ecological and Therapeutic Perspective*, 72 Ind. L.J. 775, 798 (1997)).

62 Barbara A. Babb, *Fashioning an Interdisciplinary Framework for Court Reform in Family Law: A Blueprint to Construct a Unified Family Court*, 71 S. Cal. L. Rev. 469, 511 (1998).

63 Barbara A. Babb, *Fashioning an Interdisciplinary Framework for Court Reform in Family Law: A Blueprint to Construct a Unified Family Court*, 71 S. Cal. L. Rev. 469, 512 (1998).

64 Barbara A. Babb & Jeffrey A. Kuhn, Performance Standards and Measures for Maryland's Family Divisions 6 (2002); Barbara A. Babb & Jeffrey A. Kuhn, *Maryland's Family Divisions Performance Standard 5.1: A Therapeutic, Holistic, Ecological Approach to Family Law Decision Making, in* Judging in a Therapeutic Key: Therapeutic Jurisprudence and the Courts 125–27 (Bruce J. Winick & David B. Wexler eds., 2003).

> [i]ncreasing access to the family justice system; [u]sing judicial time efficiently by providing comprehensive information to judges and masters [magistrates] to assist them in making the most informed decisions possible; [d]eveloping a familiarity with each family; and [i]ncreasing cultural competency[65]

Indeed, the adversarial process, as noted previously, too often is destructive for families and children. A therapeutic approach to family law cases "mandates that family cases be expedited to minimize the trauma of litigation and to ensure safety and support for all family members."[66] Families must have the opportunity to make decisions for themselves by equipping them with educational programs, necessary services, and alternative dispute resolution techniques. Family courts have begun to realize "that because they function in many instances as a 'trauma center,' serving families in crisis, they are in a unique position to identify problems and connect those families with much needed services."[67]

Judges hearing family law cases have an opportunity to provide the families with a holistic understanding of their legal and related nonlegal issues and to fashion effective outcomes that improve families' and children's lives. This requires specialized training. "[J]udges assigned to . . . family courts must be informed about relevant social science literature, including child development and family dynamics, and about how that knowledge applies to family law decision-making."[68]

> Not only must these judges fully understand the intricacies of the entire body of family law, but they also must possess an appreciation for and understanding of the social settings within which family members function, including any problems

65 Barbara A. Babb & Jeffrey A. Kuhn, PERFORMANCE STANDARDS AND MEASURES FOR MARYLAND'S FAMILY DIVISIONS 6 (2002).

66 Barbara A. Babb & Jeffrey A. Kuhn, PERFORMANCE STANDARDS AND MEASURES FOR MARYLAND'S FAMILY DIVISIONS 48 (2002); Barbara A. Babb & Jeffrey A. Kuhn, *Maryland's Family Divisions Performance Standard 5.1: A Therapeutic, Holistic, Ecological Approach to Family Law Decision Making, in* JUDGING IN A THERAPEUTIC KEY: THERAPEUTIC JURISPRUDENCE AND THE COURTS 125 (Bruce J. Winick & David B. Wexler eds., 2003).

67 Barbara A. Babb & Jeffrey A. Kuhn, PERFORMANCE STANDARDS AND MEASURES FOR MARYLAND'S FAMILY DIVISIONS 48 (2002); Barbara A. Babb & Jeffrey A. Kuhn, *Maryland's Family Divisions Performance Standard 5.1: A Therapeutic, Holistic, Ecological Approach to Family Law Decision Making, in* JUDGING IN A THERAPEUTIC KEY: THERAPEUTIC JURISPRUDENCE AND THE COURTS 125 (Bruce J. Winick & David B. Wexler eds., 2003).

68 Barbara A. Babb, *A Unified Family* Court, *in* JUDGING IN A THERAPEUTIC KEY: THERAPEUTIC JURISPRUDENCE AND THE COURTS 295 (Bruce J. Winick & David B. Wexler eds., 2003). Natalie A. Knowlton, *The Modern Family Court Judge: Knowledge, Qualities, and Skills for Success*, INST. FOR THE ADVANCEMENT OF THE AMERICAN LEGAL SYSTEM (May 2015), http://iaals.du.edu/sites/default/files/documents/publications/the_modern_family_court_judge.pdf; Barbara A. Babb & Judith B. Moran, *Judicial Independence in Family* Courts, *in* JUSTICE IN JEOPARDY: REPORT OF THE AMERICAN BAR ASSOCIATION COMMISSION ON THE 21ST CENTURY JUDICIARY app. H at 13–14 (2003).

attendant to each of these settings, such as substance abuse and domestic violence.[69]

Cindy Lederman emphasizes the background needed for effective family court judging.

> Judges need to understand the characteristics of the people they are trying to help, including their risk factors, protective factors, and level of functioning. Judges need to understand the history of the families they see in order to understand how to help them. Judges need to know about their behavior, the traumas they have suffered, and especially their resilience.[70]

Judges with this background have the knowledge required to promote family well-being. Because family court judges must be more than triers of fact, "[f]amily law decision-makers must embrace as a goal of family law jurisprudence the need to strengthen individuals and families and to enhance their functioning."[71] According to Lederman, "our goals must really be to change human behavior, to protect, and to heal. The goals are not traditional judicial functions, which, by comparison, are simple."[72]

When the justice system serves individuals and families well and improves their functioning, the entire society benefits.

> A unified family court that comprehensively approaches the needs of families from an interdisciplinary [ecological and therapeutic] perspective and [that] is able to do so in a user-friendly way . . . [can] meet the current challenges of overburdened courts and families that desperately need their help.[73]

69 Barbara A. Babb, *Fashioning an Interdisciplinary Framework for Court Reform in Family Law: A Blueprint to Construct a Unified Family Court*, 71 S. Cal. L. Rev. 469, 514–15 (1998); *see* Sanford N. Katz & Jeffrey A Kuhn, Recommendations for a Model Family Court 5–6 (1991); Barbara A. Babb & Judith D. Moran, *Substance Abuse, Families, and Unified Family Courts: The Creation of a Caring Justice System*, 3 J. Health Pol'y & L. 1 (1999); Natalie A. Knowlton, *The Modern Family Court Judge: Knowledge, Qualities, and Skills for Success*, Instit. for the Advancement of the American Legal System (May 2015) http://iaals.du.edu/sites/default/files/documents/publications/the_modern_family_court_judge.pdf.

70 Cindy Lederman, *Science in the Courtroom: Vital to Best Interests and Reasonable Efforts*, 61 Juv. & Fam. Ct. J. 63, 65 (2010).

71 Barbara A. Babb, *An Interdisciplinary Approach to Family Law Jurisprudence: Application of an Ecological and Therapeutic Perspective*, 72 Ind. L.J. 775, 808 (1997); Barbara A. Babb & Judith B. Moran, *Judicial Independence in Family* Courts, *in* Justice in Jeopardy: Report of the American Bar Association Commission on the 21st Century Judiciary app. H at 13 (2003).

72 Cindy Lederman, *Science in the Courtroom: Vital to Best Interests and Reasonable Efforts*, 61 Juv. & Fam. Ct. J. 63, 64 (2010).

73 Barbara A. Babb, *Unified Family Courts: An Interdisciplinary Framework and a Problem-Solving Approach in* Problem Solving Courts: Social Science and Legal Perspectives 65, 82 (Richard L. Wiener & Eve M. Brank eds., 2013).

Maryland's former Chief Judge Robert Bell has articulated the need for this approach.

> [W]e have finally come to realize, that the effective resolution of legal disputes within a family requires a fundamental shift from the traditional adjudication focus to a more holistic, therapeutic model that attempts to improve the lives of families and children in substantive ways. To achieve this new paradigm, there must be a confluence of access to coordinated and comprehensive legal and social services, efficient case processing and management, and a more widely accessible court system.[74]

The need for more components

During the past several decades, we have interacted with the family justice system in many capacities: as attorneys representing clients in court, as a family court administrator, as the director of a law school family justice center, as law professors teaching law students how to practice family law, as scholars writing about reform proposals, as advocates speaking about the need for change, and as consultants providing technical assistance to various jurisdictions about how to implement family court reform. Throughout all of this work, it has become clear, as noted on the first page of Chapter 1, that family courts function much like hospital emergency rooms because family courts deal with children and families in crisis. Thus, like the hospital emergency room, we must envision the family court as a "care center." How can this happen? How can we create a caring family court?

By blending unified family courts, the ecology of human development, and therapeutic jurisprudence with an ethic of care and narrative practice, family court intervention has the potential to become an even more effective positive force in the lives of children and families. The court's problem-solving capabilities are enhanced, giving the court the capacity to do greater good. Creating the court as a care center becomes the essence of how the family justice system must operate and responds to the ultimate goal of family law as stated by Clare Huntington.

> This approach to dispute-resolution family law—restructuring families with an eye to the future, preserving and repairing relationships, and keeping family members safe—creates a framework for understanding what the government should be doing in structural family law: proactively nurturing strong, stable, positive relationships to avoid these conflicts as much as possible.[75]

This theoretical paradigm responds to the criticism of the state of affairs to date, that "reforms remain incomplete and at times actively challenged, in part because they lack an overarching framework."[76] We supply this critical construct.

74 Robert M. Bell, *Administration of Justice*, 32 Md. B.J. 2, 4 (1999).
75 Clare Huntington, Failure to Flourish: How Law Undermines Family Relationships, at xiv (2014).
76 Clare Huntington, Failure to Flourish: How Law Undermines Family Relationships 106 (2014).

Conclusion

Caring, in the words of Urie Bronfenbrenner, is "what makes human beings human."[77] According to Bronfenbrenner, "[i]n order to develop, a child needs the enduring, irrational involvement of one or more adults in care and joint activity with the child . . . . Somebody has to be crazy about that kid."[78] Judith Areen agrees with Bronfenbrenner: "Caring may well be understood as a virtue . . . indeed it may be the central virtue for sustaining human relationships."[79] Family law in particular addresses and affects relationships and emotions. Because care is so fundamental to the human condition, it must be an explicit factor in family law theory, practice, and decision-making, as well as in family court structure and operation. An ethic of care perspective views family justice as accounting for the application of relevant law but also attending to the individual and unique circumstances of each family law case. Involvement in the family justice system has the potential to alter family relationships, parental access and decision-making, and economic resources, among other outcomes. The court's immense power to change people's lives "requires bringing an ethic of care to the law through the efforts of the attorneys, judges, and staff, just as doctors and nurses would in caring for a patient in a medical setting."[80] Thus, an ethic of care must guide the behavior of legal actors and the operation of the family justice system as they together attempt to resolve families' problems.

In order to operate from a caring perspective, family court participants, including attorneys, decision-makers, court personnel, and service providers, must rely on and utilize each family's story as the foundation for fashioning an effective resolution to the legal and related nonlegal issues. Narrative theory and practice promote this enlightened view, as knowledge of each family's distinctive facts and points of view become the context from which the family justice system demonstrates its capacity to care. The family justice system must incorporate active narrative practices.

The remainder of this book charts our new prescription for family justice system reform. Chapter 3 introduces the ethic of care. It defines the ethic of care as both a theory and a practice. It traces the history of the ethic of care, discusses how it provides an approach to law, and describes how it can promote effective justice. Chapter 4 elaborates on the elements of narrative practice. It amplifies how narrative can promote an ethic of care in the family justice system, resulting in a more therapeutic approach to family law practice and decision-making. Chapter 5 presents a vision for a family justice system that incorporates into the model presented thus far—the unified family court, the ecology of human development, and therapeutic jurisprudence—principles and practices

77 *See generally* Making Human Beings Human: Bioecological Perspectives on Human Development (Urie Bronfenbrenner, ed. 2005) (an anthology of articles utilizing the ecology of human development as a research paradigm).

78 Urie Bronfenbrenner, *Who Needs Parent Education*, 74 Tchr. Coll. Rec. 774 (1978).

79 Judith Areen, *A Need for Caring*, 86 Mich. L. Rev. 1067, 1076 (1988) (reviewing Harlon L. Dalton & Scott Burris, *Aids and the Law: A Guide for the Public* (1987)).

80 Michael A. Town, *The Unified Family Court: Preventive, Therapeutic and Restorative Justice for America's Families*, Juv. & Fam. Just. Today 14, 15 (Winter 2002).

from an ethic of care orientation and from a narrative perspective. Such an approach is essential to guide necessary and effective family justice system reform, intended to accommodate and to address the very unique challenges presented by the families appearing before the court. Chapter 6 highlights innovative, caring practices currently in place in family courts and suggestions for incorporating caring components into the family justice system.

We as a society owe it to families and children to continue to strive to redesign and to improve the functioning of the family justice system. Despite innovative out-of-court practices in family law matters, "[c]ourts are likely to remain the forum to which people turn for the resolution of their family legal matters."[81] Or, as one of the authors of this book has argued, "Family courts are here to stay, so let's improve them."[82] Further justification for the viability of family courts stems from their critical functions:

> [T]he core functions of the courts are protection, enforcement, and fact-finding. Those are functions no other entity can provide. Courts *must* continue to offer protection for victims, disputed fact-finding where necessary, and enforcement of orders. They *must* also receive adequate resources to perform these functions efficiently and fairly. If choices have to be made, use of the court's time in family cases will be focused on the cases where the need for judicial intervention is the highest. Family court judges *must* have the opportunity for training and education about child development, family dynamics, and dispute resolution before they rotate in to a family court division. No amount of community involvement or service diversion will change the need for these basic services.[83]

Perhaps the most significant reason for attending to the family justice system is, as Jack Weinstein has noted, "[i]n theory, if not always in practice, everyone is equal in the courts; mechanisms exist to help redress imbalances and protect against manifest injustice."[84] Family justice system reform is a process that cannot wait. Our families and children already are in the family court emergency room in great numbers. They need and deserve effective treatment.

81 Barbara A. Babb, *Fashioning an Interdisciplinary Framework for Court Reform in Family Law: A Blueprint to Construct a Unified Family Court*, 71 S. Cal. L. Rev. 469, 527 (1998).

82 Barbara A. Babb, *Family Courts Are Here to Stay, So Let's Improve Them*, 52 Fam. Ct. Rev. 642 (2014).

83 Rebecca L. Kourlis, et al., *IAALS' Honoring Families Initiative: Courts and Communities Helping Families in Transition from Separation or Divorce*, 51 Fam. Ct. Rev. 351 (2013).

84 Jack B. Weinstein, *Some Benefits and Risks of Privatization of Justice Through ADR*, 11 Ohio St. J. on Disp. Resol. 241, 246 (1996).

3 Equipping the family justice system with the ethic of care

Introduction

> [J]ustice must be caring if it is to be just, and . . . caring must be just if it is to be caring . . . .[1]

The family justice system owes a duty to families and children to intervene effectively. Does this obligation involve the responsibility to care about families and children? "Law is best designed to deal with precise disputes: who did what to whom and when? Caring is about relationships"[2] and "is at the heart of human existence."[3] We agree with those scholars who believe that "the focus of family law should be on the promotion of caring relationships,"[4] something Naomi Cahn has characterized as the "new morality within family law."[5] The family justice system plays a critical role in the development of these caring relationships. At the same time, the main functions of family law are the following: "(1) Protective: to guard members of a family from physical, emotional or economic harm. (2) Adjustive: to help families which have broken down to adjust to new lives apart. (3) Supportive: to encourage and support family life."[6] How can the family justice system accomplish caring while carrying out its important functions?

> Feminist theorists are not alone in feeling that the old paradigms cannot adequately describe the realities that exist and that require transformation. Most of us who devote our time to thinking about these questions would agree that there needs to be a shift in our vision, so that we can see the world differently . . . . [Our] hope is to provide a glimpse into a different world, one where the daily caring of people for each other is a valued premise of human existence.[7]

1 Robin West, Caring for Justice 24 (1997).
2 Jonathan Herring, Caring and the Law 2 (2013).
3 Daniel Engster, The Heart of Justice 1 (2007).
4 Jonathan Herring, Caring and the Law 196 (2013).
5 Naomi R. Cahn, *The Moral Complexities of Family Law*, 50 Stan. L. Rev. 225, 270 (1997).
6 Jonathan Herring, Caring and the Law 190 (2013) (footnote omitted).
7 Joan Tronto, Moral Boundaries: A Political Argument for an Ethic of Care (1994).

Indeed, "[t]he world will look different if we move care from its current peripheral location to a place near the center of human life."[8] The need for care is universal, and the family alone is insufficient to supply all the care humans need. "Martha Fineman contends that all people share a common vulnerability and experience dependency at some point in their lives, that society cannot free ride on familial caregiving . . . ."[9] Fineman explains her position:

> Vulnerability is posited as the characteristic that positions us in relation to each other as human beings and also suggests a relationship of responsibility between state and individual. The nature of human vulnerability forms the basis for a claim that the state must be more responsive to that vulnerability. It fulfills that responsibility primarily through the establishment and support of societal institutions.[10]

Fineman concludes that "human vulnerability must be at the heart of our ideas of social and state responsibility."[11]

We agree that human vulnerability necessitates care. Care must become a "national political value."[12]

> We need to elevate care to this level of importance for the basic reason that it is essential to human health and balanced development. It is also crucial to developing human moral potential, to instilling and reinforcing in an individual a sense of positive connection to others. And it is this sense of connection that makes possible the whole range of mutual responsibilities that allow the people of a society to respect and work toward common goals.[13]

In order for care to become a national political value, care needs to be a significant goal of government—"creating an environment in which everyone is able to develop their basic capabilities as a human being in light of basic human needs for strong connections with others . . . ."[14]

> Caring for each other is the most basic form of civic participation. We learn to care in families, and we enlarge our communities of concern as we mature.

8 Joan Tronto, Moral Boundaries: A Political Argument for an Ethic of Care 101 (1994).

9 Clare Huntington, *Early Childhood Development and the Law*, 90 S. Cal. L. Rev. 755, 793 (2017) (citing Martha Albertson Fineman, The Autonomy Myth: A Theory of Dependency 33–38, 47–49 (2004)).

10 Martha Albertson Fineman, *The Vulnerable Subject and the Responsive State,* 60 Emory L.J. 251, 255–56 (2010).

11 Martha Albertson Fineman, *The Vulnerable Subject and the Responsive State*, 60 Emory L.J. 251, 267 (2010).

12 Mona Harrington, Care and Equality: Inventing a New Family Politics 44 (1999).

13 Mona Harrington, Care and Equality: Inventing a New Family Politics 49 (1999).

14 Mary Becker, *Caring for Children and Caretakers*, 76 Chicago-Kent L. Rev. 1495, 1540 (2001).

> Caring is the essential democratic act, the prerequisite to voting, joining associations, attending meetings, holding office, and all the other ways we sustain democracy. Care, the noun, requires families and workers who care, the verb. Caring, the activity, breeds caring, the attitude, and caring, the attitude, seeds caring, the politics.[15]

Society needs a "care movement"[16] in order for individuals to overcome their vulnerabilities. Nevertheless, "[i]t is one thing to conclude that caring should be extended beyond family relationships, and quite another to know how to apply the caring perspective in the public sphere."[17] Linda McClain finds that family policy reforms, in particular, are a valuable platform from which "to think creatively about institutional arrangements that would recognize and support care as a public value and move . . . closer to a new caregiving order."[18]

Thinking about how to incorporate caring requires that we begin with an examination of the ethic of care. What is the ethic of care? It is a moral philosophy grounded in notions of human need and vulnerability, respect for others, responsibility, and interpersonal relationships.[19] The ethic of care in a legal sense contemplates a comprehensive view of justice—one that assumes both the application of relevant law and attention to individual circumstances embodied within cases that come before the courts.[20] Obtaining justice coincides with caring about how laws may affect the persons to whom they are applied, in addition to considering litigants' co-occurring needs to which the law must respond. From an ethic of care perspective, "rather than the primary focus of the legal . . . enquiry being whether 'is [it] my right to do X?', the question should be 'what is my proper obligation within the context of this relationship?'"[21]

While this chapter addresses the role of the ethic of care, the following chapter tackles the subject of narrative and the meshing of the two notions, both of which are important elements of family justice system reform. In light of the profoundly intimate and human consequences stemming from family law adjudication, family courts must adhere to the ethic of caring for the family according to its particular circumstances. The ethic of care guides the court in determining its obligation, and narrative provides the context for the court's determination.

15 Deborah Stone, *Why We Need a Care Movement*, Nation, Feb. 23, 2000, https://www.thenation.com/article/why-we-need-care-movement/.
16 Deborah Stone, *Why We Need a Care Movement*, Nation, Feb. 23, 2000, https://www.thenation.com/article/why-we-need-care-movement/.
17 Judith Areen, *A Need for Caring*, 86 Mich. L. Rev. 1067, 1078 (1988).
18 Linda C. McClain, *Care as a Public Value: Linking Responsibility, Resources, and Republicanism*, 76 Chicago-Kent L. Rev. 1673, 1730 (2001).
19 *Care Ethics*, Internet Encyclopedia of Philosophy, http://www.iep.utm.edu/care-eth/ (last visited Oct. 12, 2017). Jonathan Herring, Caring and the Law 14 (2013).
20 *See Care Ethics*, Internet Encyclopedia of Philosophy, http://www.iep.utm.edu/care-eth/ (last visited Oct. 12, 2017).
21 Jonathan Herring, Caring and the Law 60 (2013).

In this chapter, we define the ethic of care as both a moral theory and a practical endeavor. We trace the history of the ethic of care—its roots in ancient moral philosophies, antecedents stemming from eighteenth and nineteenth century ethical theories, and interpretations contained in contemporary feminist ideology. We discuss how the ethic of care has evolved to provide a model for approaches to all aspects of law, and we attempt to reconcile the purported tensions between justice and care.

Defining care and the ethic of care

The ethic of care, while a somewhat recent concept in its application to law, is fundamental in other professional settings. Nursing and care go hand in hand; nursing care is a term that routinely describes what nurses do.[22] In medical practice, caring is an essential ethical precept,[23] as well as a very practical intervention. As one physician concludes, care is a means to "bettering the tattered state of doctor-patient relationships and to improving the outcomes of our medicine."[24] One scholar believes "[c]aring . . . is the cornerstone of ethical consideration for professionals, *all* professionals."[25] As applied to the law, Marjorie Silver characterizes the practice of law as a "healing profession."[26] According to Silver, as lawyers, "[w]hen we represent a client, we receive into our care a human being with an array of problems and possibilities, only some of which are likely to be legal."[27]

The notion of care has become a topic in policymaking and political discourse, as well.[28] The sweeping United States healthcare legislation of 2010 is known as the Patient Protection and Affordable Care Act.[29] Hillary Clinton, in a campaign speech for the Democratic party nomination in the 2016 American presidential race, has spoken of the importance of creating a network of resources in communities to address individuals' and families' need for care.[30]

22 *See, e.g.*, Vicki Lachman, *Applying the Ethics of Care to Your Nursing Practice*, 21 Ethics, L. & Pol'y 112 (2012) (noting the interconnectedness between definitions of caring and nursing); Joan McCarthy, *Principlism or Narrative Ethics: Must We Choose Between Them?*, 29 Med. Human. 65 (2003), *available at* http://mh.bmj.com/content/29/2/65.full (arguing for a more nuanced view of bioethical decision-making that considers individual narratives as instructive in ethical choices).

23 *See* Judith Areen, *A Need for Caring*, 86 Mich. L. Rev. 1067, 1081–82 (1988) (noting Lewis Thomas's recollections on physicians providing "more care than cure").

24 Rita Charon, Narrative Medicine: Honoring the Stories of Illness, at ix (2006).

25 Michelle Brenner, *On Compassion, in* Conversations on Compassion 41 (Michelle Brenner ed., 2015) (emphasis added).

26 *See generally* The Affective Assistance of Counsel: Practicing Law as a Healing Profession (Marjorie Silver ed., 2007).

27 *Introduction*, The Affective Assistance of Counsel: Practicing Law as a Healing Profession, at xix (Marjorie Silver ed., 2007).

28 Joan Tronto, Moral Boundaries: A Political Argument for an Ethic of Care (1994) (advocating for an ethic of care perspective in policymaking).

29 Patient Protection and Affordable Care Act, Pub. L. No. 111–48, 124 Stat. 119 (2010) (codified as amended in scattered sections of 21, 25, 26, 29, and 42 U.S.C.).

30 Emily Gurnon, *Where Clinton and Trump Stand on Care-Giving and Long-Term Care*, Forbes (Aug. 26, 2016, 10:59 AM), https://www.forbes.com/sites/nextavenue/2016/

What do we mean by care? "Most people agree that the world would be a better place if we all cared more for one another, but despite that initial agreement we find it hard to say exactly what we mean by *caring*."[31] "Caring is so common, we don't see it."[32] Care is defined in the dictionary as "the provision of what is necessary for the health, welfare, maintenance, and protection of someone or something"[33] or the "feeling and exhibiting [of] concern and empathy for others; showing or having compassion."[34] "Caring implies some kind of on-going responsibility and commitment."[35] It is "a universal aspect of human life."[36] "When we care, we intend to offer some positive form of response. Often our aim is to prevent harm."[37] "[T]he notion of care expands from the paralyzing injunction not to hurt others to an injunction to act responsibly toward self and others and thus sustain connection."[38]

Virginia Held has said, "There is not yet anything close to agreement among those writing on care on what exactly we should take the meaning of this term to be . . . ."[39] Nonetheless, scholars have characterized care in comprehensive terms. Annette Baier defines care as "a felt concern for the good of others and for community with them."[40] According to Joan Tronto, care in the most general sense implicates "some kind of engagement," whether positive or negative.[41] She believes, however, that "[c]are is both a practice and a disposition"[42] that "involves more than simply good intentions. It requires a deep and thoughtful knowledge of the situation . . . ."[43] The starting point for care, according to Tronto, is understanding another's needs and involves four phases: caring about, or recognizing the need to care; taking care of, or assuming responsibility to respond to the need; care-giving, or directly meeting the care need; and care-

08/26/where-clinton-and-trump-stand-on-caregiving-and-long-term-care/#b6d9494492a1.

31 Nel Noddings, Starting at Home: Caring and Social Policy 11 (2002).

32 George Kent, *On Caring, in* Conversations on Compassion 162 (Michelle Brenner ed., 2015).

33 *Care*, Oxforddictionary.com, http://www.oxforddictionaries.com/us/definition/american_english/care.

34 Vicki Lachman, *Applying the Ethics of Care to Your Nursing Practice*, 21 Ethics, L. & Pol'y 112 (2012) (citing *Caring*, Thefreedictionary.com).

35 Virginia Held, The Ethics of Care 102 (2006).

36 Joan Tronto, Moral Boundaries: A Political Argument for an Ethic of Care 110 (1994).

37 Nel Noddings, Starting at Home: Caring and Social Policy 31 (2002).

38 Carol Gilligan, In a Different Voice: Psychological Theory and Women's Development 149 (1982).

39 Virginia Held, The Ethics of Care 29 (2006).

40 Annette Baier, *The Need for More Than Justice* in Ethical Theory: An Anthology 721, 721 (Russ Shafer-Landau ed., 2d ed. 2013).

41 Joan Tronto, Moral Boundaries: A Political Argument for an Ethic of Care 102 (1994).

42 Joan Tronto, Moral Boundaries: A Political Argument for an Ethic of Care 104 (1994).

43 Joan Tronto, Moral Boundaries: A Political Argument for an Ethic of Care 136 (1994).

receiving, or the recipient's response to the care received.[44] For Tronto, "[p]roviding an integrated, holistic way to meet concrete needs is the ideal of care."[45] Thus, "[t]hose who engage in a care process must make judgments . . . ."[46] Held, while claiming definitions of care vary, identifies features of care as a habit of mind and caring an activity.[47] She joins others in describing care as an aspect of human relatedness, using by way of example the cautionary words in common parlance, to "take care."[48] Such a statement implies one's concern for another. Kim Treiger-Bar-Am also views care as comprised of feelings and action: "Care signifies the feelings of affection, or love" and "is shown by treatment that is demonstrated in actions and conduct."[49]

Judith Areen defines three characteristics of care, one of which concerns relatedness. For Areen, "[f]irst, a caring person is responsive to the reality of the person receiving care."[50] This fosters autonomy and inhibits paternalism. "Second, a caring person also cares about herself sufficiently to sustain the physical, mental, and emotional resources needed to care for others."[51] Finally, Areen points out that "caring does not always begin or end by choice."[52]

Matthew Kavanagh also highlights the relatedness aspect of care. "Families and communities are characterized by systems of care—intersecting webs of people who give care, people who receive care, and, primarily, people who both give *and* receive care. These systems are active in everyday life in obvious ways, such as the work of parenthood, and in less visible ways, such as those whose work makes it possible for parents to care for their children."[53]

Susan Daicoff defines care as

> a decision-making preference that emphasizes interpersonal harmony and mercy. It is contextual and its adherents make decisions by avoiding harm, seeking to maintain and restore relationships, protecting others from hurt, and assessing the relative harm of various choices to and the vulnerabilities of, the parties involved.[54]

44 Joan Tronto, Moral Boundaries: A Political Argument for an Ethic of Care 105–07 (1994).
45 Joan Tronto, Moral Boundaries: A Political Argument for an Ethic of Care 109 (1994).
46 Joan Tronto, Moral Boundaries: A Political Argument for an Ethic of Care 137 (1994).
47 Virginia Held, The Ethics of Care 29–30 (2006).
48 Virginia Held, The Ethics of Care 29–30 (2006).
49 Kim Treiger-Bar-Am, *In Defense of Autonomy: An Ethic of Care*, 3 N.Y.U. J.L. & Liberty 548, 550 (2008).
50 Judith Areen, *A Need for Caring*, 86 Mich. L. Rev. 1067, 1075 (1988).
51 Judith Areen, *A Need for Caring*, 86 Mich. L. Rev. 1067, 1075 (1988).
52 Judith Areen, *A Need for Caring*, 86 Mich. L. Rev. 1067, 1075 (1988).
53 Matthew M. Kavanagh, *Rewriting the Legal Family: Beyond Exclusivity to a Care-Based Standard*, 16 Yale J.L. & Feminism 84 (2004).
54 Susan Daicoff, *Lawyer, Be Thyself: An Empirical Investigation of the Relationship Between the Ethic of Care, the Feeling Decision-making Preference, and Lawyer Well-being*, 16 Va. J. Soc. Pol'y & L. 87, 115 (2008).

The attributes of caring to which Daicoff refers compel an awareness of the other and her particular circumstances resulting in a connection between the carer and the cared about.[55] In this regard, Daicoff also sees care as relational.

Likewise, Nel Noddings' standpoint on care corresponds with relational views: "Close attention to the feelings, needs, desires, and thoughts of those cared for, and a skill in understanding a situation from that person's point of view, are central to caring for someone."[56] Noddings distinguishes between two types of care. "Whereas caring for occurs in the 'face-to-face occasions in which one person, as carer, cares directly for another, the cared-for,' caring-about 'moves us from the face-to-face world into the wider public realm' where institutions and policies serve to establish and promote 'the conditions under which caring-for can flourish.'"[57] Noddings believes "[c]are, properly, involves an 'engrossment' in the life of the other . . ." enabling the capacity to "receive and feel with the other,"[58] characterized in psychological literature as a form of empathy.[59] As we discuss in Chapter 4 on the relationship between caring and narrative competency, empathy is one of the interpersonal skills enabled through narrative engagement.[60] Noddings' definition of caring supports the need to incorporate a narrative approach, as the capacity to "receive and feel with another" happens by listening to someone's life account—the crux of narrative practice.

Daniel Engster defines caring as either a virtue or a practice. "When caring is defined as a virtue, the focus is on the inner traits, dispositions, and motivations of the caring person."[61] On the other hand, "[w]hen caring is defined as a practice, . . . the focus is on a person's external actions and their consequences."[62] Engster finds these views compatible: "Virtue-based definitions usually acknowledge some role for actions, and practice-based definitions generally recognize some role for internal dispositions and relational virtues."[63]

55 *See* Virginia Held, The Ethics of Care 30 (2006).
56 Virginia Held, The Ethics of Care 31 (2006) (citing Nel Noddings, Feminine Approach to Ethics and Moral Education (1986)).
57 Daniel Engster, The Heart of Justice 75 (2007) (citing Nel Noddings, Starting at Home: Caring and Social Policy (2002)).
58 Robert White, *Care and Justice*, 16 Ethical Persp. 459, 466 (2009) (citing Nel Noddings, Caring: A Feminine Approach to Ethics and Moral Education 30 (2d ed. 2003)).
59 Robert White, *Care and Justice*, 16 Ethical Persp. 459, 466 (2009) (citing Michael Slote, The Ethics of Care and Empathy 12 (2007) in explaining that the "engrossment" to which Noddings refers is labeled as "mediated associative empathy" in psychological discourse).
60 *See, e.g.*, Rita Charon, Narrative Medicine: Honoring the Stories of Illness 132 (2006). *Id.* Charon has delineated three narrative competencies, including attention. *Id.* She maintains that in order to care for patients, the physician must first pay meticulous attention to the patient's narrative: "attention," she explains "connotes the emptying of self so as to become an instrument for receiving the meaning of another."
61 Daniel Engster, The Heart of Justice 21 (2007).
62 Daniel Engster, The Heart of Justice 21 (2007).
63 Daniel Engster, The Heart of Justice 21 (2007).

We turn now to the incorporation of caring into what is known as the ethic of care, although some scholars refer to the plural, ethics of care, instead.[64] The ethic of care, as noted earlier, is a moral philosophy and is characterized and described in various ways. Nel Noddings, following David Hume's position that "morality is founded upon and rooted in feeling,"[65] has described the ethic of care as comprised of two "sentiments." "[N]atural caring"[66] is the first sentiment—which Noddings suggests is reflected in "situations where we act on behalf of the other because we want to do so . . . ."[67] The second sentiment arises from memories of one's own experiences of caring and being cared for.[68] Rita Charon similarly views emotions and feelings "as an important part of . . . care ethics . . . ."[69] She has said that "emotions of empathy or compassion are recognized to be a source of care."[70] Robin West has stated in a related vein that "caregiving is importantly tied to affect and inclination."[71]

Carol Gilligan, a historically significant figure in launching the modern ethic of care discourse[72] and an avatar of the feminist movement that has embraced it,[73] has framed her definition in terms of insight, connectedness, and particularity: "a way of knowing . . . emphasiz[ing] people's mutual connections rather than their solitary autonomy . . . . [and] eschew[ing] sweeping principles in favor of sincere effort to respond to the particular context in which moral choice must be made."[74] Gilligan goes on to say,

> The morality of rights is predicated on equality and centered on the understanding of fairness, while the ethic of responsibility relies on the concept of equity, the recognition of differences in need. While the ethic of rights is a manifestation of equal respect, balancing the claims of other and self, the ethic of responsibility rests on an understanding that gives rise to compassion and care.[75]

64 *See, e.g.*, Virginia Held, The Ethics of Care 169 n. 1 (2006) (explaining that she uses the plural form "to suggest that there are multiple versions of this ethic, though they all have much in common, making it understandable that some prefer 'the ethic of care,'" as we have chosen to do).

65 Nel Noddings, *An Ethic of Caring, in* Ethical Theory: An Anthology 699 (Russ Shafer-Landau ed., 2d ed. 2013).

66 Nel Noddings, *An Ethic of Caring, in* Ethical Theory: An Anthology 699 (Russ Shafer-Landau ed., 2d ed. 2013).

67 Nel Noddings, *An Ethic of Caring, in* Ethical Theory: An Anthology 699 (Russ Shafer-Landau ed., 2d ed. 2013).

68 *See* Nel Noddings, *An Ethic of Caring, in* Ethical Theory: An Anthology 699 (Russ Shafer-Landau ed., 2d ed. 2013).

69 Rita Charon et al., The Principles and Practice of Narrative Medicine 128 (2017).

70 Rita Charon et al., The Principles and Practice of Narrative Medicine 129 (2017).

71 Robin West, Caring for Justice 34 (1997).

72 *See, e.g.*, Carol Gilligan, In a Different Voice: Psychological Theory and Women's Development (1982). This book is Gilligan's foundational text on moral reasoning, which embraces a contextual and relational approach.

73 *See, e.g.*, Robin West, Caring for Justice 7 (1997) (noting that Gilligan's premise inspired a following of "relational feminists").

74 Stephen Ellmann, *The Ethic of Care as an Ethic for Lawyers*, 81 Geo. L.J. 2665, 2668 (1992).

75 Carol Gilligan, In a Different Voice: Psychological Theory and Women's Development 164–65 (1982).

Joan Tronto, in concert with Gilligan, has viewed ethical obligations from the standpoint of relatedness. Tronto's four essential elements of caring—attentiveness, responsibility, competence, and responsiveness[76]—are characteristic of an interdependent, responsibility-based ethical scheme. These attributes align her with Gilligan in diverging from the philosophers in the Kantian mold, who have looked to abstract, universal, rational principles to resolve ethical quandaries.[77] In this way, both Tronto and Gilligan have championed the proposition that the relationship with others is the point from which an ethic of care analysis must launch. As Tronto herself has claimed, "[p]erhaps the most important characteristic of an ethic of care is that, within it, moral situations are defined not in terms of rights and responsibilities but in terms of relationships of care."[78]

Jonathan Herring advances the discourse on the meaning and attributes of the ethic of care in offering a four-part definition, or the "four markers of care," including meeting needs, respect, responsibility, and relationality.[79] Herring considers that care is first and foremost action-oriented.[80] He distinguishes "caring for" from "caring about."[81] The responsibility prong in Herring's definition of care is one in which the quality of caring is selfless—providing care "even where that was not one's preference."[82] It is an act one takes responsibility to render—one which is chosen. While Herring sees care as a choice, albeit a responsible one, Carrie Menkel-Meadow points out that, historically, care has rested in the hands of a subservient class of individuals—those who bear the responsibility for it, but who are not in a position to make the choice to do it.[83]

Joan Tronto also defines "caring for" and "caring about," two of her four phases discussed previously. "Caring about refers to less concrete objects; it is characterized by a more general form of commitment. Caring for implies a

76 Joan Tronto, Moral Boundaries: A Political Argument for an Ethic of Care 127 (1994).

77 *See, e.g.*, Joan Tronto, Moral Boundaries: A Political Argument for an Ethic of Care 26 (1994) ("[For] the majority of later philosophical writers [e.g., John Rawls] . . . ethics is defined as a subject in Kantian terms."); Virginia Held, The Ethics of Care 63 (2006) (noting that, while utilitarian moral theorists differed in their views, the "similarities between Kantian and utilitarian theories are of more significance than the differences . . . both are theories of right action aimed at recommending rational choices . . . .").

78 Joan Tronto, *Beyond Gender Difference to a Theory of Care*, *in* An Ethic of Care: Feminist and Interdisciplinary Perspectives 240, 249 (Mary Jeanne Larrabee ed., 1993).

79 *See* Jonathan Herring, Caring and the Law 14–25 (2013).

80 *See* Jonathan Herring, Caring and the Law 15 (2013) (noting that "caring relationships usually involve an action").

81 Jonathan Herring, Caring and the Law 19 (2013); *see also* Vicki Lachman, *Applying the Ethics of Care to Your Nursing Practice*, 21 Ethics, L. & Pol'y 112 (2012) ("[C]aring is a feeling that also requires an action.").

82 Jonathan Herring, Caring and the Law 19 (2013).

83 Carrie Menkel-Meadow, *What's Gender Got to Do with It? The Politics and Morality of an Ethic of Care*, 22 N.Y.U. Rev. L. & Soc. Change 265, 280 (1996) (noting that care was historically "the work of slaves, servants and women").

specific, particular object that is the focus of caring."[84] Tronto suggests a role for the justice system in "caring for:"

> [T]he particular structures involving caring for grow especially out of the family; caring professions are often construed as a buttress to, or substitute for, care that can no longer be provided within a family. The family may no longer be intact, as a result of death, divorce, distance. Or the family may not be able to provide help; some caring requires expertise. The family may be or may be seen as the source of the problem—for example, families with patterns of substance abuse, incest, violence.[85]

Ruth O'Brien has distilled four shared principles from among the many descriptions of a care ethic.[86] These "pillars" of care theory, as she refers to them, include, first, the relational aspect—that "the self . . . is deeply situated in relationships," to the extent that our "desires, wants, and needs" stem from and are meaningful only in the context of a social milieu.[87] Second, care theory anticipates both public and private domains incorporating both societal and personal issues. This "pillar" applies to all persons, whether imbued with specific articulated rights or whether those rights are associated, as with children, whose care is not guaranteed specifically by law but whose well-being is "considered vital in a civil society."[88] Third, the ethic of care appreciates unique needs, elevating the individual to a position worthy of consideration and respect. Finally, valuing individual differences, an ethic of care "takes into account particular peoples with their own specific histories."[89] Consequently, individual stories are essential for a conception of care ethics. We devote the following chapter to the central relationship between the ethic of care and narrative, or the personal histories to which O'Brien refers.

A compelling feature of the ethic of care is its universality.

> Since all people depend upon some rather fixed forms of caring for their survival, development, and functioning, all people can be said. . . to recognize caring as a moral good. Care theory should therefore be able to generate a theory of justice that is universally acceptable across different cultural, religious, and moral communities.[90]

84 Joan C. Tronto, *Women and Caring: What Can Feminists Learn about Morality from Caring?, in* Justice and Care 103 (Virginia Held ed., 1995).
85 Joan C. Tronto, *Women and Caring: What Can Feminists Learn about Morality from Caring?, in* Justice and Care 103 (Virginia Held ed., 1995).
86 Ruth O'Brien, Bodies in Revolt: Gender, Disability, and a Workplace Ethic of Care 61–62 (2005).
87 Ruth O'Brien, Bodies in Revolt: Gender, Disability, and a Workplace Ethic of Care 61 (2005).
88 Ruth O'Brien, Bodies in Revolt: Gender, Disability, and a Workplace Ethic of Care 61 (2005).
89 Ruth O'Brien, Bodies in Revolt: Gender, Disability, and a Workplace Ethic of Care 62 (2005).
90 Daniel Engster, The Heart of Justice 16 (2007).

The universality of the ethic of care renders it an appropriate attribute of family justice system reform.

In sum, the ethic of care privileges needs above rights, relationships above autonomy, and individuality above abstraction. "An ethic of care does not reject the concept of rights, but it logically construes rights as originating in and anchored in needs."[91] The principles of the ethic of care compel empathy for and service to others, and they exist within an environment that is relational rather than self-focused. Definitions of the ethic of care have evolved as contemporary theorists have embraced, interpreted, and applied it to law, medicine, and socio-political movements. The ethic of care now exists as both a moral theory and a practice, adaptable to many human endeavors.[92]

Historical background

How did the ethic of care emerge? There are two views. One version argues that it is rooted in writings of the ancient philosophers.[93] Joan Tronto explains: "Contextual moral theories [such as the ethic of care] have a long history; indeed, it is a history almost as old as Western philosophy itself, finding an original formulation in the writings of Aristotle."[94] Aristotle has characterized care as a virtue—"that a virtuous actor will know what constitutes right action . . . ."[95] Arguably, Aristotle's stance, that goodness is grounded in the virtue of engaging in benevolent acts, fits squarely within ethic of care parameters.[96] As Tronto summarizes, Aristotle's perspective on caring is that which requires a distinct "disposition" toward a "moral imagination, character, and actions [in response] to the complexity of a given situation."[97] It is precisely this given situation that provides the context to

91 Nel Noddings, Starting at Home: Caring and Social Policy 53 (2002).

92 *See*, e.g., Vicki Lachman, *Applying the Ethics of Care to Your Nursing Practice*, 21 Ethics, L. & Pol'y 112 (2012) (demonstrating care ethics as it pertains to nursing practice); Rita Charon, Narrative Medicine: Honoring the Stories of Illness, at ix (2006) (applying the ethic of care to medical practice).

93 *See* Jonathan Herring, Caring and the Law 47 n.6 (2013) (citing Ruth Groenhout, Connected Lives: Human Nature and an Ethics of Care (2004) for the notion that ethic of care perspectives "can be traced much further back" than those espoused by contemporary philosophers).

94 Joan Tronto, Moral Boundaries: A Political Argument for an Ethic of Care 27 (1994); *but see* Rosalind Hursthouse and Glen Pettigrove, *Virtue Ethics*, Stanford Encyclopedia Phil., http://plato.stanford.edu/entries/ethics-virtue/ (last updated Dec. 8, 2016) (explaining that virtue ethics' roots in Chinese philosophy are even more ancient).

95 Judith Areen, *A Need for Caring*, 86 Mich. L. Rev. 1067, 1976 (1988) (noting, however, that contemporary philosophers "consider his theory naïve").

96 *See, e.g.*, Rosalind Hursthouse and Glen Pettigrove, *Virtue Ethics*, Stanford Encyclopedia Phil., http://plato.stanford.edu/entries/ethics-virtue/ (last updated Dec. 8, 2016) (defining the virtue ethicist as one who views the act of helping someone in need as "charitable or benevolent").

97 Joan Tronto, *Beyond Gender Difference to a Theory of Care, in* An Ethic of Care: Feminist and Interdisciplinary Perspectives 240, 248 (Mary Jeanne Larrabee ed., 1993).

which an ethic of care approach applies. Later moralists—Kant most notably—have sidelined the attributes of virtue theory and have insisted instead on a rationalist position, such "that the morality of particular acts can be determined only by reasoning from moral principles."[98]

Similar ways of thinking about ethics in relation to care are attributable to St. Augustine,[99] Socrates, and Plato.[100] Augustinian philosophy "emphasizes from beginning to end that humans are not able to care for themselves, that humans cannot take full responsibility for themselves, and that human knowledge is unavoidably dependent on human relationships."[101] Socrates, in discussing what constitutes a moral life, refers to the importance of attentiveness,[102] a signal characteristic of caring as Rita Charon describes it in her discussion of ethical approaches to caring for the sick.[103] "In Book I of the Republic, Socrates and his cohorts briefly mention that unless one is willing to listen, [to attend] the philosopher can have no effect."[104] The attention given yields insight into the care required. Plato, along with Aristotle, also is characterized as a proponent of care as a virtue.[105] The two both view caring for others as a righteous enterprise. Due to their inclusion of the relational and contextual components to an ethical existence, the ancients are foundational in the development of the ethic of care.

Moving forward to the seventeenth century, Benedict de Spinoza influenced the construction of a care ethic to the extent that he maintained that the basis for rendering care to another person lies in the relationship that one has with the other.[106] Eighteenth century Scottish Enlightenment theorists, including Francis Hutcheson, David Hume, and Adam Smith, contributed to the development of

98 Judith Areen, *A Need for Caring*, 86 MICH. L. REV. 1067, 1076 (1988).

99 JONATHAN HERRING, CARING AND THE LAW 47 n.6 (2013) (citing RUTH GROENHOUT, CONNECTED LIVES: HUMAN NATURE AND AN ETHICS OF CARE (2004)).

100 *See* Carrie Menkel-Meadow, *What's Gender Got to Do with It? The Politics and Morality of an Ethic of Care*, 22 N.Y.U. REV. L. & SOC. CHANGE 265, 270 n.14 (1996) (citing MARILYN FRIEDMAN, WHAT ARE FRIENDS FOR? FEMINIST PERSPECTIVES ON PERSONAL RELATIONSHIPS AND MORAL THEORY (1993) and VIRGINIA HELD, FEMINIST MORALITY: TRANSFORMING CULTURE, SOCIETY, AND POLITICS (1993)); *but see* VIRGINIA HELD, THE ETHICS OF CARE 9 (2006) (distinguishing Aristotelian virtue ethics from ethic of care morality).

101 RUTH E. GROENHOUT, CONNECTED LIVES: HUMAN NATURE AND ETHICS OF CARE, AUGUSTINE AND CARE 75 (Rowman & Littlefield Publishers, Inc. 2004).

102 JOAN TRONTO, MORAL BOUNDARIES: A POLITICAL ARGUMENT FOR AN ETHIC OF CARE 129 (1994).

103 RITA CHARON, NARRATIVE MEDICINE: HONORING THE STORIES OF ILLNESS 132 (2006) ("Any effort to provide health care begins by bestowing attention on the patient . . . . [A]ttention connotes the emptying of self so as to become an instrument for receiving the meaning of another.").

104 JOAN TRONTO, MORAL BOUNDARIES: A POLITICAL ARGUMENT FOR AN ETHIC OF CARE 129 (1994).

105 *See* Rosalind Hursthouse and Glen Pettigrove, *Virtue Ethics*, STANFORD ENCYCLOPEDIA PHIL., http://plato.stanford.edu/entries/ethics-virtue/ (last updated Dec. 8, 2016) (noting, however, that Aristotle was foremost).

106 RUTH O'BRIEN, BODIES IN REVOLT: GENDER, DISABILITY, AND A WORKPLACE ETHIC OF CARE 66 (2005).

the ethic of care, as well.[107] They presented an emotional basis for ethicality in which sentiments such as sympathy inspired caring.[108]

Hutcheson "was the first prominent proponent of . . . moral-sentiment or common-sense philosophy."[109] He claimed this moral sensibility was a God-given quality "that we might or might not activate."[110] Because Hutcheson conceived of sympathy as an inborn trait, it was thus "practically innate"[111] and presumably relied upon to prompt ethicality without external provocation. Hume differed in that he suggested sympathy for another person was motivated by interpersonal interaction; therefore, external circumstance initiated ethical actions.[112] Adam Smith enlarged upon Hume and Hutcheson's notions of a sympathetic response by asking "when and how . . . can [we] imagine ourselves in the situation of another, such that we may overcome our usual focus on ourselves?"[113] Carrie Menkel-Meadow interpreted Smith's question as an attempt to explore empathy.

Overall, the sentiment-based theories of the enlightenment philosophers, with the exception of Hutcheson, were united in the belief that affiliation with others was necessary to develop an ethical sensitivity.[114] Regardless of whether these philosophers conceived of an innate capacity for sympathetic feelings, as did Hutcheson, or believed sympathy occurred due to circumstances of affiliation, the notion that emotions matter in ethical decision-making emerged. As one commenter on Scottish Enlightenment thinkers summarized, an ethic of care

107 *See* Carrie Menkel-Meadow, *What's Gender Got to Do with It? The Politics and Morality of an Ethic of Care*, 22 N.Y.U. Rev. L. & Soc. Change 265, 266 (1996) (citing Joan Tronto's review of the "historical and philosophical basis for an ethic of care, derived from the Scottish Enlightenment, which she claims originally knew no gender basis.").

108 *See* Carrie Menkel-Meadow, *What's Gender Got to Do with It? The Politics and Morality of an Ethic of Care*, 22 N.Y.U. Rev. L. & Soc. Change 265, 270 (1996).

109 Joan Tronto, Moral Boundaries: A Political Argument for an Ethic of Care 39 (1994).

110 *See* Carrie Menkel-Meadow, *What's Gender Got to Do with It? The Politics and Morality of an Ethic of Care*, 22 N.Y.U. Rev. L. & Soc. Change 265, 271 (1996); *see also* Joan Tronto, Moral Boundaries: A Political Argument for an Ethicof Care 39 (1994); Jonathan Herring, Caring and the Law 15 (2013) (demonstrating that Hume presaged Herring's view of care as ethics' action-orientation).

111 Joan Tronto, Moral Boundaries: A Political Argument for an Ethic of Care 40 (1994).

112 Menkel-Meadow, *What's Gender Got to Do with It? The Politics and Morality of an Ethic of Care*, 22 N.Y.U. Rev. L. & Soc. Change 265, 272 (1996); Joan Tronto, Moral Boundaries: A Political Argument for an Ethic of Care 40 (1994).

113 *See* Carrie Menkel-Meadow, *What's Gender Got to Do with It? The Politics and Morality of an Ethic of Care*, 22 N.Y.U. Rev. L. & Soc. Change 265, 272–73 (1996); *see also* Joan Tronto, Moral Boundaries: A Political Argument for an Ethic of Care (1994); Robert White, *Care and Justice*, 16 Ethical Persp. 459, 464–65 (2009) (citing Michael Slote, The Ethics of Care and Empathy 13 (2007) in explaining the roots of empathy—that the moral sentimentalists, Smith among them, "likely referred to sympathy instead because there was no word for empathy until the 20th century.").

114 Nel Noddings, *An Ethic of Caring*, *in* Ethical Theory: An Anthology 699, 711 (Russ Shafer-Landau ed., 2d ed. 2013) (explaining that ethicality is not entirely our own doing as "we depend upon each other even for our own goodness.").

orientation as they envisioned it was "receptive-intuitive" in that "understanding the needs of those cared for depends more on feeling with them rather than on rational cognition,"[115] another reference to empathy.

At the same time the enlightenment philosophers voiced their ideas about sentiment-based ethics, Emmanuel Kant proposed an alternative view—that universal principles, rather than individual responses based upon feelings, were the foundation of a moral life.[116] One contemporary ethicist argued that even Kant's rational, universalist standpoint reconciled with the ethics of caring and was thus consistent with care theory. Kant's categorical imperative, "to act in a manner that respects other individuals' existences as ends in themselves," or to "'do unto others as you would have them do unto you,'"[117] was congruent with ethic of care precepts.

Feeling-inspired morality declined at the end of the eighteenth century.[118] This development was an outgrowth of emerging social norms that skewed toward self-interest rather than "genuine virtue, genuine friendship, and heroic deeds."[119] As "the strength of self-interest . . . became increasingly powerful . . . it required less of a rich social setting for individuals."[120] Thus, the relational component of ethics embraced by the Scottish moralists fell from favor. "By the end of the eighteenth century, Scottish moralists writing in the popular press were lamenting the passage of"[121] these by-gone hallmarks of their ethical framework.

Philosophers writing in the early- to mid-twentieth century have contributed to ethic of care discussions by grappling with intersubjectivity—"the situation that occurs when two subjects, or two authentic selves, meet."[122] The concept of two beings and their relationship to one another is explained by the phenomenologists Edmund Husserl and Martin Heidegger. Husserl writes of existing in the world not only in the sense of the self, but in a conjoint existence with others, thus "grant[ing] fellowship to its cohabitants, in both their mutual regard of its objects and their becoming objects for one another's regard and experience."[123]

115 Virginia Held, The Ethics of Care 31 (2006) (discussing Nel Noddings, Caring: A Feminine Approach to Ethics and Moral Education 14–19 (1984)).

116 *See* Carrie Menkel-Meadow, *What's Gender Got to Do with It? The Politics and Morality of an Ethic of Care*, 22 N.Y.U. Rev. L. & Soc. Change 265, 270 (1996) (citing features of Kantian ethics).

117 Kim Treiger-Bar-Am, *In Defense of Autonomy: An Ethic of Care*, 3 N.Y.U. J.L. & Liberty 548, 550 (2008).

118 *See* Joan Tronto, Moral Boundaries: A Political Argument for an Ethic of Care 50 (1994) ("As the distance among individuals grew, the reliability of controlling the influences on individuals became a more urgent problem. The strength of self-interest as a regulator of human activity became increasingly powerful because it required less of a rich social setting for individuals." (footnote omitted)).

119 Joan Tronto, Moral Boundaries: A Political Argument for an Ethic of Care 50 (1994).

120 Joan Tronto, Moral Boundaries: A Political Argument for an Ethic of Care 50 (1994).

121 Joan Tronto, Moral Boundaries: A Political Argument for an Ethic of Care 50 (1994).

122 Rita Charon, Narrative Medicine: Honoring the Stories of Illness 51 (2006).

123 Rita Charon, Narrative Medicine: Honoring the Stories of Illness 51 (2006).

"Heidegger proposes care as the fundamental trait of human existence."[124] His concept of the human experience comprises being and time. He construes it is through being that we are present with others in "works, deeds, sacrifices, and sayings,"[125] and time allows the opportunity to involve oneself in such caring enterprises. Emmanuel Levinas promotes ethics[126] that obligate a mutual responsibility for one another. In his view, presence and need compel our ethical task. To illustrate presence, he writes of being "summoned" by the "other" in a confrontation with her face.[127] Further, Levinas characterizes human need as vulnerability—a defining aspect of all persons that supports the contention that the ethical responsibility to care is a social imperative.[128]

In contrast to the long view of ethic of care history is the assertion that the ethic of care is an outgrowth of the modern feminist movement.[129] While we have demonstrated its historical prominence, most commentators likely agree that the first wave of contemporary expositions of the ethic of care date to the work of Carol Gilligan.[130] Gilligan's landmark book, *In a Different Voice*,[131] features a counter-argument to the conventional belief, embodied in the work of Lawrence Kohlberg,[132] that women's moral development is inferior to that of men.[133]

124 Mihaela Czobor-Lupp, *Heidegger's Contribution to an Ethic of Care and Responsiveness* 3 (Paper Presented at the Annual Meeting of the American Political Association, Washington, D.C., Sept. 2–5, 2010).

125 Mihaela Czobor-Lupp, *Heidegger's Contribution to an Ethic of Care and Responsiveness* 4 (Paper Presented at the Annual Meeting of the American Political Association, Washington, D.C., Sept. 2–5, 2010).

126 Rita Charon, Narrative Medicine: Honoring the Stories of Illness 51 (2006).

127 *See* Rita Charon, Narrative Medicine: Honoring the Stories of Illness 135 (2006).

128 *See* Jonathan Herring, Caring and the Law 50 (2013) (citing Levinas' statement, "'The I, from head to foot and to the bone marrow, is vulnerability.'")(footnote omitted).

129 *See* Jacqueline Fox, *Book Review: Caring and the Law, Jonathan Herring*, 35 J. Legal Med. 337, 338 (2014) (reviewing Jonathan Herring, Caring and the Law (2013)) ("In its earliest stages of development, the ethics of care was referred to as feminist ethics."). *See* Carrie Menkel-Meadow, *What's Gender Got to Do with It? The Politics and Morality of an Ethic of Care*, 22 N.Y.U. Rev. L. & Soc. Change 265, 293 (1996) (critiquing Tronto's view of the ethic of care because of its origin in the work of male philosophers).

130 *See, e.g.*, Jonathan Herring, Caring and the Law 47 (2013) ("It is widely agreed that contemporary understandings of an ethic of care arise from the work of Carol Gilligan . . . .").

131 *See* Jonathan Herring, Caring and the Law 47 n.7 (2013) (citing Carol Gilligan, In a Different Voice: Psychological Theory and Women's Development (1982)); Vicki Lachman, *Applying the Ethics of Care to Your Nursing Practice*, 21 Ethics, L. & Pol'y 112 (2012) ("Gilligan was the first to move moral theorizing from a position where selves were seen as independent to a position where selves are interconnected and interdependent.").

132 *See, e.g.*, Robin West, Caring for Justice 34 (1997) (explaining the Kohlbergian ideal as one that privileged "principled, deductive, or simply reasoned moral decision-making," characteristic of the "moral maturity" and superiority he attributed to men).

133 Jacqueline Fox, *Book Review: Caring and the Law, Jonathan Herring*, 35 J. Legal Med. 337, 338 (2014) (reviewing Jonathan Herring, Caring and the Law (2013)) (noting the several contributions of feminist scholars to contemporary ethic of care discourse in an effort to repudiate "the academic assertion that women were incapable of developing the highly functioning morality of men."); *see* Jonathan Herring, Caring and the Law 47 (2013).

Gilligan has suggested, instead, that women approach ethical questions differently—that they, in determining what is right, seek answers that stem from the relational aspect of the issue rather than from abstract moral principles.[134] Gilligan bolsters her thesis with empirical evidence gathered from a study she conducted on men and women's moral reasoning. She has

> found that women are more likely to consider others, to consider the people in the problem in relation to each other, and to seek solutions that minimize pain to all, rather than to find universal principles that reflexively determine an issue.[135]

For Gilligan, ethics center on caring and compassion for others.

According to the ethicist Maria Drakopoulou, Gilligan's most important contribution is that it offers a new vision—one that features the "primacy of human connectedness . . . [embedded in a society] where emotions, peaceful co-operation, empathy, friendship and responsibility are aspired to rather than universal, abstract, rational principles (autonomy, freedom, justice, equality and rights)."[136] Gilligan and her colleagues in the feminist ethic of care enterprise[137] are responsible for positioning "the act of caring for others" such that it has "a virtue of its own."[138]

Other ethic of care proponents have appealed for broader parameters for the ethic of care.[139] Joan Tronto urges feminists to rethink their positions regarding a gendered perspective on care.[140] To support her position, Tronto draws upon the work of Scottish Enlightenment philosophers, who, as we have discussed, maintain that human connectedness is not the sole province of women. "According to Scottish Enlightenment thinkers, eighteenth century men exhibited the senses of connection, moral sensibility, attachment to others and to community that are often attributed to women."[141] Tronto posits that care is a "universal, moral imperative,"[142] one that engages both genders.

134 *See* Jonathan Herring, Caring and the Law 47 (2013).
135 Carrie Menkel-Meadow, *Portia Redux: Another Look at Gender, Feminism, and Legal Ethics*, 2 Va. J. Soc. Pol'y & L. 75, 78 (1994).
136 Jonathan Herring, Caring and the Law 48 (2013).
137 *See, e.g.*, Annette Baier, *Caring About Caring: A Reply to Frankfurt*, 53 Synthese 273 (1982); Carrie Menkel-Meadow, *What's Gender Got to Do with It? The Politics and Morality of an Ethic of Care*, 22 N.Y.U. Rev. L. & Soc. Change 265 (1996); Nel Noddings, Caring: A Feminine Approach to Ethics and Moral Education (1984); Sara Ruddick, Maternal Thinking: Toward a Politics of Peace (1989).
138 Jacqueline Fox, *Book Review: Caring and the Law, Jonathan Herring*, 35 J. Legal Med. 337, 338 (2014) (reviewing Jonathan Herring, Caring and the Law (2013)).
139 *See* Jonathan Herring, Caring and the Law 49 (2013).
140 *See* Joan Tronto, Moral Boundaries: A Political Argument for an Ethic of Care (1994); Carrie Menkel-Meadow, *What's Gender Got to Do with It? The Politics and Morality of an Ethic of Care*, 22 N.Y.U. Rev. L. & Soc. Change 265 (1996).
141 Joan Tronto, Moral Boundaries: A Political Argument for an Ethic of Care 57 (1994).
142 Carrie Menkel-Meadow, *What's Gender Got to Do with It? The Politics and Morality of an Ethic of Care*, 22 N.Y.U. Rev. L. & Soc. Change 265, 267 (1996).

Tronto also maintains that ethicality must extend beyond the individual person to the society at large to enable political and social systems to operationalize caring on a larger scale. She explains "that if we focus on caring relationships and the relationships between power and caring practices, such as bringing up children and caring for the sick, a radically different set of social arrangements will ensue."[143] Carrie Menkel-Meadow critiques Tronto's perspective for its attribution of caring to male philosophers and for its dismissal of empirical evidence of women's prominence in providing care.[144] Menkel-Meadow does credit Tronto with raising important questions about the ethic of care, including its origins and the extent to which women engage in its practice, and allows that, once they are resolved, it "can emerge as a fully humanist and political philosophy."[145] Menkel-Meadow concludes that in "locat[ing] [her] argument in feminist theory, Tronto inevitably reconnects an ethic of care to women's experiences and the theories of feminist philosophers and strategists."[146] Even Carol Gilligan, however, despite her feminist perspective, claims that

> the contrasts between male and female voices [which she uses to define the ethic of care] are presented . . . to highlight a distinction between two modes of thought and to focus a problem of interpretation rather than to represent a generalization about either sex.[147]

While Tronto does not completely disconnect from the feminists, she contributes to propelling the movement to disentangle care ethics from feminist rhetoric. By acknowledging the contributions of other philosophers to the ethic of care discourse—those espoused in Aristotle's virtue ethics as well as the views expressed by Scottish Enlightenment philosophers—Tronto contributes to the more universal perspectives on the ethic of care.

Although Gilligan and Tronto may diverge on the gender-specific nature[148] and the personal versus global scope of caregiving, one scholar suggests that both distinguish obligation-based ethics from responsibility-based ethics, with the former grounded upon universal principles and duties and the latter on relationships, as

143 Vicki Lachman, *Applying the Ethics of Care to Your Nursing Practice*, 21 ETHICS, L. & POL'Y 112 (2012).

144 Carrie Menkel-Meadow, *What's Gender Got to Do with It? The Politics and Morality of an Ethic of Care*, 22 N.Y.U. REV. L. & SOC. CHANGE 265, 293 (1996).

145 Carrie Menkel-Meadow, *What's Gender Got to Do with It? The Politics and Morality of an Ethic of Care*, 22 N.Y.U. REV. L. & SOC. CHANGE 265, 267 (1996).

146 Carrie Menkel-Meadow, *What's Gender Got to Do with It? The Politics and Morality of an Ethic of Care*, 22 N.Y.U. REV. L. & SOC. CHANGE 265, 269 (1996).

147 CAROL GILLIGAN, IN A DIFFERENT VOICE: PSYCHOLOGICAL THEORY AND WOMEN'S DEVELOPMENT 2 (1982).

148 *But see* Stephen Ellmann, *The Ethic of Care as an Ethic for Lawyers*, 81 GEO. L.J. 2665, 2665–67 (1992) (suggesting that Gilligan herself acknowledges "that the ethic of care is also characteristic of at least some men. As she presents it, the ethic of care is a form of moral reasoning that should play a part in the moral understanding of every mature person . . . [and] in the moral understanding of every lawyer.").

embraced by ethic of care theorists.[149] Nel Noddings integrates obligation within a caring construct in suggesting that "[t]he source of my obligation is the value I place on the relatedness of caring."[150] Caring in Noddings's view is partly natural inclination—an "internal sense of feeling, which nature has made universal in the whole species . . . ."[151] It is fixed in "[t]his memory of our own best moments of caring and being cared for . . . ."[152] When faced with an obligation, Noddings claims that the motivation to respond with care derives from "the more fundamental and natural desire to be and to remain related."[153] It is at this juncture that caring, based upon human need and relatedness as an alternative to abstract notions of right and wrong, mobilizes.

Virginia Held later joined Tronto's gender-inclusive perspective of caring[154] and succeeded Tronto in ushering in a twenty-first century vision. Like Tronto, Held conceived of care ethics in a more universal context, pertaining to individuals both male and female, political entities, and the global world. Held proposed a comprehensive theory that supplanted feminist approaches and made a more successful case than Tronto for freeing the ethic of care from gender, paving the way for broader interpretations.

In the vein of Tronto and Held's global intentions for the ethic of care, the notion of caring as an ethical act has prompted those who provide care in distinctly professional contexts to contribute to ethic of care scholarship. The narrative medicine movement, about which we write in more detail in Chapter 4, has incorporated principles and practices from the ethic of care canon into healthcare practice. The physician Rita Charon has offered much to this enterprise, in addition to nurses who have written on the topic.[155] As one scholar points out, the demographic shift in

149 Vicki Lachman, *Applying the Ethics of Care to Your Nursing Practice*, 21 ETHICS, L. & POL'Y 112 (2012).

150 Nel Noddings, *An Ethic of Caring, in* ETHICAL THEORY: AN ANTHOLOGY 699, 701 (Russ Shafer-Landau ed., 2d ed. 2013).

151 Nel Noddings, *An Ethic of Caring, in* ETHICAL THEORY: AN ANTHOLOGY 699, 701 (Russ Shafer-Landau ed., 2d ed. 2013)

152 Nel Noddings, *An Ethic of Caring, in* ETHICAL THEORY: AN ANTHOLOGY 699 (Russ Shafer-Landau ed., 2d ed. 2013). *See also* M. L. STEDMAN, THE LIGHT BETWEEN OCEANS 78 (2012), for a more poetic interpretation of how memory influences caring. Stedman writes, "In the shed, he looked at the pieces of the rocking chair he was planning to make for Isabel. He had tried to remember the one on which his own mother had rocked him and told him stories. His body remembered the sensation of being held by her . . . ." *Id.*

153 Nel Noddings, *An Ethic of Caring, in* ETHICAL THEORY: AN ANTHOLOGY 699, 701 (Russ Shafer-Landau ed., 2d ed. 2013).

154 VIRGINIA HELD, THE ETHICS OF CARE 29 (2006).

155 *See especially* Jacqueline Fox, *Book Review: Caring and the Law, Jonathan Herring*, 35 J. LEGAL MED. 337, 338 (2014) (reviewing JONATHAN HERRING, CARING AND THE LAW (2013)). Nurses and philosophers have written much of the scholarship in this area. Joan McCarthy, *Principlism or Narrative Ethics: Must We Choose Between Them?*, 29 MED. HUMAN. 65 (2003), *available at* http://mh.bmj.com/content/29/2/65.full (describing, as a nurse, a case compelling a bio-ethical resolution and advocating for an outcome that comprehends the application of both general ethical norms (principles) and narrative ethics (contextual features) to achieve an ethical outcome); Vicki Lachman, *Applying the Ethics of Care to Your*

healthcare workers beginning in the 1970s itself has yielded a different view about gendered roles in caring for the sick. Since that time, more women have begun working as doctors, while the cohort of males employed as nurses also has increased in number. "In short, men, as well as women, care for others, and no single gender owns the right to, or the burden of, care."[156] This break with traditional views of caregivers in healthcare settings contributes to a less gendered, more collective responsibility to render care in line with Tronto's and Held's aspirations. Ruth O'Brien has suggested that the notion of women as the sole arbiters of the moral reasoning attendant to the ethic of care[157] has given way to a more inclusive agenda, in that "most studies exploring a care ethic had moved away from the sex/gender debate . . . ."[158] The gender issue with respect to caring largely has disappeared.

The ethic of care and the law

The ethic of care has made its way into legal scholarship.[159] It also has influenced an overall approach to thinking about law in the abstract and more specifically to applications that are evident in the realms of law reform, legal advocacy, and jurisprudence.[160] "Legal regulations and the messages from them force or nudge people in various ways. They provide generalised guidance as to how people arrange their interactions. Court cases are but a small part of how the law operates. Law can therefore be used powerfully to encourage people to act in a way which will promote caring relationships."[161]

Similar to ethic of care theory, ethic of care applications to law have advanced over time. Judith Areen has opined several decades ago that we have yet to fashion the philosophy of caring.[162] Since then, conceptions of the ethic of care are by and large a matter of perspective and degree.

Carol Gilligan is the likely progenitor of the movement to incorporate the ethic of care into the legal arena, despite the fact that she does not address legal implications specifically. Her theory of female difference has influenced a host of

Nursing Practice, 21 Ethics, L. & Pol'y 112 (2012) (discussing "care ethics to help nurses determine if they are applying this theory effectively in their practice.").

156 Jacqueline Fox, *Book Review: Caring and the Law, Jonathan Herring*, 35 J. Legal Med. 337, 338 (2014) (reviewing Jonathan Herring, Caring and the Law (2013)).

157 Ruth O'Brien, Bodies in Revolt: Gender, Disability, and a Workplace Ethic of Care 60 (2005).

158 Ruth O'Brien, Bodies in Revolt: Gender, Disability, and a Workplace Ethic of Care 60 (2005).

159 *Care Ethics*, Internet Encyclopedia of Philosophy, http://www.iep.utm.edu/care-eth/, (last visited Oct. 12, 2017); *see also* Stephen Ellmann, *The Ethic of Care as an Ethic for Lawyers*, 81 Geo. L.J. 2665, 2667 (1993); Jonathan Herring, *Compassion, Ethics of Care and Legal Rights*, 13 Int'l J. of L. in Context 158, 158 (2017).

160 *Care Ethics*, Internet Encyclopedia of Philosophy, http://www.iep.utm.edu/care-eth/, (last visited Oct. 12, 2017); *see also* Stephen Ellmann, *The Ethic of Care as an Ethic for Lawyers*, 81 Geo. L.J. 2665, 2719–22 (1993).

161 Jonathan Herring, Caring and the Law 85 (2013).

162 *See* Judith Areen, *A Need for Caring*, 86 Mich. L. Rev. 1067, 1076 (1988) (noting that "the philosophic analysis of caring is in its early stages").

followers inclined to use it "to transform law . . . ."[163] Leslie Bender has said of Gilligan's contributions to furthering justice: "I believe an ethic of care derived from women's cultures is a unique way to solve problems, work with people, locate truths, and foster justice that has been absent from our law."[164] Bender speculates that an ethic of care has the ability to usher in a new legal regime.[165] "Caregiving, cooperation and an orientation toward interpersonal responsibility can be socially and legally promoted as easily as economic efficiency, competitive hierarchies, and self-interest have been."[166]

As Gilligan's influence coalesced, it inspired law professors like Leslie Bender and others to consider how Gilligan's conclusions about the inconsistencies between men and women's moral reasoning figured in their approach to lawyering.[167] After publication of Gilligan's *In A Different Voice*, "legal scholars were quick to apply an ethic of care to the widely disparate disciplines of civil procedure, contract law, constitutional law, and judicial behavior."[168] Carrie Menkel-Meadow explored "how gender differences might affect the ways in which lawyers performed their tasks, structured their work, made ethical decisions, and interpreted and enforced the law."[169] The article led her and similarly inclined colleagues[170] to endorse the concept that women were prone to analyze legal issues with a "care perspective,"[171] focused on people, in contrast to the way in which men applied universal principles to achieve a just outcome.

Menkel-Meadow may have launched the most prominent conversation about the ethic of care and law. Her ongoing work in exploring the ethic of care has evolved from an essentialist view (that the care ethic is exclusive to women) to a

163 Leslie Bender, *From Gender Difference to Feminist Solidarity: Using Carol Gilligan and an Ethic of Care in Law*, 15 VT. L. REV. 1, 3 (1990).

164 Leslie Bender, *From Gender Difference to Feminist Solidarity: Using Carol Gilligan and an Ethic of Care in Law*, 15 VT. L. REV. 1, 45 (1990).

165 Leslie Bender, *From Gender Difference to Feminist Solidarity: Using Carol Gilligan and an Ethic of Care in Law*, 15 VT. L. REV. 1, 48 (1990).

166 Leslie Bender, *From Gender Difference to Feminist Solidarity: Using Carol Gilligan and an Ethic of Care in Law*, 15 VT. L. REV. 1, 42 (1990).

167 *But see* Judith Areen, *A Need for Caring*, 86 MICH. L. REV. 1067, 1073 n.25 (1988) (explaining that "critics have complained that Gilligan's data do not support the assertion that caring is biologically determined" and "Gilligan has answered that her intent was to highlight different modes of thought rather than to generalize about either sex.").

168 Carrie Menkel-Meadow, *What's Gender Got to Do with It? The Politics and Morality of an Ethic of Care*, 22 N.Y.U. REV. L. & SOC. CHANGE 265, 291–92 (1996).

169 Carrie Menkel-Meadow, *Portia Redux: Another Look at Gender, Feminism, and Legal Ethics*, 2 VA. J. SOC. POL'Y & L. 75 (1994).

170 *See* Carrie Menkel-Meadow, *Portia Redux: Another Look at Gender, Feminism, and Legal Ethics*, 2 VA. J. SOC. POL'Y & L. 75, 76 n.8 (1994) (citing colleagues who have engaged in a similar discourse on the relationship between law and caring).

171 *See* Carrie Menkel-Meadow, *Portia Redux: Another Look at Gender, Feminism, and Legal Ethics*, 2 VA. J. SOC. POL'Y & L. 75, 76 n.8 (1994) (citing Judith Areen's article, *A Need for Caring*, 86 MICH. L. REV. 1067 (1988), which "highlight[s] the use of the parent-child relationship as the paradigm for a new approach to moral issues based on Gilligan's work establishing a 'care perspective.'").

more generalized perspective—that care is an attribute common to both sexes. Evidence of her thinking has spanned the last decade of the twentieth century to nearly two decades into the twenty-first. During this period, Menkel-Meadow has wrestled with the question of the primacy of gender in the ethic of care movement[172] and has incorporated her thinking about the reach of the ethic of care into the realm of law. Menkel-Meadow has proposed, "The significance of an ethic of care for law practice is itself a difficult and important question, which could be explored independent of its connection to gender."[173] She has pondered "whether law can be made a site of encouraging more positive, peace seeking, non-violent, and pro-social behaviors."[174] Menkel-Meadow reconciles the gender debate by claiming that both men and women can and should engage in a joint effort toward a jurisprudence of peace, which embodies the very essence of the ethic of care as evidenced in her words: "a sense of responsibility toward others to be cared for and to prevent harm."[175]

Robin West has joined the discussion on care ethics, locating her thoughts explicitly within a justice system framework. She argues that caring "should be central to the meaning of legal justice."[176] While West does not jettison feminist principles and their influence on the development of the ethic of care,[177] she takes a more integrated approach when applying a care ethic to the courts. She explains that the two competing views of justice—one involving universal rules (the male-oriented viewpoint) and the other contemplating a situational standpoint calling for caring (the feminist perspective)—can and should be joined, and that both men and women are capable of embracing them. She argues, "[j]udges should aim for justice, but if they hope to achieve it, then they must *also* aim for care. An uncaring decision will *for that very reason* be unjust."[178] Further, according to West, "[i]f the caring response *is* the moral response, then our public life and public decision-making should obviously be caring as well."[179]

172 *See, e.g.*, Carrie Menkel-Meadow, *What's Gender Got to Do with It? The Politics and Morality of an Ethic of Care*, 22 N.Y.U. Rev. L. & Soc. Change 265, 293 (1996) ("[W]e cannot strategically hide the influence of women in both the conceptualization and practice of care. I would prefer to acknowledge the important role of women, and men, where they have contributed to this enterprise . . . .").

173 Carrie Menkel-Meadow, *Portia Redux: Another Look at Gender, Feminism, and Legal Ethics*, 2 Va. J. Soc. Pol'y & L. 75, 77 (1994).

174 Carrie Menkel-Meadow, *Toward A Jurisprudence of Law, Peace, Justice, and a Tilt Toward Non-Violent and Empathic Means of Human Problem Solving*, 8 Unbound: Harv. J. Legal Left 79, 80 (2013).

175 Carrie Menkel-Meadow, *Toward A Jurisprudence of Law, Peace, Justice, and a Tilt Toward Non-Violent and Empathic Means of Human Problem Solving*, 8 Unbound: Harv. J. Legal Left 79, 108 (2013).

176 Robin West, Caring for Justice 9 (1997).

177 Robin West, Caring for Justice 20 (1997) (explaining that while the two views are equally defensible and applicable, "this universalizing ambition does not require us to ignore the genesis of the ethic [of care] in women's lives.").

178 Robin West, Caring for Justice 24 (1997).

179 Robin West, Caring for Justice 34–35 (1997).

In addition to jurisprudence, ethic of care ideology has prompted law reform and the interpretation of existing laws to remedy situations that call for care-informed justice. Ruth O'Brien has written about this phenomenon, specifically, the potential for the Americans With Disabilities Act (ADA) to promote caring in the workplace. O'Brien discusses how the ADA enables the accomplishment of work within a framework that anticipates individual needs stemming from physical limitations. She states emphatically that the ADA "is the first civil rights law that embodies an ethic of care."[180] She explains that such a model mirrors ethic of care philosophies signaling the strength in joining with other persons in a common endeavor of care and concern to maximize human potential on the job.[181] Joan Williams and Stephanie Bornstein write about opportunities to use employment discrimination law in cases of "discrimination against people based on their caregiving responsibilities—whether for children, elderly parents, or ill partners."[182] Barbara White applies an ethic of care to business law, where she suggests replacing the traditional cost-benefit analysis to an approach based on fairness and meeting needs.[183]

With regard to an ethic of care and its relationship to family law in particular, Milton Regan argues that marriage and parenthood both involve and rely on an ethic of care due to "the interdependence that characterizes a shared life."[184] For Regan, marriage is more than a social contract, and obligations arising from marriage continue beyond divorce, particularly where children are involved.

Jonathan Herring's foundational text, *Caring and the Law*, is the first exhaustive exploration of the ethic of care as it pertains to laws governing families, children, the aged, otherwise disabled members of society, and those who care for them. Herring notes ethic of care attributes, such as "trust, sympathy, empathy, [and] sensitivity"[185] as particularly appropriate to this area of the law, because these descriptive qualities lie at the heart of the ethic of care as a relational enterprise.[186] As hallmarks of caring relationships, these traits stand in stark contrast to the purely rational and largely conventional model for legal analysis that is characteristic of how the law treats issues related to caregiving and resolving family law disputes—generally without regard to caring.

180 Ruth O'Brien, Bodies in Revolt: Gender, Disability, and a Workplace Ethic of Care 58 (2005).

181 Ruth O'Brien, Bodies in Revolt: Gender, Disability, and a Workplace Ethic of Care 149 (2005) (citing Spinoza's theory of the maximizing potential of human interconnectedness: "If we are 'joined to one another, they compose an individual twice as powerful as each one.'").

182 Joan C. Williams & Stephanie Bornstein, *Caregivers in the Courtroom: The Growing Trend of Family Responsibilities Discrimination*, 41 U.S.F. L. Rev. 171, 171 (2006).

183 *See generally* Barbara Ann White, *Economic Efficiency and the Parameters of Fairness: A Marriage of Marketplace Morals and the Ethic of Care*, 15 Cornell J.L. & Pub. Pol'y 1 (2005); *see also* Barbara Ann White, *Feminist Foundations for the Law of Business: One Law and Economics Scholar's Survey and (Re)View*, 10 UCLA Women's L.J. 39 (1999).

184 Milton C. Regan, Jr., *Boundaries of Care: Constructing Community After Divorce*, 31 Hous. L. Rev. 425, 434 (1994).

185 Jonathan Herring, Caring and the Law 57 (2013).

186 Jonathan Herring, Caring and the Law 59 (2013).

Herring "contends that the law does not properly recognize the importance of caring."[187] His project is to imbue family law with such sentiment. He claims that without "caring practices" embedded in family law jurisprudence, there is no possibility of ensuring liberty and equality for parents, children, the elderly and infirm, and those who provide them with assistance. Herring's position is that laws and legal decision-making must reorient to address the realities of care and family life in the twenty-first century. His thesis supports our assertion that the family justice system must be a co-participant with other civic structures in such an undertaking. Without such involvement by the family justice system, the ultimate end of valuing care and ensuring that it is part of the social contract is likely to fail.

Although not a lawyer herself, Joan Tronto's views on the intersection between political structures and the ethic of care have implications for the justice system. Tronto posits that embracing care as a political issue makes large-scale reforms possible,[188] which certainly can extend to the manner in which courts operate. While Tronto never explicitly mentions the impact of an ethic of care on law, she frequently refers to social justice, which is within the province of the justice system. Because legal proceedings, especially those that pertain to family law, address human needs, meeting those needs requires implementing ethic of care principles and practices.

In recent years, there has been a more wholesale acceptance of the notion that caring and the law are linked inextricably. Former president of the American Bar Association Karen Mathis has urged lawyers, "Caring is as much a part of the legal profession as intelligence . . . . [I]t is *every* lawyer's responsibility in *every* setting to serve others."[189] Kevin Worthen, former Dean of the J. Reuben Clark Law School at Brigham Young University, also envisions law as a caring enterprise. Worthen suggests that owing to the "complex nature of law in our society, people are required to trust lawyers with their hopes, their dreams, their fortunes, their rights, and sometimes even their lives."[190] As a consequence of safeguarding "those precious commodities," Worthen believes it is incumbent upon lawyers to "learn to really care enough about the human condition."[191] Likewise, a practicing lawyer

187 Jacqueline Fox, *Book Review: Caring and the Law, Jonathan Herring*, 35 J. Legal Med. 337 (2014) (reviewing Jonathan Herring, Caring and the Law (2013)).

188 Carrie Menkel-Meadow, *What's Gender Got to Do with It? The Politics and Morality of an Ethic of Care*, 22 N.Y.U. Rev. L. & Soc. Change 265, 284 (1996) ("[F]or Tronto, making care a central concern of political theory, as well as practical politics, and not just a question of private morality, offers the possibility of effecting greater social and political change . . . .").

189 Kristin B. Gerdy, *The Heart of Lawyering: Clients, Empathy, and Compassion, in* Life in the Law: Religious Conviction 189 (Jane H. Wise, Scott W. Cameron, & Galen L. Fletcher eds., 2013), *available at* http://digitalcommons.law.byu.edu/life_law_vol3/24.

190 Kristin B. Gerdy, *The Heart of Lawyering: Clients, Empathy, and Compassion, in* Life in the Law: Religious Conviction 196 (Jane H. Wise, Scott W. Cameron, & Galen L. Fletcher eds., 2013), *available at* http://digitalcommons.law.byu.edu/life_law_vol3/24.

191 Kristin B. Gerdy, *The Heart of Lawyering: Clients, Empathy, and Compassion, in* Life in the Law: Religious Conviction 196 (Jane H. Wise, Scott W. Cameron, & Galen L. Fletcher eds., 2013), *available at* http://digitalcommons.law.byu.edu/life_law_vol3/24.

has noted that "the quality that elevates us from being a great lawyer and moves us into the next level is *simply caring*."[192]

Stephen Ellmann also considers the lawyer's relationship to an ethic of care. He asks,

> For whom should the caring lawyer care? One answer to this question might be that the caring lawyer—that is, the lawyer for whom considerations of care are central to moral judgment—should care for everyone involved in the situation.[193]

Ellmann admits that the caring lawyer need not care for all people equally,[194] and he concludes that lawyering with an ethic of care coincides with existing codes of professional conduct.[195] For Ellmann, "the ethic of care . . . enriches lawyer-client relations."[196]

The ethic of care versus the ethic of justice

In discussing the ethic of care, we must address the tension between what appear as two conflicting moral philosophies[197]—the ethic of care on the one hand and the ethic of justice on the other. While we are not attempting to replace an ethic of justice with an ethic of care,

> [a] series of questions can be raised about the central concepts of justice and care: Are they compatible? Are they alternative and incompatible . . . , and if so, how can we decide which should guide us? . . . . Should care supplement justice, or justice supplement care—is one or the other more fundamental?[198]

Following upon our discussion of the various definitions of care and the ethic of care, we now offer a brief description of justice as a moral-ethical precept. "Justice,

192 Kristin B. Gerdy, *The Heart of Lawyering: Clients, Empathy, and Compassion*, *in* LIFE IN THE LAW: RELIGIOUS CONVICTION 197 (Jane H. Wise, Scott W. Cameron, & Galen L. Fletcher eds., 2013) (citing Robert F. Blomquist, *Ten Vital Virtues for American Public Lawyers*, 39 IND. L. REV. 493, 508 (2006)), *available at* http://digitalcommons.law.byu.edu/life_law_vol3/24.

193 Stephen Ellmann, *The Ethic of Care as an Ethic for Lawyers*, 81 GEO. L.J. 2665, 2679 (1993).

194 Stephen Ellmann, *The Ethic of Care as an Ethic for Lawyers*, 81 GEO. L.J. 2665, 2680 (1993).

195 Stephen Ellmann, *The Ethic of Care as an Ethic for Lawyers*, 81 GEO. L.J. 2665, 2709 (1993).

196 Stephen Ellmann, *The Ethic of Care as an Ethic for Lawyers*, 81 GEO. L.J. 2665, 2711 (1993).

197 *See* Cheshire Calhoun, *Justice, Care, and Gender Bias*, *in* ETHICAL THEORY: AN ANTHOLOGY 713 (Russ Shafer-Landau ed., 2d ed. 2013), for an explanation of Carol Gilligan's perspective. Calhoun states, "[t]he ethics of justice, on her [Gilligan's] view, excludes some dimensions of moral experience, such as contextual decision-making, special obligations, the moral motives of compassion and sympathy . . . ." *Id.*

198 *Introduction*, *in* JUSTICE AND CARE 2 (Virginia Held ed., 1995).

at the most general level, is a matter of giving people their due, of treating them appropriately."[199] There is common ground between the ethic of care and the ethic of justice.[200] While we find that definitions of care and the ethic of care are somewhat comparable among scholars, definitions of justice are many and varied, depending upon the outlook of those who have described its attributes. Aristotle's vision of justice, put simply, is that it is a component of virtue or goodness—"a halfway point between the two extremes of excess and deficiency."[201] This concept, known as the "Golden Mean,"[202] evokes a vision of the scales of justice—so often emblematic of how judges reach a decision[203]—and is relevant to a discussion of justice as an ethical ideal in law. As a counterpoint to Aristotle, Emmanuel Kant defines justice as a set of abstract principles, "capable of being universal laws" that "create 'categorical imperatives'" for human behavior.[204]

According to Daniel Engster,

> [t]here would be no individual liberty or equality, community values or good life without the caring practices necessary to sustain and foster human life and society. As such, the aims and virtues of caring may be said to precede and underlie all theories of justice.[205]

Thus, "the concepts of care and justice are mutually compatible. People who treat each other justly can also care about each other."[206] Further, "[w]here care is perhaps most prominent—within the family and in the contexts of health and welfare—justice is surely needed as well."[207] Carol Gilligan describes the importance of and relationship between justice and care.

> The experiences of inequality and interconnection, inherent in the relation of parent and child, then give rise to the ethics of justice and care, the ideals of human relationship—the vision that self and other will be treated as of equal worth, that despite differences in power, things will be fair; the vision

199 Marilyn Friedman, *The De-Moralization of* Gender, *in* Justice and Care 66 (Virginia Held ed., 1995).

200 *See, e.g.*, Cheshire Calhoun, *Justice, Care, and Gender Bias, in* Ethical Theory: An Anthology 713 (Russ Shafer-Landau ed., 2d ed. 2013) (proposing that some have argued "there is no incompatibility between the two . . . . Correctly applying moral rules and principles, for instance, requires rather than excludes knowledge of contextual details [which are among the hallmarks of care ethics].").

201 Raymond Wacks, Justice 13 (2017).

202 Raymond Wacks, Justice 13 (2017).

203 *See, e.g.*, Robin West, Caring for Justice 29 (1997) ("[T]he scales of balance . . . [are] perhaps the image we most often associate with legal justice . . . .").

204 Raymond Wacks, Justice 190 (2017).

205 Daniel Engster, The Heart of Justice 5 (Oxford U. Press 2007).

206 Marilyn Friedman, *The De-Moralization of* Gender, *in* Justice and Care 66 (Virginia Held ed., 1995).

207 *Introduction, in* Justice and Care 1–2 (Virginia Held ed., 1995).

> that everyone will be responded to and included, that no one will be left alone or hurt.[208]

"[J]ustice is needed to frame caring relationships and . . . care for others is the value implicit in impartiality."[209] In short, "care theory defines the heart of justice."[210]

For some, however, justice and care seem incompatible.

> Justice thinking often prides itself on being objective precisely insofar as it distances itself from the self and particular relationships and dismisses care thinking as subjective and therefore unreliable precisely because successful caring by definition involves particular relations between carers and those cared-for.[211]

More contemporary visions of justice become apparent, as we have noted, with the advent of feminist thinkers. For advocates promoting a more humanistic ideal for attaining fair results, justice is a correlative of care.[212] Feminist scholars suggest that justice occurs by taking into account individual circumstances—the human component. Carol Gilligan believes that this requires a change in orientation. "Rather than seeking to establish whose rights take precedence in a contest of rights, the question becomes how to act in a network of mutuality where what affects one directly affects all indirectly."[213] Further, "[a]ttention is devoted to the context of disputes, not the principles for which they stand. And the judicial ideal is captured by the judge who works carefully—and caringly . . . ."[214] Yet, for Gilligan, there is a difference between the two. "While an ethic of justice proceeds from the premise of equality—that everyone should be treated the same—an ethic of care rests on the premise of nonviolence—that no one should be hurt."[215]

Political theorists also have advanced the position that justice and care are not inconsistent principles. Joan Tronto delineates three distinctions between the two. She describes care as concerned with "responsibility and relationships rather than rights and rules"[216] of the justice perspective. She finds that care is "tied to

208 Carol Gilligan, In a Different Voice: Psychological Theory and Women's Development 62–63 (1982).

209 Alison M. Jaggar, *Caring as a Feminist Practice of Moral Reason, in* Justice and Care 184 (Virginia Held ed., 1995).

210 Daniel Engster, The Heart of Justice 5 (Oxford U. Press 2007).

211 Alison M. Jaggar, *Caring as a Feminist Practice of Moral Reason, in* Justice and Care 191 (Virginia Held ed., 1995).

212 *See, e.g.*, Annette Baier, *The Need for More Than Justice*, *in* Ethical Theory: An Anthology 721, 721 (Russ Shafer-Landau ed., 2d ed. 2013) (explaining that theories of justice evolved as feminists approached the concept in light of "an enlarged moral vocabulary, which draws on what Gilligan calls the ethics of *care* as well as that of *justice*").

213 Carol Gilligan, *Revisiting "In a Different Voice,"* 39 Harbinger 19, 25 (2015).

214 Robin West, Caring for Justice 205 (1997).

215 Carol Gilligan, In a Different Voice: Psychological Theory and Women's Development 174 (1982).

216 Joan Tronto, Moral Boundaries: A Political Argument for an Ethic of Care 79 (1994).

concrete circumstances rather than being formal and abstract."[217] Finally, care "is best expressed not as a set of principles but as an activity, the 'activity of care.'"[218] Tronto proposes that while the ethic of justice and the ethic of care are described differently, there is some compatibility. Tronto acknowledges that "an ethic of care necessarily rests on a different set of premises about what a good moral theory is."[219] Tronto argues, however, that they are not irreconcilable, asserting that to distinguish care from justice creates a false dichotomy. She contends that justice and care are intertwined:

> The separation of care and justice grows out of using the old moral boundaries as a starting point for describing moral life. But with a different sense of the relationship of how humans are interdependent, how human practices inform human rationality, and therefore how human activity can change what we accept as rational, the relationship between justice and care can be a relationship of compatibility rather than hostility.[220]

"Another possible way of trying to reconcile justice and care is to think of justice as setting moral minimums . . . , whereas care deals with questions of the good life or of human value over and above the obligatory minimums of justice."[221] For Jonathan Herring,

> [c]are is the most primary value as it is essential to meet people's most basic survival needs, without that talk of justice would be meaningless. We need to support and enable care, so that justice can be considered. To be blunt we could survive in a society which was not just, but we could not survive in a society in which there was no care.[222]

For Nel Noddings, justice derives from "caring about," or "caring about people who are at a distance from us in terms of social status, culture, physical distance, or time—that is, the future."[223] In other words,

> [w]hen we cannot care directly *for* others but wish that we could—when, that is, we sincerely care about the well-being of others—we rely on principles of justice that approximate . . . the actions we would perform if we could . . . .[224]

217 Joan Tronto, Moral Boundaries: A Political Argument for an Ethic of Care 79 (1994).
218 Joan Tronto, Moral Boundaries: A Political Argument for an Ethic of Care 79 (1994).
219 Joan Tronto, Moral Boundaries: A Political Argument for an Ethic of Care 248 (1994).
220 Joan Tronto, Moral Boundaries: A Political Argument for an Ethic of Care 167 (1994).
221 *Introduction, in* Justice and Care 3 (Virginia Held ed., 1995).
222 Jonathan Herring, Caring and the Law 67 (2013) (footnote omitted).
223 Nel Noddings, Starting at Home: Caring and Social Policy 3 (2002).
224 Nel Noddings, Starting at Home: Caring and Social Policy 3 (2002) (emphasis added).

For Noddings, "caring about" links the concepts of care and justice, as "caring supplies the basic good in which the sense of justice is grounded."[225]

Virginia Held has considered whether it is possible to accommodate both the moralities of care and justice and has concluded that:

> As conceptions of how justice and care ought to be integrated become more developed, there may be possibilities for agreement on the priorities that ought to govern in different domains . . . . Choices need constantly to be made about whether to interpret various issues as primarily matters of justice and rights or primarily matters to be approached from the perspective of care.[226]

Held's position is particularly salient insofar as family justice is concerned. Because family law cases are not resolved entirely by applying legal rules, statutory guidance is, for the most part, incomplete in guiding family law decision-making. Family law litigants need help with a panoply of other nonlegal problems that require caring interventions.[227] Consequently, justice for families and children requires perspective taking, as Held remarks, in rendering what is a just result. "Within a justice construction, care becomes the mercy that tempers justice; or connotes the special obligations or . . . duties that arise in personal relationships . . . ."[228] Further, in family law cases, detachment, which "is considered the hallmark of mature moral thinking within a justice perspective,"[229] likely may work against judging from a care perspective. "From a care perspective, detachment *is* the moral problem."[230]

"[T]he 'justice perspective' might be said to rest, at bottom, on the assumption that the best way to *care* for persons is to respect their rights, and to accord them their due . . . ."[231] Yet "[b]oth orientations take account of relationships in some way; both may legitimately incorporate a concern for justice and for care, and both aim to avoid harm to others and . . . to the self."[232] We agree with Sarah Ruddick: "No matter how multifaceted the rendering of family justice, it will never constitute the whole of family morality. Within the framework I adopt, justice is always seen in tandem with care."[233]

225 Nel Noddings, Starting at Home: Caring and Social Policy 22 (2002).
226 Virginia Held, The Ethics of Care 146–47 (2006).
227 *See, e.g.*, Barbara A. Babb & Judith D. Moran, *Substance Abuse, Families, and Unified Family Courts: The Creation of a Caring Justice System*, 3 J. Health Care L. & Pol'y 125 (1999) (suggesting that family law cases involve legal and nonlegal problems, both of which deserve the court's attention).
228 Carol Gilligan, *Moral Orientation and Moral Development*, *in* Justice and Care 36 (Virginia Held ed., 1995).
229 Carol Gilligan, *Moral Orientation and Moral Development*, *in* Justice and Care 43 (Virginia Held ed., 1995).
230 Carol Gilligan, *Moral Orientation and Moral Development*, *in* Justice and Care 43 (Virginia Held ed., 1995).
231 Marilyn Friedman, *The De-Moralization of* Gender, *in* Justice and Care 71 (Virginia Held ed., 1995).
232 Marilyn Friedman, *The De-Moralization of* Gender, *in* Justice and Care 71 (Virginia Held ed., 1995).
233 Sara Ruddick, *Injustice in Families: Assault and Domination*, *in* Justice and Care 217 (Virginia Held ed., 1995).

Conclusion

When viewed through the lens of history, the ethic of care perspective has flourished in response to the compelling issues facing humankind. Carol Gilligan herself reflects on "[w]hat made the 'different voice' different:"[234]

> The difference arose from the integration of thought with emotions and self with relationships. It was a voice that spoke from a premise of connectedness rather than of separateness; our lives are embedded in a network of relationships, as humans we are interdependent. It's the understanding of the human condition that Martin Luther King articulates in his letter from the Birmingham jail: "We are caught in an inescapable network of mutuality, tied in a single garment of destiny. What affects one directly affects all indirectly.[235]

We confront many questions of how best to address the human problems that characterize our early twenty-first century world. We face dilemmas regarding our responsibilities toward the diaspora of migrants fleeing war torn countries,[236] poverty,[237] the environment,[238] healthcare,[239] the care of dependent children and adults,[240] and access to justice to remedy issues, many of which are distinctly related to care and caring.[241] The proliferation of the ethic of care approach to include "not only . . . the so-called private realms of family and friendship but [also] . . . medical practice, law, political life, the organization of society, war and

234 Carol Gilligan, *Revisiting "In a Different Voice,"* 39 Harbinger 19, 22 (2015).
235 Carol Gilligan, *Revisiting "In a Different Voice,"* 39 Harbinger 19, 22 (2015).
236 *See, e.g.*, Mihaela Czobor-Lupp, *Heidegger's Contribution to an Ethic of Care and Responsiveness* 2 (Paper Presented at the Annual Meeting of the American Political Association, Washington, D.C., Sept. 2–5, 2010) (proposing that care is "an essential category of ethics and politics" and as an approach, the ethic of care enables, "in a world of increasing displacements," a response to the need to "create a home for refugees").
237 *See, e.g.*, Salmon Masood, *At Least 150 Killed in Tanker Blast in Pakistan*, N.Y. Times, June 26, 2017, at A6 (reporting on what was characterized by a Pakastani parliamentary representative as attributable to "poverty 100%" because the spilled fuel was a source of a free "high value commodity" which could be put to domestic use or sold for profit); Justin Davidson, *Flames of Contempt*, N.Y. Mag., June 26–July 9, 2017, at 80 (commenting on the overwhelming need for government to fix the deplorable conditions in public housing projects, most recently brought to the public's attention by the Grenfell Tower fire in London).
238 Zach Wichter, *Too Hot to Fly? Climate Change May Take a Toll on Air Travel*,N. Y.Times (June 20, 2017), https://www.nytimes.com/2017/06/20/business/flying-climatechange.html?action=click&contentCollection=U.S.&module=RelatedCoverage&region=Marginalia&pgtype=article, (concluding that global climate change portends perils for air travelers).
239 Editorial, *The Health Care Hoax Exposed*, N.Y. Times, June 28, 2017, at A26 (explaining the results of the review of the most recent proposed healthcare legislation conducted by the Congressional Budget Office that indicate "the measure would leave 22 million more Americans without [health] insurance by 2026.").
240 *See, e.g.*, Jonathan Herring, Caring and the Law 13–25 (2013).
241 *See* Jonathan Herring, Caring and the Law 13–25 (2013).

international relations"[242] supports the notion that there is a pervasive need for the infusion of an ethic of care in multiple realms—from the personal to the political, from the home front to the community at large. In an essay commenting on what he considers America's fundamental values, "such as decency, reason and compassion,"[243] the physician and ethicist Atul Gawande suggests that care is a founding principle of our national enterprise. He asserts that "[t]o a large extent . . . institutions closer to home are what secure and sustain" these values, and "[t]his is the time to strengthen those institutions . . . ."[244] One can infer from Gawande's remarks a clarion call for innovative reforms to local government agencies. Among the institutions requiring such attention are the nation's family courts, where "decency, reason and compassion" are necessary elements of the caring justice our world requires. The ethic of care is at the vanguard of a movement to incorporate these ideals. As we discuss further in Chapter 4, one of the hallmarks of care ethics is that ethical questions are considered in light of narrative circumstances. We also suggest specific approaches to incorporate an ethic of care, grounded in narrative theory and practice, into the family justice system. The context of our world and the families and children who inhabit it compel caring now more than ever.

242 Virginia Held, The Ethicsof Care 9 (2006).

243 Atul Gawande, *Health of the Nation*, New Yorker (Nov. 21, 2016), https://www.newyorker.com/magazine/2016/11/21/aftermath-sixteen-writers-on-trumps-america#gawande.

244 Atul Gawande, *Health of the Nation*, New Yorker (Nov. 21, 2016), https://www.newyorker.com/magazine/2016/11/21/aftermath-sixteen-writers-on-trumps-america#gawande.

4 Family narratives and caring justice

Introduction

> Since we are temporal beings whose lives play out as series of events (mental and physical), we by definition unfold as stories . . . . We must thus grasp narrative for self-understanding, for understanding others, and for understanding how others view us and those depending on us.[1]
>
> Telling stories can move us to care . . . .[2]

Narrative theory and practice figure prominently in our prescription for family justice system reform because these endeavors are critical to the ethic of care needed for family courts to perform optimally. We have explained that the ethic of care is a context-driven calculation—one that presupposes a narrative foundation or underlying story upon which to base caring.[3] Thus, caring depends on narrative.[4] "[C]are ethics aims [sic] to meet the concrete needs of individuals in context-specific and responsive ways."[5] "The way people talk about their lives is of significance . . . the language they use and the connections they make reveal the world that they see and in which they act."[6] Because of the highly personal nature of family law—with so much of it focused on the law's attempt to meet the family's evident needs as revealed by the family's story—the perspectives of both the ethic of care and narrative are essential elements in our family justice system reform agenda. The family's narrative supplies the context that enables the court to determine an effective legal resolution fashioned with care.

1 Harold Anthony Lloyd, *Narrative in Law and Life: Some Frequently Asked Questions*, Second Draft, Fall 2015, at 1, *available at* http://ssrn.com/abstract=2609406.
2 Toni Massaro, *Empathy, Legal Storytelling, and the Rule of Law: New Words, Old Wounds?*, 87 Mich. L. Rev. 2099, 2105 (1989).
3 *See Care Ethics*, Internet Encyclopedia of Philosophy, http://www.iep.utm.edu/care-eth /, (last visited Oct. 12, 2017).
4 Virginia Held, The Ethics of Care 15 (2006) ("An ethic of care focuses on . . . narrative nuance, and cultivating caring relations.").
5 Daniel Engster, The Heart of Justice 2 (2007).
6 Carol Gilligan, In a Different Voice: Psychological Theory and Women's Development 2 (1982).

In this chapter, we elaborate on the role of narrative and how it relates to promoting an ethic of care perspective in the family justice system. Narrative practice and the ethic of care, itself a practice, are interdependent elements that must be part of family law jurisprudence and the overall work of family courts. Knowledge of a family's unique story enables a nuanced standpoint for decision-making that is both caring and just. Family courts owe families who seek their help a duty to honor the stories they "carry with them"[7] and to consider these narratives in fashioning outcomes. Justice needs to correspond to the best interests of the family based on the circumstances that each family presents to the court. While discourse frequently addresses narrative in relation to lawyering,[8] narrative also promotes a more therapeutic approach to family law decision-making; the court learns from the stories litigants tell so that it can extend to these litigants the *care* that is fundamental to resolve effectively their family law issues. Our view of narrative is distinct from that of other theorists,[9] as we propose incorporating active narrative practices[10] into family justice system structure, policies, and procedures. When a family court embraces the parallel principles associated with both narrative and the ethic of care, the family story becomes the context from which the court can fashion an ethical, caring, and legally appropriate solution to the family's problems.[11]

This chapter defines narrative, traces its history in law, explains the capacities it enables (the why of narrative), and describes its practices (the how of narrative).

Defining narrative

Steven Winter "has determined that narrative derives both from the Latin 'narrare,' to tell, and 'gnarus,' having knowledge or experience."[12] The terms

7 *See* Robert Coles, The Call of Stories: Teaching and the Moral Imagination 30 (1989) (quoting William Carlos Williams: "Their story, yours, mine—it's what we all carry with us on this trip we take, and we owe it to each other to respect our stories and learn from them.").

8 *See, e.g.*, Anthony G. Amsterdam & Jerome Bruner, Minding the Law (2000) (writing an account of their experience teaching lawyering skills using a narrative-based approach); Philip N. Meyer, Storytelling for Lawyers (2014) (describing the features of narrative and its application to lawyering).

9 *See, e.g.*, Binny Miller, *Telling Stories About Cases and Clients: The Ethics of Narrative*, 14 Geo. J. Legal Ethics 1, 2 (2000) (noting instances in which storytelling is used to advance critical race theory, feminist theory, and gay and lesbian theory); Anthony G. Amsterdam & Jerome Bruner, Minding the Law (2000) (examining the role of narrative in interpreting and practicing the law); Philip N. Meyer, Storytelling for Lawyers (2014) (exploring the use of narrative as a persuasive technique in legal advocacy).

10 *See, e.g.*, Rita Charon, Narrative Medicine: Honoring the Stories of Illness (2006).

11 *See* Joan McCarthy, *Principlism or Narrative Ethics: Must We Choose Between Them?*, 29 Med. Human. 65, 69 (2003), *available at* http://mh.bmj.com/content/29/2/65.full ("[narrative] provides a method and vocabulary for interpreting and respecting the unique and personal stories of individuals.").

12 Christine Metteer Lorillard, *Stories that Make the Law Free: Literature as a Bridge Between the Law and the Culture in Which It Must Exist*, 12 Tex. Wesleyan L. Rev.

"narrative" and "story," while distinct in a strictly literary sense,[13] "are sometimes used interchangeably,"[14] as we do in our discussion. Narrative is defined as "a telling of some true or fictitious event," consisting "of a set of events (the story) recounted in a process of narration (or discourse) in which the events are selected and arranged in a particular order (the plot)."[15] Others have said that "narratives are a construction"[16] of the "raw material of personal experience."[17] By contrast, a story is a creative form; it is a composition of what happened and involves sequencing "imagined events that we reconstruct from the actual arrangement of a narrative (or dramatic) plot."[18] The teller or narrator shapes stories from a set of occurrences. "The storyteller says, 'this is what really happened to me, and this is how it felt.'"[19]

The narrative medical scholar Rita Charon observes that "narrative knowledge enables one individual to understand particular events befalling another individual as a singular and meaningful situation."[20] As applied to law, narrative is a powerful perspective from which to consider and to understand a litigant's circumstances and the legal issues that stem from them.

The court process is enhanced when family court attorneys and judges seek stories from litigants and then factor the circumstances gleaned from them into strategies for advocacy and judicial decision-making. Because the stories reflect litigants' individual situations, a hallmark of family law jurisprudence, the court must consider the effects of its decisions on family life.[21] The family's narrative as presented to the court follows a trajectory. First, the family members themselves construct the story; then lawyers retell the story to gain an adversarial advantage; ultimately judges reconstruct it once more when they decide the case.[22]

251, 254 (2005) (citing to Steven L. Winter, *The Cognitive Power of the* Agon *Between Legal Power and Narrative Meaning*, 87 Mich L. Rev. 2225, 2230 (1980)).

13 Binny Miller, *Telling Stories About Cases and Clients: The Ethics of Narrative*, 14 Geo. J. Legal Ethics 1, 1 (2000) (distinguishing narrative from story and stating that "a story describes an account of a happening, while a narrative denotes a broader theme or meaning.").

14 Binny Miller, *Telling Stories About Cases and Clients: The Ethics of Narrative*, 14 Geo. J. Legal Ethics 1, 1 (2000).

15 Chris Baldick, Oxford Dictionary of Literary Terms 219 (2008).

16 Binny Miller, *Telling Stories About Cases and Clients: The Ethics of Narrative*, 14 Geo. J. Legal Ethics 1, 1 (2000) (citing Patricia Ewick & Susan Silbey, The Common Place of Law (1997)).

17 Binny Miller, *Telling Stories About Cases and Clients: The Ethics of Narrative*, 14 Geo. J. Legal Ethics 1, 1 (2000).

18 Chris Baldick, Oxford Dictionary of Literary Terms 317 (2008). For the purposes of this discussion the terms narrative and story will be used interchangeably.

19 Christine Metteer Lorillard, *Stories that Make the Law Free: Literature as a Bridge Between the Law and the Culture in Which It Must Exist,* 12 Tex. Wesleyan L. Rev. 251, 254 (2005).

20 Rita Charon, Narrative Medicine: Honoring the Stories of Illness 9 (2006).

21 *See* Family Law Stories (Carol Sanger ed., 2008) (chronicling the stories behind landmark family law cases).

22 Anthony G. Amsterdam & Jerome Bruner, Minding the Law 110 (2000) (charting the trajectory of legal storytelling).

Narrative accounts (and the stories they become) consist of several elements: plot, timeframe, setting, character, and point of view.[23] These features of narrative are the building blocks from which a story is created. The plot drives the story, while timeframe provides a temporal orientation to the events that make up the plot.[24] The characters in the context of family law storytelling are the family members and others involved in the legal matter. Point of view refers to how the litigants experience their situations (the setting). The sum of these components is fundamental to caring. Without narrative attention paid to court-involved families, including who they are (the characters), their situations (the plots, timeframes, and settings), and how they experience the events that propelled them into court (their points of view), caring is not possible. In the following section, we expand upon the connection between the family story and its capacity to enable caring in court—a concept central to our family justice system reform agenda.

Narrative law

Narrative law, by definition, uses the features of narrative both as a perspective on the law itself (how legal rules come into being)[25] and as a means to effective practice.[26] The late narrative legal scholar Jerome Bruner, commenting on the former aspect, has said that laws are constructs of cultural ways of being—an outgrowth of stories transmitted among members of a society, which, in turn, have prompted solutions to the problems they present. He uses by way of example the United States Supreme Court's decision in *Brown v. Board of Education*,[27] which demonstrates the evolution of the Court's jurisprudence from the separate but equal doctrine of *Plessy v. Ferguson* [28] to the *Brown* mandate for integration in public education. As Bruner notes, the stories of children who felt inferior because of their skin color influenced the *Brown* Court.[29] The stories told from these children's points of view convinced the Court that segregated schools contributed

23 *See* Judith D. Moran, *Families, Law, and Literature: The Story of a Course on Storytelling*, 49 U.S.F. L. Rev. 1, 4–5 (2015).

24 *See* Judith D. Moran, *Families, Law, and Literature: The Story of a Course on Storytelling*, 49 U.S.F. L. Rev. 1, 4 (2015).

25 *See generally* Oscar Chase, Law, Culture, and Ritual: Disputing Systemsin Cross-Cultural Context (2005); Jerome Bruner, Making Stories: Law, Literature, Life (2002); Arthur Graesser, Brent Olde, & Bianca Klettke, *How Does the Mind Construct and Represent Stories?, in* Narrative Impact: Social and Cognitive Foundations 229 (Melanie Green, Jeffrey Strange, & Timothy Brock eds., 2002) (explaining that the generational transmission of stories "reflect[s] the conflicts, solutions to problems [cultural practices/laws], humor, and values of a culture").

26 *See generally* Philip N. Meyer, Storytelling for Lawyers (2014) (applying the techniques of narrative to lawyering).

27 Brown v. Bd. of Educ., 347 U.S. 483 (1954).

28 Plessy v. Ferguson, 163 U.S. 537 (1896).

29 *See* Jerome Bruner, Making Stories: Law, Literature, Life 53–55 (2002) (commenting on the narrative impact of stories of segregation on the Supreme Court's decision-making).

to the children's negative self-image.[30] Other scholars have proposed that the power of storytelling to influence cultural mores lies in the ease with which listeners recall stories—stories are more memorable than mere factual recitations.[31] The influential power of stories, in this regard, is surely a factor in judicial decision-making.

Anthony Amsterdam and Jerome Bruner advance a rationale for applying narrative theory and practice to law in their foundational text, *Minding the Law*. They justify narrative law in this way: "Law lives on narrative"[32] because, among other reasons, "law is awash in storytelling."[33] They say that the nature of the lawyer-client relationship is such that clients tell their stories to lawyers, who then must construct a coherent and compelling account of what happened[34] in order to represent their clients effectively. That story then is related to judges and jurors, and the telling and retelling is at the heart of lawyering.[35] In the same vein, Philip Meyer explains, "Make no mistake about it—lawyers are storytellers."[36] In law, it follows that judges and jurors are the listeners. While the stories are part and parcel of a legal case, these personal accounts also enable the family justice system to operate with care.

Narrative practice

Narrative practice is a set of skills[37] that, when applied, support the caring function necessary for family justice system reform.[38] The narrative method incorporates a

30 *See* Toni Massaro, *Empathy, Legal Storytelling, and the Rule of Law: New Words, Old Wounds?*, 87 MICH. L. REV. 2099, 2100 (1989), for arguments supporting "individualized justice," citing Brown v. Board of Education as an example. "Cases like Brown v. Board of Education, it is argued, should be seen as a simple truth about the harm in segregation that any ten-year-old black child understands. Lawyers should argue this simple truth. Judges should respect it." *Id. See also Segregation Ruled Unequal, and Therefore Unconstitutional*, AM. PSYCHOL. ASS'N (May 28, 2003), http://www.apa.org/research/action/segregation.aspx (chronicling the study conducted by the psychologists Kenneth and Mamie Clark, demonstrating that segregated schools contributed to black children's negative self-image).

31 *See, e.g.*, Arthur Graesser, Brent Olde, & Bianca Klettke, *How Does the Mind Construct and Represent Stories?, in* NARRATIVE IMPACT: SOCIAL AND COGNITIVE FOUNDATIONS 229 (Melanie Green, Jeffrey Strange, & Timothy Brock eds., 2002) ("Narrative is the primary genre of oral discourse and it may be the easiest genre to remember," citing Arthur Graesser & Victor Ottati, *Why Stories? Some Evidence, Questions, and Challenges, in* KNOWLEDGE AND MEMORY: THE REAL STORY 121–32 (R.S. Wyer & T.K. Srull eds., 1996)).

32 ANTHONY G. AMSTERDAM & JEROME BRUNER, MINDING THE LAW 110 (2000).

33 ANTHONY G. AMSTERDAM & JEROME BRUNER, MINDING THE LAW 110 (2000).

34 ANTHONY G. AMSTERDAM & JEROME BRUNER, MINDING THE LAW 110 (2000).

35 ANTHONY G. AMSTERDAM & JEROME BRUNER, MINDING THE LAW 110 (2000).

36 PHILIP N. MEYER, STORYTELLING FOR LAWYERS 2 (2014).

37 *See, e.g.*, RITA CHARON, NARRATIVE MEDICINE: HONORING THE STORIES OF ILLNESS 186 (2006) (noting that narrative involves a sequence of practical aspects).

38 *See, e.g.*, VIRGINIA HELD, THE ETHICS OF CARE 10 (2006) (caring involves attention to "contextual nuance and particular narratives . . . ."); RITA CHARON, NARRATIVE MEDICINE: HONORING THE STORIES OF ILLNESS 186 (2006).

relational aspect, which, as we have explained, is a foundational principle of the ethic of care.[39] The skills that pertain to narrative practice are listening to[40] and acting on the stories[41] that are told to the prospective carer. These hallmarks of caring embody the ethic of care's relational quality. Rita Charon says these narratively focused activities "enable one person to receive and understand the stories told by another."[42]

The term narrative practice appears in literature devoted to narrative medicine, a discipline that teaches doctors, nurses, and allied healthcare workers how better to serve their patients.[43] The narrative medicine movement describes the enterprise in this way:

> The care of the sick unfolds in stories. The effective practice of healthcare requires the ability to recognize, absorb, interpret, and act on the stories and plights of others. Medicine practiced with narrative competence is a model for humane and effective medical practice . . . . [I]t acknowledges the power of narrative to change the way care is given and received.[44]

In law, scholars have coined the term relational lawyering,[45] which comprises aptitudes akin to those adopted by the healthcare professions.[46] Susan Brooks refers to these methods as "relational competencies, such as empathy, self-awareness, listening skills, and practical judgment."[47] Relational lawyering methods provide a means to ascertain the client's story and are an adjunct to narrative law in that respect. The required narrative features (plot, timeframe, setting, character, and point of view) become known through relational legal practice. The documentation that stories contribute to effective advocacy strategies and promote

39 *See* JONATHAN HERRING, CARING AND THE LAW 14 (2013) (proposing four markers of care: Meeting needs, Respect, Responsibility, Relationality).

40 *See, e.g.*, JONATHAN HERRING, CARING AND THE LAW 18 (2013) (discussing respect in the context of caring and emphasizing listening as an aspect of respect). *See also* RITA CHARON, NARRATIVE MEDICINE: HONORING THE STORIES OF ILLNESS 58 (2006) (discussing the importance of listening to the teller—the quest for the authentic story the teller has to tell, and good listeners are "instrument(s) of the speaker.").

41 *See, e.g.*, RITA CHARON, NARRATIVE MEDICINE: HONORING THE STORIES OF ILLNESS 55 (2006) (explaining that the "receiver of another's narrative" owes a duty to the teller, implicating that some sort of action is required).

42 RITA CHARON, NARRATIVE MEDICINE: HONORING THE STORIES OF ILLNESS 3 (2006).

43 JEROME BRUNER, MAKING STORIES: LAW, LITERATURE, LIFE 106 (2002) (citing the narrative medicine scholar and physician, Rita Charon, in describing narrative medicine practice).

44 *Narrative Medicine: Master of Science*, COLUMBIA U. SCH. PROF. STUD., http://sps.columbia.edu/narrative-medicine (last visited July 15, 2016).

45 *See* Susan L. Brooks, *Using a Communication Perspective to Teach Relational Lawyering*, 15 NEV. L.J. 477 (2015).

46 *See* Susan L. Brooks, *Using a Communication Perspective to Teach Relational Lawyering*, 15 NEV. L.J. 477 (2015).

47 Susan L. Brooks, *Using a Communication Perspective to Teach Relational Lawyering*, 15 NEV. L.J. 477, 478 (2015).

empathetic and ethical practice is so extensive that legal scholars have embraced Applied Legal Storytelling as a methodology to explore how to use narrative in legal advocacy.[48] Narrative law precepts are singularly important to promote the infusion of an ethic of care to family courts. [49]

Narrative and the law: An historical perspective

The narrative tradition emerged in early history.[50] "Stories were the primary way our ancestors transmitted knowledge and values."[51] Before there were written versions of events, there were oral recitations.[52]

Narrative scholars maintain that narrative "is the primary genre of oral discourse and the easiest genre to remember."[53] Jerome Bruner points to the fact that early rites of celebration included storytelling.[54] Further, he suggests that because young children are capable of relating narrative accounts, evidence of this primitive capacity for narration bolsters the claim that it existed in early man—"that if little kids understand story almost as soon as they grasp remoteness and arbitrariness and some primitive case grammar, maybe early *Homo sapiens* did?"[55] The tradition of storytelling persists in many cultures. Commentators on African culture have observed that nomadic tribes tell stories to one another as they wander the desert in search of food.[56] A single word, ***kataribe*** (storyteller), illustrates the storytelling tradition in Japan. The term refers to a category of survivors of Hiroshima and Nagasaki who "'came out' . . . about the atom bomb, reminding people of the

48 Steven Johansen, *Was Colonel Sanders a Terrorist? An Essay on the Ethical Limits of Applied Legal Storytelling*, 7 J. Ass'n Legal Writing Directors 63, 63 n.2 (2010) (explaining that "applied legal storytelling" came into being "as a way to distinguish the exploration of how narrative theory is integral to the practice of law from the broader traditions of law and literature.").

49 *See* Virginia Held, The Ethics of Care 10 (2006) (delineating the features of an ethic of care as a "mosaic of insights . . . sensitive to contextual nuance and particular narratives . . . ."); Thomas B. Lawrence & Sally Maitlis, *Care and Possibility: Enacting an Ethic of Care Through Narrative Practice*, 37 Acad. Mgmt. Rev. 641, 642 (2012), *available at* http://dx.doi.org/10.5465/amr.2010.0466 (citing "research on a wide range of narrative practices that suggests they provide an important means through which care can be enacted.").

50 *See* Cynthia Ozick, *The Novel's Evil Tongue*, N.Y. Times, Dec. 20, 2015, at BR1 (explaining that "[w]hen the World was just new, Story came into being . . . .").

51 Drew Westen, Op-Ed., *What Happened to Obama?*, N.Y. Times, Aug. 7, 2011, at SR1.

52 Jon Sutherland, *Book People*, N.Y. Times Book Rev., Jan. 7, 2018 at 1 (stating that "Storytelling is as human as breathing . . . . it has 'shaped the lives of most humans on the planet earth.'").

53 Arthur Graesser, Brent Olde, & Bianca Klettke, *How Does the Mind Construct and Represent Stories?, in* Narrative Impact: Social and Cognitive Foundations 229 (Melanie Green, Jeffrey Strange, & Timothy Brock eds., 2002).

54 *See* Jerome Bruner, Making Stories: Law, Literature, Life 97 (2002) (noting that early stories were "a staple in marking special occasions").

55 Jerome Bruner, Making Stories: Law, Literature, Life 97 (2002).

56 Henning Mankell, Op-Ed., *The Art of Listening*, N.Y. Times, Dec. 11, 2011, at SR4.

horrors of nuclear war . . . . ,"[57] using their narrative accounts to depict what happened on the day of the atomic bombing of their cities.

Historical chronicles of early legal education describe antecedents of narrative legal studies. Narrative Law, as it has come to be known, has its origins in the Law and Literature movement begun in the eighteenth century, when a lawyer's education included a solid grounding in the classical Greek and Latin literary canon.[58] The narrative strand of Law and Literature is the most recent version; the strands that predate it are Law as Literature[59] and Law in Literature.[60] These fields of inquiry demonstrate that law and literature are linked inextricably in that we can view law through a literary lens. The language of the law itself often is the subject of literary critique,[61] while numerous works of fiction involve legal themes.[62] Narrative Law, including Law as Literature and Law in Literature, surely has influenced the study of narrative as a theoretical and practical means to enhance lawyering and to further the ends of justice.

While trends in legal education embodied in the Law and Literature movement led to the incorporation of narrative theory into legal practice, the evolution of jurisprudence in the early twentieth century also contributed to generating a narrative bent in legal reasoning. The dawn of legal realism at that time began to erode the purely analytical approach to legal analysis that characterized judicial decision-making in the mid-nineteenth century.[63] Legal realism differed in that it encouraged a way of thinking about law that acknowledged the salience of its social milieu. As a consequence, the use of legal principles alone to determine the law fell from favor. "Legal 'realists' began to question whether only legal

57 Ian Buruma, *Under a Cloud*, N.Y. TIMES, Aug. 2, 2015, at BR9 (reviewing SUSAN SOUTHARD, NAGASAKI: LIFE AFTER NUCLEAR WAR (2015)).

58 *See* AMY D. RONNER, LAW, LITERATURE, AND THERAPEUTIC JURISPRUDENCE 7 (2010) (referencing James Kent, "who lectured at Columbia College in 1794," and "advised American lawyers to master Greek and Latin classics and said that only those 'well read in the whole circle of the arts and sciences' could form 'an accurate acquaintance with the general principles of Universal Law'").

59 *See* Stacey A. Tovino, *Incorporating Literature into a Health Law Curriculum*, 9 MICH. ST. J. MED. & L. 213, 228 (2005) (explaining that the *Law as Literature* strand applies "rigorous principles of literary criticism to legal writing in order to identify literary features of statutes, regulations, judicial opinions, contracts, and other forms of legal or jurisprudential writings.").

60 *See* AMY D. RONNER, LAW, LITERATURE, AND THERAPEUTIC JURISPRUDENCE 13 (2010) (describing the *Law in Literature* approach as an "analysis and criticism of literary works that have legal themes, portray lawyers, or depict legal practice.").

61 *See* Stacey A. Tovino, *Incorporating Literature into a Health Law Curriculum*, 9 MICH. ST. J. MED. & L. 213, 228 (2005) (describing the *Law as Literature* strand as that which applies "rigorous principles of literary criticism to legal writing in order to identify literary features of statutes, regulations, judicial opinions, contracts, and other forms of legal or jurisprudential writings.").

62 *See, e.g.*, CHARLES DICKENS, BLEAK HOUSE (1853); ANTHONY TROLLOPE, ORLEY FARM (1861); HERMAN MELVILLE, BILLY BUDD (1924); JOHN GRISHAM, THE CLIENT (1993).

63 *See* AMY D. RONNER, LAW, LITERATURE, AND THERAPEUTIC JURISPRUDENCE 9 (2010) (noting the effect of the case method instituted by Langdell in promoting a rational approach to legal decision-making).

principles should dictate or explain outcomes, and literature was identified as one field that could supplement, enrich, or correct legal principles."[64] Moreover, "legal realists always have emphasized the importance of stories . . . ."[65] In light of this movement to embed the law with human experience, narrative law was destined to materialize as a discipline unto itself.

Family law issues are especially well suited to a narrative template. Many, if not most, legal issues in this area of law require complex fact-based considerations. The best-interests-of-the-child standard[66] in custody proceedings illustrates this point. Among other factors, the standard often requires the court to consider the family members, the quality of their relationships, the household circumstances, and the family routines. In narrative parlance, such facts become the characters, their points of view, the setting, and the plot. These elements comprise the family story. When presented in a narrative format, they are instructive for judges and family court service providers because they depict the family's situation in ways that are compelling.[67] It is for this reason—the influential quality of narrative presentations—that stories are persuasive in informing judicial decisions and making strategic connections to services for troubled families.[68] In the family justice system, however, litigants' stories often are not sought and considered in any systematic way. Narrative practice, on the other hand, entails a very specific and deliberate way of engaging with litigants and the stories they tell.[69] The results of

64 Stacey A. Tovino, *Incorporating Literature into a Health Law Curriculum*, 9 MICH. ST. J. MED. & L. 213, 226 (2005).

65 Binny Miller, *Telling Stories About Cases and Clients: The Ethics of Narrative*, 14 GEO. J. LEGAL ETHICS 1, 1.

66 N.J. REV. STAT. § 9:2-4a (2015) ("[I]n any action concerning children undertaken by a State department, agency, commission, authority, court of law, or State or local legislative body, the best interests of the child shall be a primary consideration."); ME. REV. STAT. tit. 19-A, § 1653(3) (2015) ("The court, in making an award of parental rights and responsibilities with respect to a child, shall apply the standard of the best interest of the child. In making decisions regarding the child's residence and parent-child contact, the court shall consider as primary the safety and well-being of the child. In applying this standard, the court shall consider the following factors: A. The age of the child; B. The relationship of the child with the child's parents and any other persons who may significantly affect the child's welfare; C. The preference of the child, if old enough to express a meaningful preference . . . .").

67 *See, e.g.*, Evan R. Seamone, *Educating Family Court Judges on the Front Line of Combat Readjustment: Toward the Formulation and Delivery of a Core Curriculum on Military Family Issues*, 52. FAM. CT. REV. 458, 69 (2014) (citing a recommendation that family court judges would benefit from exposure to narratives of military families as told from the "perspectives of spouses themselves in overcoming the challenges of a unique military culture.").

68 Steven Johansen, *Was Colonel Sanders a Terrorist? An Essay on the Ethical Limits of Applied Legal Storytelling*, 7 J. ASS'N LEGAL WRITING DIRECTORS 63, 63 (2010) ("This much we know: stories can change people's minds. Literally hundreds of studies have found that stories are effective narrative tools. No study has found otherwise," citing KENDALL HAVEN, STORY PROOF: THE SCIENCE BEHIND THE STARTLING POWER OF STORY 4 (2007)).

69 *See, e.g.*, RITA CHARON, NARRATIVE MEDICINE: HONORING THE STORIES OF ILLNESS 67 (2006). Charon has said, for example, that "relationship-centered care [a stand-in for

such directed inquiry and analysis must drive family law decision-making if it is to be both caring and just.[70]

The importance of narrative

Jerome Bruner has said that "[n]arrative . . . is indeed serious business."[71] Narrative competence, or the ability to integrate into professional practice a narrative intention, improves the way in which lawyers represent their clients. Numerous legal scholars and practicing lawyers attest to the value of storytelling.[72] Carrie Menkel-Meadow has said that "law teachers and lawyers have discovered the power of case stories and narratives to accomplish many things."[73] Menkel-Meadow expands the reach of narrative in claiming that the narrative framework can teach students "about lawyering, decision-making, the social impact of law and legal ethics."[74] Andrea McArdle advocates for judging through a narrative lens.[75] Judges themselves have endorsed a narrative perspective in judicial decision-making.[76] The same holds true in the family justice system—that shining a light on litigants' stories makes a difference—that the story can encourage caring in court.

narrative practice] require[s] relationships . . . that come about through attentive and creative listening." *Id.* These are deliberate activities, which are hallmarks of narrative practice.

70 See Shawn C. Marsh & Mari Kay Bickett, *Trauma-Informed Courts and the Role of the Judge*, Judges' Page Newsl. (Nat'l CASA Ass'n & Nat'l Council of Juvenile & Family Court Judges, Washington, D.C.), Feb. 11, 2015, *available at* https://www.ncjfcj.org/trauma-informed-courts-and-role-judge, for a discussion of practices recommended to promote more informed approaches to court-involved children and families. One recommendation is for judges to adopt a narrative form of inquiry, e.g., "asking 'What happened to you?' versus 'What is wrong with you?' in their interactions with parties." *Id.* This form of questioning clearly harks to a narrative format.

71 Jerome Bruner, Making Stories: Law, Literature, Life 107 (2002).

72 *See, e.g.*, Anthony G. Amsterdam & Jerome Bruner, Minding the Law (2000); Philip N. Meyer, Storytelling for Lawyers (2014); Adam Liptak & Matt Flegenheimer, *After Rocky Start, Cruz Had Success Before Justices*, N.Y. Times, Feb. 17, 2016, at A13 (explaining that Senator Cruz, in mentoring the current Texas solicitor general, counseled that "every case is really about a story").

73 Carrie Menkel-Meadow, *Telling Stories in School: Using Case Studies and Stories to Teach Legal Ethics*, 69 Fordham L. Rev. 787, 787 (2000).

74 Carrie Menkel-Meadow, *Telling Stories in School: Using Case Studies and Stories to Teach Legal Ethics*, 69 Fordham L. Rev. 787, 787 (2000).

75 *See* Andrea McArdle, *Using a Narrative Lens to Understand Empathy and How It Matters in Judging*, 9 Legal Comm. & Rhetoric: JALWD 173, 181 (2012) (explaining the need for judicial decision-making that incorporates an empathetic perspective which is derived from "one's identity, experience, and appreciation of narrative facts . . . .").

76 *Nomination of Elena Kagan to be an Associate Justice of the Supreme Court of the United States: Hearing before the S. Comm. on the Judiciary*, 111th Cong., 2d Sess. (2010) (statement of Elena Kagan: "[W]hat it means to decide an actual case or controversy is to think about the application of law to facts, and what that requires is that you really understand the facts, that you really-that you delve through the record, that you get your absolute best sense of what the actual conditions and circumstances of the parties are.").

Because family law stories illuminate the facts of a case and make them memorable, they can promote the development of reasoned outcomes that fit the circumstances featured in the narrative set before the court.[77] A litigant's story can elicit a host of considerations that may not fall within the parameters of a strictly legal issue, but which, if known and considered, certainly can affect the legal outcome. For example, families with legal issues also may suffer from substance abuse, mental health issues, and problems associated with poverty, including inadequate housing or homelessness, unsafe neighborhoods, and lack of food, among others.[78] When the court understands these complexities, the determination may include connections to much-needed therapeutic interventions.[79] In this way, the synergistic effect of narrative and law increases the likelihood of a just and caring result for troubled families.

Narrative attributes

The power of narrative stems from its three main attributes: Narrative is potent,[80] instructive,[81] and ethical.[82] Jointly, these characteristics contribute to furthering the capacities that narrative engenders—empathy, decision-making, and ethicality.

Narrative is a potent force because it heightens awareness of others' plights, thus enabling an empathic regard—the ability to feel with and for another human being. Stories told from the point of view of a character (a litigant for our purpose) provide a perspective on the whys and wherefores of what happened that otherwise may remain unknown to the listener. This enlightened standpoint can counter negative judgments about the story subject by providing a detailed context that prompts a deeper attention to the human condition beneath it.

77 *See* Robin West, Caring for Justice 205 (1997) (explaining that judicial decision-making requires attention to the stories underlying the legal case).

78 *See, e.g.*, Barbara A. Babb & Judith D. Moran, *Substance Abuse, Families, and Unified Family Courts: The Creation of a Caring Justice System*, 3 J. Health Care L. & Pol'y 1, 19 (1999) (listing some of the nonlegal problems associated with family court cases).

79 *See, e.g.*, Barbara A. Babb & Judith D. Moran, *Substance Abuse, Families, and Unified Family Courts: The Creation of a Caring Justice System*, 3 J. Health Care L. & Pol'y 1, 23–33 (1999) (describing the court services available in the Family Division of the Circuit Court for Baltimore City, which is comprised largely of litigants with a diverse array of nonlegal problems in need of practical solutions). *Id.*

80 *See* Rita Charon, Narrative Medicine: Honoring the Stories of Illness 58 (2006) (describing narrative as a "potent force" that must be understood for its benefits as well as its risks).

81 *See, e.g.*, J. Christopher Rideout, *Storytelling, Narrative Rationality, and Legal Persuasion*, 14 Legal Writing: J. Legal Writing Inst. 53, 57 (2008) (proposing that narratives are compelling, "most probably because narratives are a natural mode for understanding human experience").

82 Carrie Menkel-Meadow, *Telling Stories in School: Using Case Studies and Stories to Teach Legal Ethics*, 69 Fordham L. Rev. 787, 793 (2000) (commenting that storytelling acumen is "significant for those seeking to make good moral and ethical choices").

Akin to the potent capacity to "feel" with and for another person stimulated by a narrative account is the notion that narratives also are instructive. Kenworthey Bilz explains this particular narrative attribute: "[P]eople have a hard time understanding information when it is removed from its context. But when context—especially sensible narrative—is supplied, they are actually quite capable and efficient at recalling it and giving it its appropriate weight."[83] Bilz uses the term "sensible narrative" to suggest that such a framework, when put forth in court, enables decision-makers to recall the evidentiary facts and derive a well-reasoned outcome from the narrative incorporating them.[84] Jerome Bruner proposes that narrative is sense-making and informative in another way. According to Bruner, personal accounts or stories provide a viewpoint on a set of facts which "helps us to make sense of things when they don't."[85] Bruner adds that narrative domesticates reality so that what seems incomprehensible becomes explicable. For example, in legal cases, criminal acts and civil disputes involving highly-contested family matters arise from behavior beyond the normal course; effective advocacy involves explanation of the unexpected and the unusual.[86] In this way, the instructive nature of stories prompts understanding and compassion for those whose behavior is otherwise confounding.[87]

Lastly, commentators on professional ethics suggest that narrative enables ethical approaches to legal outcomes.[88] Since narrative is ethically informative, it aids in the quality of the legal decision-making.[89] Narrative illuminates what is right

83 Kenworthey Bilz, *We Don't Want to Hear It: Psychology, Literature and the Narrative Model of Judging*, 2010 U. ILL. L. REV. 429, 437 (2010).

84 Kenworthey Bilz, *We Don't Want to Hear It: Psychology, Literature and the Narrative Model of Judging*, 2010 U. ILL. L. REV. 429, 437 (2010) (explaining a model of narrative judging that reconciles evidentiary exclusionary requirements with a narrative approach to lawyering, but in so doing acknowledges the psychological potency of storytelling in legal advocacy). *But cf.* Toni Massaro, *Empathy, Legal Storytelling, and the Rule of Law: New Words, Old Wounds?*, 87 MICH. L. REV. 2099, 2105 (1989) (noting the "call to context" which has been taken up by proponents of legal storytelling, but cautioning that such context (stories) can also compromise judicial decision-making).

85 JEROME BRUNER, MAKING STORIES: LAW, LITERATURE, LIFE 28 (2002).

86 *See generally* JEROME BRUNER, MAKING STORIES: LAW, LITERATURE, LIFE (2002).

87 *See* Craig Brown, *Finding Clients by Telling Stories*, LAWVISION INSIGHTS BLOG (Feb. 4, 2016), http://lawvisiongroup.com/finding-clients-by-telling-stories/?print-pdf (citing scientific studies that "conclude that good, character-driven stories actually cause the brain to produce oxytocin, which increases trust, generosity, charitability, and compassion.").

88 *See, e.g.*, Carrie Menkel-Meadow, *Telling Stories in School: Using Case Studies and Stories to Teach Legal Ethics*, 69 FORDHAM L. REV. 787, 792 (2000) (remarking on the value of using narrative contexts for teaching legal ethics; "many legal educators now suggest that the telling of stories is a way to deepen legal and ethical reasoning.").

89 Richard Delgado & Jean Stefancic, *Norms and Narratives: Can Judges Avoid Serious Moral Error?*, 69 TEX. L. REV. 1929, 1952, 1932 (1991) (reviewing cases marked by serious moral error and concluding that "most serious judicial mistakes result from the judge's inability to empathize with the litigants or their circumstances" and "narrative might plausibly have saved the judge from serious moral error.").

and just in accordance with the litigants' circumstances. How, then, does narrative work? What can facilitate narrative competence?

How narrative works: Narrative competence and narrative capacities

Narrative competence

Rita Charon cautions, "Achieving narrative competence . . . is not a trivial goal . . . ." and it "is not attained without considerable effort and commitment."[90] The means to narrative proficiency involve multiple skills. They include imagination, empathy, ethical awareness, and attentiveness,[91] all of which require dedication to a specific way of addressing professional practice. While Charon directs her remarks to a largely medical audience, her observations merit consideration from the legal profession, as well. Narrative competence translates into practice-based capacities. The capacities engendered by narrative competence that are most relevant to a discussion of promoting the ethic of care in the family justice system are empathy, decision-making, and ethical awareness.[92]

Narrative capacities

Empathy

Narrative makes empathy possible. As one scholar explains:

> Stories tend to work directly from 'experiential understanding' . . . . Consequently, narrative may be a particularly powerful means of facilitating empathic understanding: a concrete story comes closest to actual experience and so may evoke our empathic distress response more readily than abstract theory. Telling stories can move us to care, and hence pave the way to action.[93]

The role that narrative competence and practice play in the application of an ethic of care to the work of the family justice system hinges on empathy. One commentator on empathy has said, "Empathy is about deepening connections."[94]

90 Rita Charon, Narrative Medicine: Honoring the Stories of Illness ix (2006).
91 Rita Charon, Narrative Medicine: Honoring the Stories of Illness 107 (2006).
92 Narrative competence has also been shown to enhance legal analysis. *See generally* Richard H. Weisberg, *Wigmore and the Law and Literature Movement*, 21 L. & Literature 129, 136–37 (2009) (noting that lessons learned from narrative may be applied to legal analysis); Anthony G. Amsterdam & Jerome Bruner, Minding the Law (2000) (narrative proficiency aids in the construction of compelling legal arguments and law reform); Judith D. Moran, *Families, Law, and Literature: The Story of a Course on Storytelling*, 49 U.S.F. L. Rev. 1, 3–4 (2015) (demonstrating the impact of personal stories on legislation, using name-based laws as an example).
93 Toni Massaro, *Empathy, Legal Storytelling, and the Rule of Law: New Words, Old Wounds?*, 87 Mich. L. Rev. 2099, 2105 (1989).
94 Anna Holmes, *Who Gets to Tell Other People's Stories?*, N.Y. Times, May 29, 2016, at BR27.

Definitions of empathy are abundant and may overlap with terms such as compassion, sympathy, and pity.[95] We focus on definitions that feature the capacity[96] to understand another person's point of view: "a procedure by which a person centrally imagines the narrative (the thoughts, feelings and emotions) of another person."[97] Similarly, empathy is seen as "a capacity for understanding the desires, goals and intentions of others."[98] The term has its roots in the Greek words *en* (in) and *pathos* (suffering or experience).[99]

Other commentators suggest that imagination is a condition for empathic feelings.[100] For example, Derek Matravers claims that in order to express empathy, "it is necessary that I have a grasp of the narrative which I can imaginatively enact, with the other as narrator."[101] Along these lines of thought, empathy is the end result in a sequence of behaviors, beginning with narrative attention, prompting imagination, and culminating with an empathetic response.[102]

95 Susan A. Bandes, *Compassion and the Rule of Law*, 13 INT'L J.L. CONTEXT 184, 185 (2016), *available at* https://ssrn.com/abstract=2887374. Bandes notes, *id.* and we have explained in Chapter 3, *supra* Chapter 3, that the term empathy evolved from what was once called sympathy.

96 Some definitions categorize empathy as a "capacity" or "skill." *See, e.g.*, Andrea McArdle, *Using a Narrative Lens to Understand Empathy and How It Matters in Judging*, 9 LEGAL COMM. & RHETORIC: JALWD 173, 178 (2012) (citing Susan A. Bandes, *Empathetic Judging and the Rule of Law*, 2009 CARDOZO L. REV. DE NOVO 133, 136 (2009)) (noting that "[e]mpathy, as Bandes recently described it, is the 'capacity' to 'understand what others are thinking, feeling, or perceiving . . . .'"); Dominic McIver Lopes, *An Empathic Eye*, in EMPATHY: PHILOSOPHICAL AND PSYCHOLOGICAL PERSPECTIVES 19 (Amy Coplan & Peter Goldie, eds., 2011) (describing empathy as a skill).

97 Derek Matravers, *Empathy as a Route to Knowledge, in* EMPATHY: PHILOSOPHICAL AND PSYCHOLOGICAL PERSPECTIVES 123, 124 (Amy Coplan & Peter Goldie, eds., 2011) (also characterizing empathy as a "skill"—"having whatever cognitive wherewithal is implicated in empathic response.").

98 Susan A. Bandes, *Compassion and the Rule of Law*, 13 INT'L J.L. CONTEXT 184, 185 (2016), *available at* https://ssrn.com/abstract=2887374.

99 Charles Siebert, *Of a Feather*, N.Y. TIMES MAG., Jan. 31, 2016, at MM40, MM57. *See also* Carrie Menkel-Meadow, *Telling Stories in School: Using Case Studies and Stories to Teach Legal Ethics*, 69 FORDHAM L. REV. 787, 791 n.12 (2000) (referencing the German derivation of empathy—"'einfuhlung,' literally translated as 'feeling into'").

100 *See, e.g.*, Toni Massaro, *Empathy, Legal Storytelling, and the Rule of Law: New Words, Old Wounds?*, 87 MICH. L. REV. 2099, 2100 (1989) (noting that "Feminist jurisprudence in particular . . . argues that feeling and imagination also are important aspects of . . . understanding"); Helen Riess, *Like-Minded*, NEW YORKER, June 3, 2013, at 3 ("Empathy is a complex capacity that includes cognitive, emotional, moral and behavioral processes, not only to feel another's pain but to imagine how one could alleviate his suffering . . . .").

101 Derek Matravers, *Empathy as a Route to Knowledge, in* EMPATHY: PHILOSOPHICAL AND PSYCHOLOGICAL PERSPECTIVES 19, 19 (Amy Coplan & Peter Goldie, eds., 2011); Toni Massaro, *Empathy, Legal Storytelling, and the Rule of Law: New Words, Old Wounds?*, 87 MICH. L. REV. 2099, 2105 (1989) (noting that empathy and storytelling are related).

102 *See, e.g.*, Derek Matravers, *Empathy as a Route to Knowledge, in* EMPATHY: PHILOSOPHICAL AND PSYCHOLOGICAL PERSPECTIVES 19 (Amy Coplan & Peter Goldie, eds., 2011); Carrie Menkel-Meadow, *Telling Stories in School: Using Case Studies and Stories to Teach Legal Ethics*, 69 FORDHAM L. REV. 787, 791–92 (2000); Andrea McArdle, *Using a Narrative Lens to Understand Empathy and How It Matters in Judging*, 9 LEGAL

In addition to commentary by legal scholars and ethicists on the value of empathy, it has become a subject of scientific inquiry, as well. Outcomes from empirical research with animals affirm that empathy is very real, indeed. In laboratory experiments, rats have been observed "free[ing] a trapped companion before munching on a food treat."[103] Researchers also have demonstrated a "shared neuronal circuitry that has now been mapped across species, from us to the other primates to elephants and whales . . . ."[104] and even birds. This concern for others is ascribed to an empathetic proclivity.[105] In humans, cognitive brain studies have yielded evidence of "mirror neurons"—structures in the brain that are capable of absorbing emotive information from another person.[106] These neurons, in turn, allow the observer or listener to experience the same set of emotions experienced by the other, as if "the person had experienced the event personally."[107] As empathy is now an identifiable cross-species trait, neuroscientists have considered that it may be a "bioevolutionary tool for survival."[108] It is possible, for example, that the ability to feel a "fellow being's" fear may prompt action to avoid the potential harm.[109] As neuroscience literature documenting experiments with animals and humans suggests that empathy binds them together in a shared emotive network,[110] it

COMM. & RHETORIC: JALWD 173, 180 (2012) (supporting the view that "empathy is centrally connected with narrative"). *See also* JAMES BOYD WHITE, THE LEGAL IMAGINATION (1985). White's textbook was used in a course he taught for many years (by the same name) at the University of Michigan Law School.

103 Nicholas Kristof, Op-Ed., *How Do We Increase Empathy?*, N.Y. TIMES, Jan. 29, 2015, at A27.

104 Charles Siebert, *Of a Feather*, N.Y. TIMES MAG., Jan. 31, 2016, at MM40, MM59.

105 *See* Charles Siebert, *Of a Feather*, N.Y. TIMES MAG., Jan. 31, 2016 at MM40 (documenting the parrot's capacity for empathy and explaining how parrots are being used for therapeutic interventions in treating PTSD patients).

106 *See* Susan L. Brooks & Robert G. Madden, *Epistemology and Ethics in Relationship-Centered Legal Education and Practice*, 56 N.Y. L. SCH. L. REV. 331, 362 (2011/12), *available at* http://papers.ssrn.com/sol3/papers.cfm?abstract_id=1932831. *See also* Elayne Greenberg, *Bridging Our Justice Gap with Empathic Processes that Change Hearts, Expand Minds About Implicit Discrimination*, 32 OHIO ST. J. ON DISP. RESOL. 425, 439 (2017), *available at* https://ssrn.com/abstract=3016617 ("Starting at birth, we see newborns exhibit empathetic distress or crying when other newborns cry.").

107 *See* Susan L. Brooks & Robert G. Madden, *Epistemology and Ethics in Relationship-Centered Legal Education and Practice*, 56 N.Y. L. SCH. L. REV. 331, 362 (2011/12), *available at* http://papers.ssrn.com/sol3/papers.cfm?abstract_id=1932831.

108 Charles Siebert, *Of a Feather*, N.Y. TIMES MAG., Jan. 31, 2016, at MM40, MM57.

109 *See* Charles Siebert, *Of a Feather*, N.Y. TIMES MAG., Jan. 31, 2016 at MM57; Paul J. Zak, *How Stories Change the Brain*, GREATERGOOD.BERKELEY.EDU (Dec. 17, 2013) http://greatergood.berkeely.edu/article/itme/how_stories_change_brain (explaining that the neural mechanism associated with empathy "allow[s] us to rapidly forecast if people around us are angry or kind, dangerous or safe, friend or foe" . . . thereby "keep[ing] us safe").

110 *See* Paul J. Zak, *How Stories Change the Brain*, GREATERGOOD.BERKELEY.EDU (Dec. 17, 2013), http://greatergood.berkeely.edu/article/itme/how_stories_change_brain (explaining "transportation," the neural mechanism that enables empathy, and consequently causes humans to form relationships based upon shared emotional responses); *See also* Elayne Greenberg, *Bridging Our Justice Gap with Empathic Processes that Change*

"can be thought of as the source of all emotion, the one without which the others would have no register."[111]

Other research shows that empathy in humans is greatest when individuals are presented with a subjective narrative—the story of a single person.[112] "We struggle to care when the numbers get big," investigators have surmised.[113] Personal stories tug at the human heart, and, when they arise from a family law case, the stories are quite likely to induce empathy.[114] In family law cases, which are invariably complex and often involve children, empathy matters a lot.

Empathy as a predicate for judging, however, is controversial.[115] Those who question its relevance to judicial decision-making are concerned with the extent to which empathy is a factor in determining legal outcomes.[116] Despite the controversy, the case for empathic judges has emerged in a very public arena:

Hearts, Expand Minds About Implicit Discrimination, 32 Ohio St. J. on Disp. Resol. 425, 442 (2017), *available at* https://ssrn.com/abstract=3016617 (citing Jeremy Rifkin, The Empathic Civilization: The Race to Global Consciousness in a World in Crisis (2010), for the idea that "our need to belong is our number one empathic drive").

111 *See* Charles Siebert, *Of a Feather*, N.Y. Times Mag., Jan. 31, 2016, at MM40, MM57.

112 *See* Scott Slovic & Paul Slovic, Op-Ed., *The Arithmetic of Compassion*, N.Y. Times, Dec. 6, 2015, at SR10 (describing research that "[o]ur sympathy for suffering and loss declines precipitously when we are presented with increasing numbers of victims" and noting that the story of the dead Syrian child washed up on the beach during his family's attempt to escape the ravages of their war torn country was more powerful in inspiring empathy for refugees than accounts of greater losses of life during other migrations); Carrie Menkel-Meadow, *What's Gender Got to Do With It? The Politics and Morality of an Ethic of Care*, 22 N.Y.U. Rev. L. & Soc. Change 265, 272 (1996) (noting evidence supporting that "our feelings and capacities to care are most activated by those nearest us . . . based in kinship altruisim" and other relationships based upon similarity); Joan Tronto, Moral Boundaries: A Political Argument for an Ethic of Care 127 (1994); Jeanne Marie Laskas, *The Mail Room*, N.Y. Times Mag., Jan. 22, 2017, at MM31, MM61 (chronicling the work of White House staffers who read the President's mail and how the individual stories contained in the letters sent to then President Obama moved him to not only make caring interventions on a singular level, but "the mail grew into something else; letters informed policy proposals and speeches.").

113 Scott Slovic & Paul Slovic, Op-Ed., *The Arithmetic of Compassion*, N.Y. Times, Dec. 6, 2015, at SR10.

114 *See* Family Law Stories (Carol Sanger ed., 2008); Judith D. Moran, *Families, Law, and Literature: The Story of a Course on Storytelling*, 49 U.S.F. L. Rev. 1, 43 (2015) (noting students' attestations to the power of specific stories to engender empathy for otherwise unsympathetic characters, such as Cholly in Toni Morrison, The Bluest Eye (1970)).

115 *See generally* Elayne Greenberg, *Bridging Our Justice Gap with Empathic Processes that Change Hearts, Expand Minds About Implicit Discrimination*, 32 Ohio St. J. on Disp. Resol. 425, 449 (2017), *available at* https://ssrn.com/abstract=3016617 (discussing an overall concern about introducing empathy "into the interpretation of the rule of law . . . .").

116 *See, e.g.*, Toni Massaro, *Empathy, Legal Storytelling, and the Rule of Law: New Words, Old Wounds*, 87 Mich. L. Rev. 2099, 2126 (1989) (expressing concerns that empathy will spawn "unguided emotion" in law, advocating instead for a balanced approach that takes into consideration the formalism of law along with attention to the effects on the persons to whom it is applied); *See also* Andrea McArdle, *Using a Narrative Lens to Understand Empathy and How It Matters in Judging*, 9 Legal Comm. & Rhetoric: JALWD 173 (2012) (advising that empathy must be used sparingly in judicial decision-making).

> In 2009, President Obama announced that his criteria for selecting a Supreme Court Justice included evidence of a capacity for empathy . . . . [H]e described the approach to judging called for by the difficult cases that reached the Court. Such cases, he averred, "can only be determined on the basis of one's deepest values, one's core concerns, one's broader perspectives on how the world works, and the depth and breadth of one's empathy."[117]

Following subsequent United States Supreme Court confirmation hearings, judicial empathy became the subject of a highly contested political debate.[118] Nonetheless, former President Barak Obama continued to press his empathy agenda: "When he nominated . . . [now Justice Elena Kagan], he called her someone who understands the law 'as it affects the lives of ordinary people,'"[119] a likely endorsement of the importance of empathy in judicial decision-making.

Lynne Henderson also has argued for empathy in judging. "Empathy aids both processes of discovery—the procedure by which a judge . . . reaches a conclusion—and processes of justification—the procedure used by a judge . . . to justify the conclusion . . . ."[120] While Henderson's endorsement of empathy does not mention narrative per se, the processes of discovery and justification to which she refers imply attention to litigants' stories.

In sum, empathy is scientifically verifiable. The feelings for others that it inspires emanate from the stories people tell. Judges must rely sparingly on empathy so as not to tip the scales of justice, although the nature of the court process is itself a safeguard in that the court considers and hears stories on both sides. Empathy counts in family law jurisprudence and family court practices, where enhanced caretaking is necessary to respond effectively to the needs of litigants. To foster the ethic of care in the family court arena, judges, most certainly, as well as lawyers and court personnel, must draw on narrative to power the empathic process. "[J]udging

117 Andrea McArdle, *Using a Narrative Lens to Understand Empathy and How It Matters in Judging*, 9 Legal Comm. & Rhetoric: JALWD 173, 173 (2012).

118 *See* Andrea McArdle, *Using a Narrative Lens to Understand Empathy and How It Matters in Judging*, 9 Legal Comm. & Rhetoric: JALWD 173, 173 (2012); *See also* Alexander Burns, Maggie Haberman, & Ashley Parker, *Trump Struggles in Feud with Fallen G.I.'s Family*, N.Y. Times, Aug. 1, 2016, at A1, A7 (reporting on the 2016 U.S. political campaign in which the Republican candidate made a disparaging comment about a Muslim family who had lost a son in the Iraq war. The family responded by saying that the candidate, Donald Trump, "lacked the moral character and empathy to be president," suggesting that the president must have empathy); Elayne Greenberg, *Bridging our Justice Gap With Empathic Processes that Change Hearts, Expand Minds About Implicit Discrimination*, 32 Ohio. St. J. on Disp. Resol. 425, 451, https://ssrn.com/abstract=3016617 (explaining that, "For some the empathy issue has become a political buzzword that divides liberals from conservatives, and depending on which point of view is in control, could facilitate or bar judicial appointment.").

119 Sheryl Gay Stolberg, *Top Issues At Kagan Hearings May Be Obama and Roberts,* N.Y. Times, June 27, 2010, at A1.

120 Lynne N. Henderson, *Legality and Empathy*, 85 Mich. L. Rev. 1574, 1576 (1987).

is and ought to be an empathic, as well as a rational, act, informed by a sympathetic engagement with the lives and interests of the competing litigants, tempered with mercy, and guided by care."[121]

Decision-making

In our discussion of empathy, we have suggested that the emotive signal to care is narrative because this format facilitates empathy and related feelings, such as compassion and caring.[122] "Through stories, emotions that can help inspire decision-making are engaged."[123] Stories provide context—an underlying narrative describing the family's circumstances. A judge inclined to think contextually attends to the features of the family's story to ensure that both the legal and situational aspects of the case factor into her decision. A decision-making framework—one that takes the litigant's story into account—has the potential to activate an ethic of care through empathic regard for the litigant.[124] Owing to this interdependent relationship between narrative and empathy, we propose that judges deliberate in family law matters with a view toward the narrative perspective. A judge who is guided by a family story likely is a more caring and ethical jurist, one who can reconcile the legal with the contextual aspects of the case.[125]

Recently, the application of narrative to judging has gained momentum and credibility from the legal storytelling movement:

121 Robin West, Caring for Justice 207 (1997).

122 *See, e.g.*, Andrea McArdle, *Using a Narrative Lens to Understand Empathy and How It Matters in Judging*, 9 Legal Comm. & Rhetoric: JALWD 173, 179–80 (2012) (suggesting that a narrative perspective makes empathy possible). *See also* Virginia Held, The Ethics of Care 10 (2006) (supporting the notion that care derives from emotive responses that stories inspire and explaining that moral decisions about whether to care are facilitated by "such emotions as sympathy, empathy, sensitivity and responsiveness . . . .").

123 Craig Brown, *Finding Clients by Telling Stories*, LawVision INSIGHTS Blog (Feb. 4, 2016), http://lawvisiongroup.com/finding-clients-by-telling-stories/?print-pdf.

124 *See, e.g.*, Julia Driver, *Mill, Moral Sentimentalism, and the Cultivation of Virtue*, *in* Cultivating Virtue 56, 56 (Nancy E. Snow ed., 2015) ("training in perspective taking [ascertaining another's point of view] is important to the development of a good character in human beings and for the ability to make proper moral judgements . . . . Perspective-taking . . . allows us to get information [a narrative account for our purpose] that is crucial to effective moral agency—one cannot help another without some understanding of what the other considers good or desirable.") As such, the connection between narrative inquiry and the virtue of caring is consequential.

125 *See* Andrea McArdle, *Using a Narrative Lens to Understand Empathy and How It Matters in Judging*, 9 Legal Comm. & Rhetoric: JALWD 173, 176 (2012) (referencing now Justice Sotomayor's comments during the Senate Judiciary Confirmation hearings about her family background and "its potentially positive contribution to judging"—while these comments "raised concerns about bias and thus about the nominee's qualification to serve.") Her remarks also support the use of narrative in judicial decision-making. *Id.*

> Those who encourage legal storytelling and those who favor empathic decision-making seem to share at least two concerns. One concern is that legal theory and legal discourse often are too removed from individual experience . . . . Stories can shock them [judges and lawyers] back into sensation, into life as it *is* versus how we talk about it.[126]

Anthony Amsterdam and Jerome Bruner contend that narrative is more of a help than a hindrance to judicial reasoning. "The value of narrative, in their view, is that it is flexible, and responsive to different ways of understanding and interpreting experience."[127] Kenworthey Bilz states that "a narrative format enables a decision-maker to process information effectively in a way that contributes to the objective quality of a judgment."[128] In calling for judging that is attuned to stories, feminist legal scholars have made known their support for the notion that narrative prompts humane jurisprudence.[129] These views demonstrate that the judicial deliberative process is enhanced by taking litigants' stories into account. "Concrete human stories add so much more to our understanding of the issues than abstract legal principles."[130]

Judges are steeped in narrative from internal stimuli, as well. In writing about judicial decision-making and its impact on the development of constitutional interpretation, Richard Weisberg notes that judges' "assumptions about the world, the values they were likely to put into the text they interpreted . . ."[131] are prompted by their own familiar narratives.[132] The internalized stories to which Weisberg refers sometimes result in judicial reasoning that runs afoul of optimal outcomes for litigants. Linda Berger illustrates Weisberg's observation with a

126 Toni Massaro, *Empathy, Legal Storytelling, and the Rule of Law: New Words, Old Wounds?*, 87 Mich. L. Rev. 2099, 2105 (1989).

127 Andrea McArdle, *Using a Narrative Lens to Understand Empathy and How It Matters in Judging*, 9 Legal Comm. & Rhetoric: JALWD 173, 181 (2012).

128 Kenworthey Bilz, *We Don't Want to Hear It: Psychology, Literature and the Narrative Model of Judging*, 2010 U. Ill. L. Rev. 429, 437 (2010).

129 Robin West, Caring for Justice 205 (1997) (noting that feminists cast the role of a judge as one whose interpretive project is aimed less at the examination of "conflicting textual rules and principles," but more specifically focused on diverging stories). *See also* Margaret Thornton & Heather Roberts, *Women Judges, Private Lives: (In)visibilities in Fact and Fiction*, 40 UNSW L.J. 761, 768 (2017) (Austrl.) for an overview of a fictional account of a "woman judge" described in Ian McEwan's *The Children Act*. Thornton and Roberts write: "'The Children Act' shows that storytelling is important as a judicial method. Rather than judges writing their judgments at a high level of abstraction, storytelling is a reminder of the human concerns that affect the people who come before them." *Id.*

130 Jane C. Murphy, *Lawyering for Social Change: The Power of Narrative in Domestic Violence Law Reform*, 21 Hofstra L. Rev. 1243, 1258 (1993).

131 Richard H. Weisberg, *Wigmore and the Law and Literature Movement*, 21 L. & Literature 129, 136 (2009).

132 *See, e.g.*, Joan McCarthy, *Principlism or Narrative Ethics: Must We Choose Between Them?*, 29 Med. Human. 65, 68 (2003), *available at* http://mh.bmj.com/content/29/2/65.full (explaining that moral decision-making is affected by "our self conceptions . . . constructed within culturally available narratives which both enable and limit the kind of people we can imagine ourselves to be.").

family law example. She asserts that judicial decisions in family law are compromised by the fact that "family law remains tethered to culturally embedded stories and symbols."[133] Berger argues that these antiquated views with respect to the best interests of children in contested custody cases[134] subvert optimal family law adjudication. She states, "While so bound, family law will fail to serve individual families and a society whose family structures diverge sharply by education, race, class and income."[135] Berger's position highlights the need for judges to listen to the actual stories presented in the courtroom and to remain mindful of outmoded narratives that may influence personal biases. [136]

While Weisberg and Berger comment on a specific concern about undue narrative influence and its empathy-inducing potential, additional reservations emanate from other legal scholars,[137] judges,[138] and legislators.[139] Overall, their misgivings pertain to the degree to which empathy, narrative (or context as it is sometimes called), and

133 *See* Linda L. Berger, *How Embedded Knowledge Structures Affect Judicial Decision Making: A Rhetorical Analysis of Metaphor, Narrative, and Imagination in Child Custody Disputes,* 18 S. Cal. Interdisc. L.J. 259, 259 (2009).

134 *See, e.g.,* Marcia Kline Pruett & J. Herbie DiFonzo, *Closing the Gap: Research, Policy, Practice, and Shared Parenting*, 52 Fam. Ct. Rev. 152, 156 (2014) (citing the "tender years" doctrine "that allocated custody of young children to their mothers upon divorce or separation"). The authors cite the presumption as that which reflects nineteenth century views of the best interests standard, and they assert that "the doctrine weakened as court began to acknowledge that gender roles were changing." *Id.*

135 Linda L. Berger, *How Embedded Knowledge Structures Affect Judicial Decision Making: A Rhetorical Analysis of Metaphor, Narrative, and Imagination in Child Custody Disputes,* 18 S. Cal. Interdisc. L.J. 259, 259 (2009).

136 *See* Robin West, Caring for Justice 211 (1997). West calls attention to the difficulties posed by "stock stories"— the mainstream narratives that form the basis for legal doctrine, but disenfranchise anyone "whose 'story' departs in significant ways from the assumed narrative which grounds" the legal rule applied to the circumstances. *Id.* West avers that stories of "typical human development" lie "at the heart of scores of legal rules" (using the story of the American family—career oriented father and stay-at-home mother as illustrative). *Id.* A stock story in this vein "obliterates the very different stor[ies] of all those—men and women—who do not fit the narrative." *Id. See also* Marcia Kline Pruett & J. Herbie DiFonzo, *Closing the Gap: Research, Policy, Practice, and Shared Parenting*, 52 Fam. Ct. Rev. 152, 156 (2014). The authors, in their discussion of the "tender years doctrine," note that "despite the nearly universal abolition of this presumption, many judges continue to prefer that the custody of young children be placed with the mother . . . ." *Id.*

137 *See generally* Toni Massaro, *Empathy, Legal Storytelling, and the Rule of Law: New Words, Old Wounds?*, 87 Mich. L. Rev. 2099 (1989).

138 *See* Andrea McArdle, *Using a Narrative Lens to Understand Empathy and How It Matters in Judging*, 9 Legal Comm. & Rhetoric: JALWD 173, 174 (2012), for a discussion on Justice Sonia Sotomayor's comment hedging her earlier position on the role of empathy in jurisprudence during her Senate confirmation hearings. When questioned about her view on empathy, now Justice Sotomayor said, "'[t]he job of a judge is to apply the law. So it's not the heart that compels conclusions in cases, it's the law.'" *Id.*

139 *See* Andrea McArdle, *Using a Narrative Lens to Understand Empathy and How It Matters in Judging*, 9 Legal Comm. & Rhetoric: JALWD 173, 173 (2012) (making note of the Congressional "debate over the attributes of empathy and its legitimacy in judicial decision-making," sparked by President Obama's announcement "that his criteria for selecting a Supreme Court Justice included evidence of a capacity for empathy . . . .").

judicial discretion factor into the decision-making equation. Toni Massaro mounts an extensive counter argument to a narrative approach to judging.[140] She cautions, "At this point, the terms 'empathy,' 'rule of law,' and 'legal storytelling' require closer scrutiny."[141] Massaro's concerns about empathy include how it works when judges are required to empathize, as a matter of course, with both parties, ultimately privileging one story above another.[142] Massaro also asserts that empathy is a construct taken from psychological literature,[143] making its application to legal reasoning misplaced.[144] Lastly, she argues that judicial discretion,[145] and by implication narrative and the empathy it encourages, already affect how judges decide cases. She notes that legal standards, such as the best interests of the child,[146] contemplate a narrative framework from which judges apply the law to the facts.[147] In the end, Massaro acknowledges that her overriding concern is that narrative and its progeny (empathy and discretion) may spawn "unguided emotion" in law.[148] She advocates a balanced approach to legal decision-making, one that takes into consideration the formalism of law along with attention to the effects on the people to whom it is applied.[149]

140 *See generally* Toni Massaro, *Empathy, Legal Storytelling, and the Rule of Law: New Words, Old Wounds?*, 87 MICH. L. REV. 2099 (1989).

141 Toni Massaro, *Empathy, Legal Storytelling, and the Rule of Law: New Words, Old Wounds?*, 87 MICH. L. REV. 2099, 2101 (1989).

142 *See* Toni Massaro, *Empathy, Legal Storytelling, and the Rule of Law: New Words, Old Wounds?*, 87 MICH. L. REV. 2099, 2107–09 (1989) (asserting that "'[l]aw' . . . cannot 'empathize' with everyone equally," but that "[o]f course, an empathic person will better 'hear' all stories . . . than one who heeds only one voice."). *But see* Andrea McArdle, *Using a Narrative Lens to Understand Empathy and How It Matters in Judging*, 9 LEGAL COMM. & RHETORIC: JALWD 173, 180 (2012) (explaining that "empathy [is] centrally connected with narrative [and] applies with equal force to the work of judging.").

143 *See* Toni Massaro, *Empathy, Legal Storytelling, and the Rule of Law: New Words, Old Wounds?*, 87 MICH. L. REV. 2099, 2107 (1989) (noting that empathy is a term "borrowed" from psychological literature).

144 *See* Toni Massaro, *Empathy, Legal Storytelling, and the Rule of Law: New Words, Old Wounds?*, 87 MICH. L. REV. 2099, 2107 (1989).

145 *See* Toni Massaro, *Empathy, Legal Storytelling, and the Rule of Law: New Words, Old Wounds?*, 87 MICH. L. REV. 2099, 2117–18 (1989) ("'[E]mpathic capacity,' as well as other relevant decision-making qualities, are unevenly discributed [sic] among human beings . . . . [O]pportunities for individualized justice and 'discretion'—explicit and implicit—already are dramatically pervasive . . . .").

146 *See, e.g.,* FLA. STAT. § 61.13 (2015) ("Determination of the best interests of the child shall be made by evaluating all of the factors affecting the welfare and interests of the particular minor child and the circumstances of that family . . . .").

147 *See* Toni Massaro, *Empathy, Legal Storytelling, and the Rule of Law: New Words, Old Wounds?*, 87 MICH. L. REV. 2099, 2111 (1989).

148 *See* Toni Massaro, *Empathy, Legal Storytelling, and the Rule of Law: New Words, Old Wounds?*, 87 MICH. L. REV. 2099, 2126 (1989).

149 *See* Toni Massaro, *Empathy, Legal Storytelling, and the Rule of Law: New Words, Old Wounds?*, 87 MICH. L. REV. 2099, 2126 (1989); *see also* ROBIN WEST, CARING FOR JUSTICE 206 (1997) (demonstrating that the feminist view of judicial decision-making, while highlighting the importance of "narrative sensibility," also takes into account that jurisprudence "require[s] immersion in the rules, principles, and lines of authority discovered in cases, statutes, and constitutions.").

Massaro's views, however, appear to be less a critique than a cautionary tale about the limits of narrative in the judicial realm, and others agree. Andrea McArdle, a confirmed advocate for narrative judging, seems comfortable with Massaro's tempered approach. McArdle avers that narrative judging, while itself an aptitude driven by narrative competence, is linked inextricably to empathy.[150] Narrative prompts empathy,[151] but empathy must not overwhelm judicial reasoning. McArdle advises that empathy does not stand alone. Judicial decisions must demonstrate "a regard for precedent and other institutional limits upon judicial function. In clear cases, presumably, precedent will dictate the outcome. In the unclear cases, empathy—informed by life experience and a capacity to appreciate others' perspectives and situations [e.g., narrative competence]—helps guide the exercise of judgment or discretion."[152]

Others, too, have counseled caution in adopting narrative or contextual approaches. "Feminists who have developed an interest in the reasoning processes of judges and other legal actors"[153] have weighed in on the role of narrative. While they are avid supporters of narrative judging, they concede the importance of "respecting the demands of abstraction and justice"[154] in decision-making that simultaneously involves "immersing [oneself] in the stories of others . . . ."[155] A commentator on bioethics provides a view on the role of narrative in the decision-making process that is equally measured in "defend[ing] narrative justification."[156] Joan McCarthy asserts that "the first person narrative is prima facie privileged. Not any tall tale will do, however, and personal stories are tested against various criteria, such as the stories of others and available documentary evidence."[157]

150 *See* Andrea McArdle, *Using a Narrative Lens to Understand Empathy and How It Matters in Judging*, 9 LEGAL COMM. & RHETORIC: JALWD 173, 180 (2012) (explaining that empathy is seen as "centrally connected with narrative [and] applies with equal force to the work of judging"); ROBIN WEST, CARING FOR JUSTICE 205 (1997) (citing Lynne Henderson, who "has argued the case for the importance of *empathy* to good judging.").

151 *See* Carrie Menkel-Meadow, *Telling Stories in School: Using Case Studies and Stories to Teach Legal Ethics*, 69 FORDHAM L. REV. 787, 792 (2000) (explaining that stories induce feelings: "'Feeling with' a character in a story or case allows us both to empathize or sympathize . . . ."). *See also* Victor D. Quintanilla, *Human-Centered Civil Justice Design*, 121 PENN ST. L. REV. 745 (2017). Quintanilla posits that human-centered justice designers, hoping to improve court systems, develop empathy for court users and stakeholders through perspective-taking gained from interviewing these constituents. *Id.* Perspective-taking, he claims, is achieved through listening to narratives of the court experience, which can then be used to drive system reforms. *Id.*

152 Andrea McArdle, *Using a Narrative Lens to Understand Empathy and How It Matters in Judging*, 9 LEGAL COMM. & RHETORIC: JALWD 173, 178 (2012).

153 ROBIN WEST, CARING FOR JUSTICE 204 (1997).

154 ROBIN WEST, CARING FOR JUSTICE 206 (1997) (citing Suzanna Sherry in commenting on "the importance of a sensitivity to the context within which each [judicial] decision is made . . . .").

155 *Id.* (citing Martha Nussbaum in commenting on "the importance of a sensitivity to the context within which each [judicial] decision is made . . . .").

156 Joan McCarthy, *Principlism or Narrative Ethics: Must We Choose Between Them?*, 29 MED. HUMAN. 65, 68 (2003), *available at* http://mh.bmj.com/content/29/2/65.full.

157 Joan McCarthy, *Principlism or Narrative Ethics: Must We Choose Between Them?*, 29 MED. HUMAN. 65, 68 (2003), *available at* http://mh.bmj.com/content/29/2/65.full.

Narratives, despite their limitations, routinely figure in how judges make decisions. Litigants' stories inevitably are embedded in cases, as the facts that form the basis for legal disputes are themselves narrative in nature. Competing narratives are the essence of litigation and are subject to the litigation process. When considered in this light, presenting a judge with counter narratives is no cause for concern.[158] Whether the applicable law is a product of a cultural narrative or a judge's personal narrative, stories always play a role in influencing judges' decisions and shaping jurisprudence. Litigants' stories merit attention from the court to determine what constitutes justice. To do justice, we need both[159]—the universal principles of law and the particular aspects of individual narratives, which provide the necessary context.[160]

Despite the qualifications regarding the use of a narrative perspective to determine legal outcomes, it is undoubtedly critical to the process. Kenneth Chestek states emphatically: "I believe that it is not only okay that judges pay attention to stories; it is imperative that they do so."[161] Chestek has conducted research to determine the effect of narrative presentations on judicial reasoning, including how a narrative format makes a difference. He has concluded,

> Narrative reasoning likely has some effect in every case, and potentially a dispositive effect in cases wherein the rules of law don't readily yield a clear answer. While not explicit, it is arguably quite certain that a judge would be remiss in not considering a narrative as would a lawyer be remiss in not framing his advocacy in this way.[162]

Chestek's standpoint on narrative reasoning is especially germane to family law. Family law statutes compel a highly fact-based interpretation.[163] In these cases, the family story is paramount in making the decision. Thus, the judge cannot ignore it.

158 *See, e.g.*, ROBIN WEST, CARING FOR JUSTICE 205 (1997) (describing the "ideal judge" who works her way through a resolution of the competing stories "carefully—and caringly").

159 *See, e.g.*, Cheshire Calhoun, *Justice, Care, and Gender Bias*, *in* ETHICAL THEORY: AN ANTHOLOGY 713, 713 (Russ Shafer-Landau ed., 2d ed. 2013) (arguing that applying principles of justice "requires, rather than excludes, knowledge of contextual details").

160 *See, e.g.*, Joan McCarthy, *Principlism or Narrative Ethics: Must We Choose Between Them?*, 29 MED. HUMAN. 65, 69 (2003), *available at* http://mh.bmj.com/content/29/2/65.full (writing about principalists versus narrativists in the bio-ethical realm, McCarthy concludes that it is possible and preferable to reconcile them when faced with a decision).

161 Kenneth D. Chestek, *Competing Stories: A Case Study of the Role of Narrative Reasoning in Judicial Decisions*, 9 LEGAL COMM. & RHETORIC: JALWD 99, 100 (2012), *available at* http://www.alwd.org/lcr/archives/fall-2012/chestek/.

162 Kenneth D. Chestek, *Competing Stories: A Case Study of the Role of Narrative Reasoning in Judicial Decisions*, 9 LEGAL COMM. & RHETORIC: JALWD 99, 135 (2012), *available at* http://www.alwd.org/lcr/archives/fall-2012/chestek/.

163 *See, e.g.*, LA. CIV. CODE ANN. art. 134 (2017) (enumerating twelve factual considerations to determine the best interest of the child, such as the emotional ties between each party and the child, the capacity of each party to give the child love and spiritual guidance, the home, school, and community history of the child, and the moral fitness of each party).

Ethical awareness

Narratives influence ethical lawyering; "the use of narrative expands the sight-lines of reality and imagination for legal and moral reasoning."[164] "Most literary critics attribute the first use of narrative for moral or political purposes to Plato."[165] Greek myths are illustrative in this way.[166] Similarly, classic fairy tales provide guidance for moral and ethical behavior.[167] Anthony Amsterdam and Jerome Bruner suggest that a culture's ethical precepts, embodied in legal rules and principles, are "identifiable in its 'stories, its genres, [and] its enduring myths.'"[168]

> "There is a peculiar and unexpected relation between the affirmation of moral law and storytelling," writes J. Hillis Miller in *The Ethics of Reading*. "Without storytelling there is no theory of ethics. Narrative examples, stories . . . are indispensable to thinking about ethics."[169]

There are two points of consideration required to address how narrative and ethical awareness intersect in telling stories. First, stories aid in developing an ethical consciousness.[170] Second, there are ethical issues involved in the act of storytelling, or, as Rita Charon describes them, "the obligations incurred in narrative acts."[171] Thus, narrative is ethically instructive, but, at the same time, narrative practice incurs its own unique ethical responsibilities (whether in court and judicial practices or lawyering).[172]

164 Carrie Menkel-Meadow, *Telling Stories in School: Using Case Studies and Stories to Teach Legal Ethics*, 69 Fordham L. Rev. 787, 793 (2000).
165 Carrie Menkel-Meadow, *Telling Stories in School: Using Case Studies and Stories to Teach Legal Ethics*, 69 Fordham L. Rev. 787, 788 n.4 (2000) (citing, e.g., Martha C. Nussbaum, Love's Knowledge: Essays on Philosophy and Literature (1990)).
166 Jerome Bruner, Making Stories: Law, Literature, Life 98 (2002) (explaining that whether the Greeks believed their myths is subject to conjecture, but "they certainly took heed of those myths in how they lived their lives and experienced their world.").
167 *See, e.g.*, Jacob Grimm & Wilhelm Grimm, Rumplestiltskin (Margaret Hunt trans., 1884); Jacob Grimm & Wilhelm Grimm, The Golden Goose (Margaret Hunt trans., 1884); Gabrielle-Suzanne Barbot de Villeneuve, Beauty and the Beast (Ernest Dowson trans., 1908); Carlo Collodi, The Adventures of Pinocchio (Carol Della Chiesa trans., 1926).
168 Andrea McArdle, *Using a Narrative Lens to Understand Empathy and How It Matters in Judging*, 9 Legal Comm. & Rhetoric: JALWD 173, 181 (2012) (citing Amsterdam & Bruner, Minding the Law 111 (2000)).
169 Rita Charon, Narrative Medicine: Honoring the Stories of Illness 55 (2006).
170 Rita Charon, Narrative Medicine: Honoring the Stories of Illness 55 (2006) (noting in her discussion of the ethical relations between the storyteller and listener that stories enable an "ethical vision"); Joan McCarthy, *Principlism or Narrative Ethics: Must We Choose Between Them?*, 29 Med. Human. 65, 68–69 (2003), *available at* http://mh.bmj.com/content/29/2/65.full (recounting the resolution of a bio-ethical issue that involved taking into account the patient's personal narrative and concluding that this approach enabled the decision-makers to determine an ethical outcome).
171 Rita Charon, Narrative Medicine: Honoring the Stories of Illness 55 (2006).
172 *See, e.g.*, Robert Weisberg, *Proclaiming Trials as Narratives: Premises and Pretenses, in* Law's Stories: Narrative and Rhetoric in the Law 65 (Peter Brooks & Paul Gewirtz eds., 1996) (claiming that "legal practice and judging are partly ethical tasks . . . .").

Feminist legal scholars have endorsed the idea without question. Robin West proposes that narrativity is at the "ethical core" of judging.[173] She explains that a judge who recognizes and considers litigants' stories works toward reaching an ethical conclusion that comports with a just result.[174] Likewise, Rebecca Lee suggests that a narrative perspective allows judges to evaluate more easily the circumstances of litigants with whom they share little common ground; thus, narratives enable a judge to enter the litigant's world and fulfill the judge's ethical responsibility to consider the multiple facets of the legal issue before her.[175] Lee asserts further that attention to the narratives on both sides of an issue demonstrates impartiality,[176] which is itself an ethical commandment for judges.[177] The link between narrative and ethicality bolsters the argument for narrativity as a component of jurisprudential considerations. Competing narrative presentations expose the ethical implications on both sides of a legal dispute, allowing judges attuned to these contrasting accounts to weigh a broad range of issues as they formulate their decisions.

While narrative helps to edify the ethical mandates of legal[178] and judicial practices[179] and the ethical impacts of legal outcomes, the narrative approach also compels corresponding responsibilities.[180] Ethical considerations apply to the act of storytelling itself, because narratives presented by lawyers are particularly persuasive.[181] Narrative accounts pose meaningful challenges to judges as they

173 Robin West, Caring for Justice 206 (1997).
174 Robin West, Caring for Justice 206 (1997).
175 *See* Rebecca K. Lee, *Judging Judges: Empathy as the Litmus Test for Impartiality*, 82 U. Cin. L. Rev. 145, 161–62 (2014) (noting that it is necessary for judges to engage in a conscious effort to understand a litigant's story, which characterizes an empathic point of view and an ethical approach, while demonstrating the impartiality of the fact-finder).
176 *See* Rebecca K. Lee, *Judging Judges: Empathy as the Litmus Test for Impartiality*, 82 U. Cin. L. Rev. 145, 161 (2014) (noting the necessity for judges to understand litigants' stories to achieve impartiality).
177 Model Rules of Prof'l Conduct r. 2.2 (Am. Bar Ass'n 2016).
178 *See* Carrie Menkel-Meadow, *Telling Stories in School: Using Case Studies and Stories to Teach Legal Ethics*, 69 Fordham L. Rev. 787, 793 (2000) (explaining that storytelling imparts contextual information about cases which enables law students and lawyers "to make good moral and ethical choices").
179 *See* Robin West, Caring for Justice 206 (1997) (suggesting that narrativity lies at the ethical core of judging).
180 *See* Binny Miller, *Telling Stories About Cases and Clients: The Ethics of Narrative*, 14 Geo. J. Legal Ethics 1 (2000), for a discussion of the ethical issues associated with telling clients' stories in the context of legal scholarship beyond compliance with client confidentiality. Miller proposes considerations respecting notice to clients about the content of the story, how the story will be used, the risks associated with self-disclosure, and whether the client should share in any monetary compensation awarded to the author. *Id.*
181 *See* J. Christopher Rideout, *Storytelling, Narrative Rationality, and Legal Persuasion*, 14 Legal Writing: J. Legal Writing Inst. 53, 54 (2008). Rideout cites research conducted by cognitive scientists concluding that "'the central cognitive process in juror decision-making is story construction.'" *Id.* Rideout states, "[T]heir research offered support for what many trial lawyers had already long known—that lawyers persuade by telling stories." *Id.*

consider evidence and balance the impacts of competing stories.[182] As Jerome Bruner has said, "Law stories are always, and are guaranteed to be, highly consequential to the parties engaged. They matter and their believability matters. It is in no sense playful storytelling."[183]

The ethical considerations specific to the practice of legal storytelling involve a discussion of three sequential activities: receiving the client's story (listening to it), reconstituting the story (refashioning it), and retelling the story in an advocacy setting. Listening carefully and deliberately is elemental to narrative practice. The reception of the teller's story is the first step in the process. The narrative practitioner must develop acute listening skills and attention to non-verbal cues.[184] Rita Charon, in detailing narrative medical practice, points to listening as an important component of narrative competence and, in turn, ethical practice.[185] This responsibility, Charon says, obligates the listener to attend fully and completely to the patient's story; mis-apprehension on a doctor's part may cause significant adverse consequences for the patient.[186]

Charon's view also applies in the legal realm, where the stakes are equally high. As physicians must focus carefully on their patients' narratives, attorneys also must pay meticulous attention to the stories their clients tell them. Without such attention, the legal case is jeopardized. Judges, too, must listen with acuity. Robin West, in describing the attributes of the ideal judge, highlights the importance of the judge's listening skills. "She must be, quintessentially, a good listener and a good teller of stories."[187] Court personnel also need to listen carefully to litigants, whether in administrative processes, such as filing court documents,[188] or during

182 *See, e.g.*, Toni Massaro, *Empathy, Legal Storytelling, and the Rule of Law: New Words, Old Wounds?*, 87 MICH. L. REV. 2099, 2107 (1989) (pointing out that conflicting stories require the judge to "'stand in the shoes of'" more than one party and in so doing the judge must choose between "competing 'voices'").

183 JEROME BRUNER, MAKING STORIES: LAW, LITERATURE, LIFE 41 (2002).

184 RITA CHARON, NARRATIVE MEDICINE: HONORING THE STORIES OF ILLNESS 67 (2006) ("Patient-centered care and relationship-centered care require respectful authentic relationships with patients that come about through attentive and creative listening.").

185 *See* RITA CHARON, NARRATIVE MEDICINE: HONORING THE STORIES OF ILLNESS 3 (2006) (describing the initiative at Columbia University College of Physicians and Surgeons to teach healthcare professionals the "skills needed to listen to narratives of illness, to understand what they mean, to attain rich and accurate interpretations of these stories, and to grasp the plights of patients in all their complexity.").

186 *See, e.g.*, JEROME BRUNER, MAKING STORIES: LAW, LITERATURE, LIFE 105 (2002) (explaining that narrative medicine came into being "in response to the increasing realization of the suffering—even deaths—attributable in part or in whole to doctors having ignored what patients told them about their illnesses."); Frank Huyler, THE BLOOD OF STRANGERS: STORIES FROM EMERGENCY MEDICINE 51 (2004) (chronicling the consequences of a physician's having ignored a single aspect of the patient's story).

187 ROBIN WEST, CARING FOR JUSTICE 206 (1997).

188 *See* Barbara A. Babb & Judith D. Moran, *Substance Abuse, Families, and Unified Family Courts: The Creation of a Caring Justice System*, 3 J. HEALTH CARE L. & POL'Y 19, 23–34 (1999), for a description of the court services available to families at the Family Division of the Circuit Court for Baltimore City where there is an effort to care for families in the justice system. The article describes training initiatives for court

evaluations of litigants for their potential participation in court services. In family courts especially, where the self-represented litigant population is substantial, families often are mired in court processes they are ill equipped to navigate. In this arena, caring is important and listening is essential.

The subsequent steps in narrative practice mentioned above (refashioning and retelling clients' stories) expand upon the ethical issues in storytelling. Refashioning the client's narrative forms the basis of the legal argument, while retelling it involves the presentation of the narrative account to a judge.[189] In both instances, lawyers must proceed with narrative attention.[190] Depending upon the type of case, the quality of the listening, refashioning, and retelling may have a profound effect on an outcome that poses serious consequences for a family. A family law litigant, for example, may lose custody or parental rights for want of an accurate and compelling story.[191] These possible adverse outcomes prompted by lapses in narrative practices, such as mis-hearing or mis-telling the client's account, further underscore the risks and responsibilities associated with legal storytelling. Judges and attorneys must take heed; the keenness and sensitivity with which a lawyer presents the case and a judge listens to the presentation matter in ensuring that justice is served.

There is another aspect of storytelling ethics related to legal advocacy. It concerns the persuasive nature of stories, which attorneys use to their clients' advantage. While narratives are a means to this end, lawyers who use stories must follow

personnel with an eye to providing specific court services to meet the unique needs of families and children. *Id.*

189 Anthony G. Amsterdam & Jerome Bruner, Minding the Law 110 (2000) (explaining the process of legal storytelling, beginning with the client interview in which "clients tell stories to lawyers who must figure out what to make of what they hear" and ending with the lawyer's presentation of the story to the court and the eventual outcome, verdict, opinion or otherwise, that is based upon the stories judges and juries "retell . . . to themselves.").

190 *See, e.g.*, Rita Charon, Narrative Medicine: Honoring the Stories of Illness 132 (2006) (describing the attention required for narrative practice as "relaxing, absorbing, making room within myself for an oceanic acceptance of what the patient offers.").

191 Statutes, especially in family law, may include factual determinations that lend themselves to narrative expositions. *See, e.g.*, Fla. Stat. § 61.13 (2016) ("Determination of the best interests of the child shall be made by evaluating all of the factors affecting the welfare and interests of the particular minor child and the circumstances of that family . . . ."); W. Va. Code § 48-6-301 (2016) ("The court shall consider the following factors in determining the amount of spousal support, child support or separate maintenance . . . . The income-earning abilities of each of the parties, . . . the physical, mental and emotional condition of each party, [and] . . . [t]he standard of living established during the marriage . . . ."); Cal. Fam. Code § 4320 (West 2016) (In ordering spousal support under this part, the court shall consider all of the following circumstances . . . . The marketable skills of the supported party; the job market for those skills . . . the extent to which the supported party contributed to the attainment of an education, training, a career position, or a license by the supporting party . . . . The needs of each party . . . .).

evidentiary mandates regulating their form, substance, and presentation.[192] Thus, persuasive techniques must adhere to these requirements, in addition to the ethical obligation that "the stories told by attorneys must be factually meticulous and truthful . . . ."[193]

Steven Johansen asserts that the growing recognition of the Applied Legal Storytelling movement, the most recent paradigm that follows a narrative tradition, requires an examination of its ethical parameters.[194] Johansen, in writing on the ethical issues involved, voices concerns about the limits of persuasion in narrative legal presentations. He maintains that these persuasive aspects highlight the lawyer's professional responsibility to contain narrative's influential power within ethical boundaries. "Specifically, questions remain about the ability of storytellers to cross the line from effective and appropriate persuasion to inappropriate manipulation."[195] One of these convincing techniques, he notes, is point of view narration,[196] which is problematic in that "other points of view are slighted or not told at all."[197] Johansen explains that a point of view perspective may result in "leav[ing] out critical parts of the story" that an ethical duty may mandate.[198] Nevertheless, Johansen asserts that a first person account also saves storytelling from the perils of persuasive manipulation. The teller of an in-court narrative is relating the story from her client's own point of view; thus, it may invite a skeptical appraisal from listeners. Such first person accounts highlight the fact that there may be other versions of the story, often told in court by opposing counsel.

Johansen's overall analysis is worthy of consideration, given the increasing recognition of legal storytelling and the proliferation of its practitioners.[199] Lawyers, however, have told stories long before the legal academy began writing about

192 *See* Philip N. Meyer, Storytelling for Lawyers 208 (2014); Anthony G. Amsterdam & Jerome Bruner, Minding the Law 46 (2000); Jerome Bruner, Making Stories: Law, Literature, Life 38 (2002) (explaining the constraints on legal storytelling).

193 Philip N. Meyer, Storytelling for Lawyers 208 (2014).

194 *See* Steven Johansen, *Was Colonel Sanders a Terrorist? An Essay on the Ethical Limits of Applied Legal Storytelling*, 7 J. Ass'n Legal Writing Directors 63 (2010). *But see* Helena Whalen-Bridge, *The Lost Narrative: The Connection Between Legal Narrative and Legal Ethics*, 7 J. Ass'n Legal Writing Directors 229, 243–44 (2010) (citing Steven Lubet's description of legal storytelling "as a noble pursuit that does not encompass misrepresentation . . . . [A] conscientious attorney 'fashions a story not to hide or distort the truth, but rather to enable a client to come closer to the truth'").

195 Steven Johansen, *Was Colonel Sanders a Terrorist? An Essay on the Ethical Limits of Applied Legal Storytelling*, 7 J. Ass'n Legal Writing Directors 63, 64 (2010).

196 Point-of-view narration is an account given from the point of view of the storyteller—otherwise known as a first person narrator.

197 Steven Johansen, *Was Colonel Sanders a Terrorist? An Essay on the Ethical Limits of Applied Legal Storytelling*, 7 J. Ass'n Legal Writing Directors 63, 64 (2010).

198 Steven Johansen, *Was Colonel Sanders a Terrorist? An Essay on the Ethical Limits of Applied Legal Storytelling*, 7 J. Ass'n Legal Writing Directors 63, 73 (2010) (using, by way of example, a prosecutor's duty to include "critical parts of the story").

199 *See Fifth Biennial Conference on Applied Legal Storytelling July 21–23, 2015, Seattle University School of Law,* (recalling opening remarks that drew attention to the growth in number and prominence of those who practice, teach, and write about legal storytelling).

narrative, and "existing ethical norms seem well suited to protect against potential abuses."[200] Johansen avers that "at least some of the unique characteristics of story create few unique ethical problems. A lawyer who chooses to use stories to persuade may look to the same ethical principles to which she has always looked."[201]

All told, narrative paves the way for ethical practice, which, in turn, informs the type of justice a court dispenses. Narrative increases the likelihood of "moral reasoning"—the capacity to "imagine" what is right and just.[202] Narrative is ethically important as a persuasive tool because it enables empathy for litigants' circumstances and augments creativity in fashioning a just and caring outcome. That said, the emotional thrust of narrative does not trump reasoned analysis. Justice requires both.[203] Without narrative underpinnings, however, courts will render justice that is bereft of caring.

Conclusion

Narrative and caring go hand in hand; they are a cooperative undertaking. In order to care for someone, you must listen to and understand her story. Narrative competence, or the capacity to elicit a person's story and from it to imagine their circumstances, is the juncture from which the ethic of care evolves. From a philosophical perspective, ". . . the responsibility to care requires participation in a collective imagery, in narratives and images that define the group's identity . . . ."[204] In the family court arena, narratives are personal. Nevertheless, they are a critical factor in dispensing caring justice.

We have set out in this chapter to demonstrate that a narrative approach to family law jurisprudence is essential to enable caring in court. Story elements, such as, plot, timeframe, setting, character, and point of view, provide the basic structure for lawyers to make convincing presentations to the court. In turn, a compelling narrative helps judges to render decisions that demonstrate caring for families and children. Without a narrative framework, judicial decision-making is limited because "a full understanding of a legal question, a legal dilemma . . . requires a humanistic analysis,"[205] which is derived from the stories told in the

200 Steven Johansen, *Was Colonel Sanders a Terrorist? An Essay on the Ethical Limits of Applied Legal Storytelling*, 7 J. Ass'n Legal Writing Directors 63, 84 (2010).

201 Steven Johansen, *Was Colonel Sanders a Terrorist? An Essay on the Ethical Limits of Applied Legal Storytelling*, 7 J. Ass'n Legal Writing Directors 63, 886 (2010).

202 Carrie Menkel-Meadow, *Telling Stories in School: Using Case Studies and Stories to Teach Legal Ethics*, 69 Fordham L. Rev. 787, 793 (2000).

203 *See* Steven Johansen, *Was Colonel Sanders a Terrorist? An Essay on the Ethical Limits of Applied Legal Storytelling*, 7 J. Ass'n Legal Writing Directors 63, 85 (2010) (explaining that emotion without reason "is not enough to justify a legal argument."); Robin West, Caring for Justice 207 (1997) (noting that "judging is and ought to be an empathic, as well as a rational, act.").

204 Mihaela Czobor-Lupp, *Heidegger's Contribution to an Ethic of Care and Responsiveness* (Paper Presented at the Annual Meeting of the American Political Association, Washington, D.C., Sept. 2–5, 2010).

205 Robin West, Caring for Justice 183 (1997).

courtroom.[206] The work of just and caring lawyering and judging relies on such narrative acts—presentations to the court contained in narrative formats and legal analysis informed by them. This practice is essential to our court reform project.

In the next chapter, Chapter 5, we combine all of our jurisprudential components—the unified family court, the ecology of human development, therapeutic jurisprudence, the ethic of care, and narrative practices. We explain how they can and must apply to the structure and function of an effective family justice system.

206 *See, e.g.*, Robin West, Caring for Justice 183 (1997) (positing the feminist view that justice must be humane and caring).

5 Applying an ethic of care to the family justice system

The transformative power of caring and narrative

Introduction

> A court that cares—a court that does not use the weapons of litigation to destroy but uses benign help to restore—is a powerful story.[1]

> [W]orking to devise a system that will better serve the needs of the public need not affect a court's ability to judge the merits of an individual case fairly.[2]

"Legal philosophers have discussed the quality of justice for thousands of years, but they have rarely, if ever, stated their conclusions specifically and concretely enough to be applied precisely by others to the everyday work of the courts."[3] How do we assess the quality of justice in family courts? Specifically, "can we define the value that [f]amily [c]ourt adds to the lives of the families it serves?"[4] As we have demonstrated, the family justice system is about more than resolving legal disputes. The system also needs to address the many related nonlegal issues and must strive to improve the lives of families and children as a result of their family court involvement.

To accomplish this, we have recounted a blueprint for and the significance of unified family courts, the ecology of human development, and therapeutic jurisprudence to our notion of justice for families. The organizational framework of unified family courts enables

> the court to hear and determine the full range of family law cases (including delinquency and dependency), to provide continuous case management, and to connect parties to necessary and appropriate nonlegal services, all under the supervision of specially trained and interested judges.[5]

1 Jane M. Spinak, *Reforming Family Court: Getting It Right Between Rhetoric and Reality*, 31 WASH. U. J.L. & POL'Y 11, 22 (2009).
2 Judith S. Kaye & Susan K. Knipps, *Judicial Responses to Domestic Violence: The Case for a Problem Solving Approach*, 27 W. ST. U. L. REV. 1, 11 (1999–2000) (footnote omitted).
3 Brian Ostrom & Roger Hanson, Achieving High Performance: A Framework for Courts 10 (Apr. 2010) (unpublished manuscript) (on file with authors).
4 Jane M. Spinak, *Adding Value to Families: The Potential of Model Family Courts*, 2002 WIS. L. REV. 331 (2002).
5 Barbara A. Babb, *Another Look at the Need for Family Law Education Reform: One Law School's Innovations*, 55 FAM. CT. REV. 59, 61 (2017).

The ecology of human development theory espouses a holistic, social science perspective to achieve optimal family functioning. It details the elements that are necessary for families and children to thrive and to participate meaningfully in contemporary society. The ecological approach depends upon an extended network of institutional and community support systems, envisioned as concentric circles surrounding the family unit. The network consists of schools, religious organizations, healthcare facilities, and court systems, among other institutions. Therapeutic jurisprudence is an approach that envisions the law and the behavior of legal actors as agents of change for the betterment of the lives of the persons whom law and its processes affect. "The sense of what constitutes a therapeutic outcome derives from the individual's own viewpoint [akin to the narrative perspective we support], which courts must attempt to honor."[6]

Many family courts have accepted and applied these constructs.[7] In order to achieve a truly effective family justice system, however, more is required. The ethic of care principle, grounded in narrative practice, can transform the family justice system into a place that demonstrates it truly has value for those it serves.

6 Barbara A. Babb & Judith D. Moran, *Substance Abuse, Families, and Unified Family Courts: The Creation of a Caring Justice System*, 3 J. Health Care L. & Pol'y 1, 16–17 (1999).

7 *See, e.g.*, Barbara A. Babb & Jeffrey A. Kuhn, Performance Standards and Measures for Maryland's Family Divisions 5–7 (2002); Judicial Council of Cal. Admin. Office of the Courts, Ctr. for Families, Children & the Courts, Unified Courts for Families Deskbook: A Guide for California Courts on Unifying and Coordinating Family and Juvenile Law Matters I-1 (2004); Department of Justice Canada, *Government of Canada Announces Judicial Appointments in Nunavut*, CISION, June 22, 2018, *available at* https://www.newswire.ca/news-releases/government-of-canada-announces-judicial-appointments-in-nunavut-686278191.html (describing Canada's dramatic expansion of unified family courts across that country's court systems and the new judicial appointments to them). *See also* Department of Justice Canada, *Government of Canada Announces Judicial Appointment in the Province of New Brunswick*, CISION, June 22, 2018, *available at* https://www.newswire.ca/news-releases/government-of-canada-announces-judicial-appointment-in-the-province-of-new-brunswick-686284921.html; Department of Justice Canada, *Government of Canada Announces Judicial Appointment in the Province of Quebec*, CISION, June 22, 2018, *available at* https://www.newswire.ca/news-releases/government-of-canada-announces-judicial-appointment-in-the-province-of-quebec-686277691.html; Department of Justice Canada, *Government of Canada Announces Judicial Appointment in the Province of Saskatchewan*, CISION, June 22, 2018, *available at* https://www.newswire.ca/news-releases/government-of-canada-announces-judicial-appointment-in-the-province-of-saskatchewan-686276961.html; Department of Justice Canada, *Government of Canada Announces Judicial Appointment to the Tax Court of Canada*, CISION, June 22, 2018, *available at* https://www.newswire.ca/news-releases/government-of-canada-announces-judicial-appointment-to-the-tax-court-of-canada- 686277301.html; Thomas Cromwell, *Access to Justice: Second Interview with Justice George Czurtin*, Law. Daily (Can.), Oct. 24, 2017, *available at* https://www.thelawyersdaily.ca/articles/4909. *The 10 Cs: Core Components of Florida's Family Court*, Fla. Courts, http://www.flcourts.org/resources-and-services/court-improvement/family-courts/judicial-toolkits/family-court-basic/core-components.stml (last visited June 1, 2018).

Is caring relevant to the operation of the family justice system? As one medical educator has counseled her student doctors, "Patients don't care how much you know . . . . [T]hey want to know how much you care."[8] Likewise in law, there are analogous situations where caring is as important as the legal outcome. In particular, caring is of great significance in family law proceedings, since legal outcomes often do not comport with clients' expectations (the resolution of a contentious custody dispute, for example).[9] In these circumstances, the care with which the judge dispenses the decision, interpreted by the attorney and supported by court service providers, may reduce the pain involved in receiving a less than desired outcome.

Matthew Kavanagh explains that "[f]amilies and communities are characterized by systems of care—intersecting webs of people who give care, people who receive care, and, primarily, people who both give *and* receive care."[10] Virginia Held is more specific in translating care theory into practice. She argues "that care is needed in such contexts of justice as . . . the courts, where persons should be treated humanely . . . ."[11] Yet, there is little discussion about whether a care ethic is an appropriate and a necessary component of the family justice system. Those scholars who write about the ethic of care are at best indirect, like Held, in applying its humanizing potential to the way courts function. A more comprehensive and deliberate project can enable family courts to care for the people who depend upon them to resolve their legal and related nonlegal issues. For the ethic of care to become a fully realized component of justice for families, it is critical to make the implicit explicit. We therefore name caring as a reform agenda and provide concrete proposals about how to implement it in family court system structure, policies, and procedures. To operationalize caring, more is required to assist justice system actors. Because caring must comport with litigants' needs, narrative practices that describe and highlight litigants' individual circumstances contribute to our reform agenda.

In this chapter, we resolve how to apply the ethic of care and narrative practice to the family justice system. In Chapter 3, we have examined the basis in political theory for an ethic of care approach to government institutions, including, from our perspective, the family justice system. In Chapter 4, we have discussed the interrelationship between a narrative viewpoint and the capacity for caring. We now propose how to infuse the family justice system with a care ethic, something that involves instilling a narrative perspective in those who work in the court—judges, lawyers, court services professionals, and administrative personnel. Our

8 Rick Rojas, *Doctor Killed in Hospital Attack Is Mourned as "Monumental Loss for Us,"* N.Y. Times, July 3, 2017, at A14.

9 *See, e.g.*, Leonard L. Riskin, *The Contemplative Lawyer: On the Potential Contributions of Mindfulness Meditation to Law Students, Lawyers, and Their Clients*, 7 Harv. Negot. L. Rev. 1, 13 (2002) (noting the discontent that is prevalent among litigants involved in matters related to divorce).

10 Matthew M. Kavanagh, *Rewriting the Legal Family: Beyond Exclusivity to a Care-Based Standard*, 16 Yale J. L. & Feminism 83, 117 (2004).

11 Virginia Held, The Ethics of Care 15 (2006).

discussion emphasizes the importance of those particular structural and theoretical components we also deem essential to enact caring, including unified family courts, the ecology of human development, and therapeutic jurisprudence. We highlight practices that embody principles of our comprehensive vision to instill caring into the ways and means of the family justice system. What matters most is a consistent and concerted effort to preserve and enhance the well-being of the families and children who seek the court's assistance to resolve their disputes.

Summarizing ethic of care and narrative concepts

As we have recounted, caring is basic to human existence. It is about relationships between and among human beings. The ethic of care, which harkens back to the earliest philosophers, has evolved to represent a comprehensive view of social policy and law. Caring thus involves both the personal and the political. It occurs on both the home front between and among family members and in the community at large, where caring is a facet of participation in civic life.

Caring in the legal sense contemplates a comprehensive view of justice. It assumes the application of relevant law, as well as attention to individual circumstances. Applied to the law, caring privileges obligations over rights, and it provides moral guidance as to what is owed to those in need. Caring thus implicates an ethical endeavor, elicited by individual encounters that compel behavior responding to the needs presented in the specific encounters. In this way, caring derives from situational contexts that involve a narrative framework. Who is in need, and what is required to meet the need? The ethic of care requires both a habit of mind and action.

Narrative competence, including the ability to imagine what is right and just under the particular circumstances after hearing an individual's story, enables caring. Narrative capacities, including empathy, informed decision-making, and ethical awareness, contribute to narrative competence. Narrative practice involves mastering a set of interpersonal skills, such as focused attention, acute listening, and empathic concern, to elicit stories from litigants. These stories or narratives provide the context for dispensing caring justice.

Narrative practice in law requires specific ethical obligations, such as respecting limits of persuasion in legal storytelling, attending properly to the stories clients and litigants tell, and retelling those stories accurately from the client's or litigant's point of view. Narrative practice, then, is a necessary aspect of both lawyering and decision-making that is caring and just.

Envisioning the family justice system as a care center

Should we incorporate an ethic of care into the operation of the family justice system? If so, how? Martha Nussbaum argues that "the judgments made in courts of law should be informed not only by legal precedent, but by the empathic knowledge we gain through the heart—what she has called 'Love's Knowledge.'"[12] Daniel Engster states, "Governments can help us to fulfill our moral duties by creating an institutional framework for supporting and accommodating caring practices . . . ."[13] Engster labels these institutional responsibilities as "secondary caring responsibilities,"[14] or those "owed to individuals with whom we share some sort of special relationship or are in a special position to help."[15] For Engster, "[t]he duty to care derives . . . from our inevitable dependency on others and the web of caring relationships that sustain us."[16]

The family justice system owes a particular duty of care, as it deals with such special relationships among and between individuals. One family law magistrate calls attention to this.

> Family law needs attorneys who are smart, certainly, but perhaps more critically, it needs attorneys who genuinely care about families . . . . You are, of course, limited in many ways: by the law, your professional responsibility, your client's wishes and those of the other side, the court and your own moral compass. But you can always choose to care about the impact your actions have on your client, your client's family, on a child, on the court, and, ultimately, on the legal system.[17]

The consequences stemming from a lack of care are dire. "Individuals who do not receive adequate care are more likely to engage in violence and crime, have difficulty finding and maintaining productive work, suffer depression and anxiety, and experience a number of other personal and health problems."[18]

> Care theory does not, however, call for anything like a revolutionary struggle to implement a new caring regime. Rather, it lends itself nicely to a gradualist or piecemeal approach to reform. If governments were to pass even a few caring policies, the long-term effect would likely be a citizen body more supportive of additional caring policies.[19]

Family courts are the perfect place to begin this piecemeal approach to the incorporation of care theory.

Courts are the one place in society where everyone is equal. Due to the numbers of individuals who utilize the court system to resolve various types of problems, courts certainly have a broad view of the community's needs. By their nature courts

12 Robin West, Caring for Justice 189 (1997) (citing Martha Nussbaum, Love's Knowledge: Essays on Philosophy and Literature (1990)).
13 Daniel Engster, The Heart of Justice 11 (2007).
14 Daniel Engster, The Heart of Justice 56 (2007).
15 Daniel Engster, The Heart of Justice 56 (2007).
16 Daniel Engster, The Heart of Justice 12 (2007).
17 Bibi Berry, *The Protector of Families*, Super Law. Mag. (Md.), 2018, at 8.
18 Daniel Engster, The Heart of Justice 15 (2007) (footnote omitted).
19 Daniel Engster, The Heart of Justice 242 (2007).

have the inherent power to integrate legal and social resources to achieve desired outcomes. Courts also have the obligation to enforce certain behavioral mores of the community and to direct the professional tone of the justice system. All of these qualify the court to act as a care center for the community. We already have discussed how family courts in particular have begun to function like hospital emergency rooms. Some even have suggested that the family justice system adopt a public health model.[20] Let us begin to insist that family courts adopt an ethic of care in their approach to family law issues so that these courts become places that care rather than places that scare.[21] As one scholar insists, "Courts are part of the healing community . . . . If we insist that [courts] meet the needs of children and families, we are saying that we value children and families . . . . Every interaction [between the court and the children and families] is an opportunity to promote healing."[22] A social worker who works with children of divorce echoes these sentiments and explains that "attorneys need to recognize the power they have to help . . . . Courts and lawyers need to be agents of healing."[23]

How can this occur? How do we equip the family justice system to operate as a care center and to effectively assist families and children? In Chapter 2, we have described how therapeutic jurisprudence is an essential theoretical foundation of the unified family court, defined in Chapter 1. Some scholars have argued that an ethic of care is the moral basis from which to consider therapeutic jurisprudence.[24] This involves "bringing an ethic of care to the law through the efforts of the attorneys, judges, and staff, just as doctors and nurses would in caring for a patient in a medical setting."[25] Further,

> therapeutic jurisprudence, incorporating significant elements of the ethics of care, uniquely redefines the role of law as a means of problem-solving and offers an alternative approach to legal practice based on a model which encourages relational intimacy, self-awareness, conciliation and restoration. As

20 Peter Salem, Irwin Sandler, & Sharlene Wolchik, *Taking Stock of Parent Education in the Family Courts: Envisioning a Public Health Approach*, 51 Fam. Ct. Rev. 131, 137 (2013).

21 *See* Marc W. Patry, David B. Wexler, Dennis P. Stolle, & Alan J. Tompkins, *Better Legal Counseling Through Empirical Research: Identifying Psycholegal Soft Spots and Strategies*, 34 Cal. W. L. Rev. 439 (1998).

22 Shawn Marsh, Dir. Of Judicial Studies & Assoc. Professor of Commc'n Studies and Soc. Psychology, Univ. of Nev., Reno, Remarks at the Association of Family and Conciliation Courts 55th Annual Conference (June 8, 2018).

23 Marcia Lebowitz, Founding Dir., Children's Divorce Ctr. & Adjunct Professor, Quinnipiac Univ., Remarks at the Association of Family and Conciliation Courts 55th Annual Conference (June 8, 2018).

24 Warren Brookbanks, *Therapeutic Jurisprudence: Conceiving an Ethical Framework*, 8 J.L.& Med. 328, 333 (2001); Michael A. Town, *The Unified Family Court: Preventive, Therapeutic and Restorative Justice for America's Families*, Juv. & Fam. Just. Today, Winter 2002, at 14–15.

25 Michael A. Town, *The Unified Family Court: Preventive, Therapeutic and Restorative Justice for America's Families*, Juv. & Fam. Just. Today, Winter 2002, at 15.

> such, therapeutic jurisprudence incorporates a conscious down-playing of the adversarial or "conflict" approach.[26]

An ethic of care approach to therapeutic jurisprudence compels a "focus on the moral perceptions, dispositions and thoughts that arise from the actual business of caring for, and advocating the interests of, people."[27] In order to engage in the business of caring,

> [t]he challenge, for lawyers as for physicians, is to be able to assist their clients to integrate the narrative of their life's experiences into an ongoing experience of life within which specific incidents of legal "trauma" may be located and understood in such a way that the client is not destroyed by the shock of legal conflict and is able to process it as an aspect, an incident, in a life well lived.[28]

An ethic of care approach to therapeutic jurisprudence "facilitates this enhancement of the emotional life in legal problem-solving . . . which . . . is better able to capture and explain the relational richness which therapeutic jurisprudence is able to express."[29] Therapeutic jurisprudence, grounded in an ethic of care, brings value to the lives of family court participants.

An ethic of care perspective requires "everyone having a voice, being listened to carefully (in their own right and on their own terms) and heard with respect."[30] These qualities significantly influence the impact of justice system actions on families and children.

> [R]esearch consistently shows positive experiences are shaped more by court users' evaluations of how they are treated and whether the process of making decisions seems fair . . . . This principle [of procedural justice] is of fundamental importance to the institutional legitimacy of a court and to the degree of trust placed in it by participants in the legal process, policy makers, and members of the public. In turn, perceptions that procedures are fair and understandable influence a host of outcome variables, including satisfaction with the process, respect for the court, and willingness to comply with court rulings and orders—even if individuals don't like the outcome.[31]

26 Warren Brookbanks, *Therapeutic Jurisprudence: Conceiving an Ethical Framework*, 8 J.L. & Med. 328, 329–30 (2001).
27 Warren Brookbanks, *Therapeutic Jurisprudence: Conceiving an Ethical Framework*, 8 J.L. & Med. 328, 333 (2001) (footnote omitted).
28 Warren Brookbanks, *Therapeutic Jurisprudence: Conceiving an Ethical Framework*, 8 J.L. & Med. 328, 339 (2001) (footnote omitted).
29 Warren Brookbanks, *Therapeutic Jurisprudence: Conceiving an Ethical Framework*, 8 J.L. & Med. 328, 341 (2001).
30 Susan L. Brooks, *Fostering Wholehearted Lawyers: Practical Guidance for Supporting Law Students' Professional Identity Formation*, 14 Univ. St. Thomas L.J. 412, 425 (2018).
31 Brian Ostrom & Roger Hanson, Achieving High Performance: A Framework for Courts 14 (Apr. 2010) (unpublished manuscript) (on file with authors).

In the family justice system context, adopting an ethic of care likewise "requires the families and children who come before the court to be treated with great civility, dignity, and patience. Efforts must be made to develop a rich source of information about their problems . . . ."[32] Once the problems are identified,

> family intervention should include prompt, front-end loaded, well-documented, and case-specific services, rather than a bureaucratic, one size fits all (or one size fits none) case plan. Consistent with due process, every effort should be made to minimize the impact of adversary court hearings so the family may continue on its way without emotional and financial devastation. This . . . may require early settlement conferences, family group conferencing, mediation, and other less adversarial forms of dispute resolution. Every effort should be made to be collegial, user friendly, and prompt. And when a contested hearing is needed, it should be conducted in a civil and productive manner.[33]

As we have recounted in Chapters 1 and 2, these are all elements of a unified family court operating from an ecological and a therapeutic framework.

Michael King's notion of solution-focused judging, discussed in Chapter 1, is an example of how an ethic of care undergirds the family justice system.

> Here the concern of the court for the party's situation and the suffering that arises from it is matched by a willingness of the court to work in collaboration with the party and a multi-disciplinary court team to address the issues underlying the party's legal problem and hence to relieve their suffering.[34]

King believes that an ethic of care must accompany traditional judicial values, such as independence, neutrality, fairness, and integrity. King defines the ethic of care in this manner as "an approach that is mindful of the effect of judicial action on the wellbeing of those taking part in or otherwise affected by judicial processes."[35] King goes on to state that an ethic of care does not mean that

> judicial officers become social workers, only that as people in authority who exercise power over citizens there is need for judicial officers to take the wellbeing

32 Michael A. Town, *The Unified Family Court: Preventive, Therapeutic and Restorative Justice for America's Families*, Juv. & Fam. Just. Today, Winter 2002, at 14–15.

33 Michael A. Town, *The Unified Family Court: Preventive, Therapeutic and Restorative Justice for America's Families*, Juv. & Fam. Just. Today, Winter 2002, at 14–15.

34 Michael King, *Compassion and the Courts: The Evolution of an Institution, in* Conversations on Compassion 215, 243 (Michelle Brenner ed., 2015).

35 Elizabeth Richardson, Pauline Spencer, & David B. Wexler, *The International Framework for Court Excellence and Therapeutic Jurisprudence: Creating Excellent Courts and Enhancing Wellbeing*, 25 J. Jud. Admin. 148, 157 (2016) (footnote omitted).

> of those people into account in determining how they conduct court processes and in how they render their decisions.[36]

Even with solution-focused judging, however, "the function remains that of judging and the boundaries of judging must be respected if the integrity of the interpersonal dimension of judging is to be maintained."[37]

Leslie Bender, in describing Carol Gilligan's ethic of care perspectives, states that

> [t]he care-oriented problem-solver examines the connections between and among people, looking at their interpersonal responsibilities and needs. Preventing hurt, preserving relationships, and developing cooperative solutions rooted in the concrete particulars of the conflict are objectives of a care-oriented ethical analysis.[38]

With her prescription that care-oriented problem solvers examine connections in people's lives, Bender advances the ecology of human development as a critical component, like we have outlined in Chapter 2.

Jill Hasday explains the importance of the need for judges to operate with an ethic of care in family courts. "Judges . . . wield the most power to decide both what the law is and what counts as a convincing argument in a judicial opinion . . . ."[39] Demonstrating a need for change, such as incorporating an ethic of care, is a tall order in the family law canon, which Hasday defines as "the dominant narratives, stories, examples and ideas that judges, lawmakers, and . . . commentators repeatedly invoke to describe and explain family law and its governing principles."[40]

> By definition, the family law canon is difficult to alter. The canon consists of deeply rooted, widely held ways of thinking about family law and its guiding principles that gain strength from their repeated invocation. Much of the family law canon's power lies in its ability to operate at the level of common sense, so that canonical narratives and modes of understanding the field appear to require no explanation or reexamination. Changing the canon requires revising fundamental, embedded assumptions about family law that legal decision-makers are accustomed to acting upon with little, if any, question or qualm. Legislators and judges, as well as scholars, lawyers, and family members, reason within the family law canon and reproduce the canon intergenerationally, instructing new generations to think about family law as their predecessors do.[41]

36 Elizabeth Richardson, Pauline Spencer, & David B. Wexler, *The International Framework for Court Excellence and Therapeutic Jurisprudence: Creating Excellent Courts and Enhancing Wellbeing*, 25 J. Jud. Admin. 148, 157 (2016) (footnote omitted).

37 Michael S. King, Monash University Faculty of Law Legal Studies Research Paper, *Realising the Potential of Judging*, 37 Monash Univ. L. Rev. (Austl.) 171, 172 (2011).

38 Leslie Bender, *From Gender Difference to Feminist Solidarity: Using Carol Gilligan and an Ethic of Care in Law*, 15 Vt. L. Rev. 1, 37 (1991).

39 Jill Elaine Hasday, Family Law Reimagined 224 (2014).

40 Jill Elaine Hasday, Family Law Reimagined 2 (2014).

41 Jill Elaine Hasday, Family Law Reimagined 221 (2014).

In order for other actors in the family justice system, including attorneys, service providers, court personnel, and policy makers, to understand the importance of a care ethic, judges must demonstrate and articulate that caring counts and must lead by example.

The role of narrative in promoting care

Former First Lady Michelle Obama emphasizes the significance of narrative: "[Former President] Barack [Obama] and I have always believed in the power of storytelling to inspire us, to make us think differently about the world around us, and to help us open our minds and hearts to others."[42] What do we mean by storytelling, and how does it relate to narrative? "Simply put: story is 'what is told' and narrative is 'how the story is transmitted.'"[43] A narrative has "a beginning, middle, and end that may differ from the story's beginning, middle, and end. Which events are included and how they are ordered in the construction of narrative are choices."[44] Further, "[s]tories simplify complexity; they are told to communicate a point, to render the conveyed ideas more accessible to an audience."[45] As one family law attorney has stated, "You can't unhear these stories once they are told to you."[46]

We have presented an exhaustive account of narrative theory in Chapter 4. How does narrative translate into practice within the family justice system? What is important about stories in the family law context? It is critical first and foremost to understand the role of lawyers as storytellers.

> Make no mistake about it—lawyers are storytellers . . . . In law practice, effective storytelling is outcome-determinative . . . . Of course, storytelling practice in law is also unlike the work of other popular storytellers. Lawyers are ethical and truthful storytellers; imagination is informed, shaped, and limited by evidence. The lawyers' voice and persona are different; the rules of, and constraints upon, formal legal storytelling are explicit and unlike those of other popular storytellers. Further, lawyers often do not tell complete stories,

42 Press Release, Netflix, Netflix Forming Storytelling Partnership with Barack and Michelle Obama (May 21, 2018) (on file with authors). *See also* George Packer, *Witnessing the Obama Presidency, From Start to Finish*, NEW YORKER (June 18, 2018), https://www.newyorker.com/magazine/2018/06/18/witnessing-the-obama-presidency-from-start-to-finish (documenting Barack Obama's belief in the power of narrative).

43 CAROLYN E. GROSE & MARGARET E. JOHNSON, LAWYERS, CLIENTS & NARRATIVE: A FRAMEWORK FOR LAW STUDENTS AND PRACTITIONERS 4 (2017).

44 CAROLYN E. GROSE & MARGARET E. JOHNSON, LAWYERS, CLIENTS & NARRATIVE: A FRAMEWORK FOR LAW STUDENTS AND PRACTITIONERS 13 (2017).

45 Jane M. Spinak, *Reforming Family Court: Getting It Right Between Rhetoric and Reality*, 31 WASH. U. J.L. & POL'Y 11, 19 (2009). *See also* JEROME BRUNER, MAKING STORIES: LAW, LITERATURE, LIFE 28 (2002) (explaining that "narrative helps to make sense of things when they don't.").

46 Samantha P. Rodier, Remarks at the Association of Family and Conciliation Courts 55th Annual Conference (June 7, 2018).

typically leaving it to others (judges, juries, decision-makers) to complete the tales and inscribe codas of meaning.[47]

In the family law arena, narrative provides the family's context, forming the basis for compelling advocacy that depicts the family's situation and corresponding needs. As such, narrative enables the court to hear the family's story and then to respond effectively to family law litigants in a manner that is both caring and just. Caring and narrative thus provide the vehicle to change the family law canon.

To examine narrative's power to facilitate caring, we begin with the judge.

> All judgments are narrative; they tell a story through facts, structure and language and it is through this storytelling method that judges seek to convince their audience that they have made the right decision. Given that cases concerning children [and families] can be amongst the most contentious, emotionally-charged, value-ridden and life-changing of cases to be dealt with by the courts, the imperative to persuade through narrative is strong.[48]

Kathryn Hollingsworth and Helen Stalford emphasize the importance of the need to understand "awareness of the particular human lives that are subjects or objects of the law, even when that particularity is subordinated to the generalizing impulse of legal regulation."[49] With regard to cases involving children, they suggest that the judge

> use facts in ways that provide a holistic and contextual account of the child's life; gives a more accurate telling of the *child's* story; better emphasises the impact of the decision on the child; and, therefore, helps to support the outcome towards which the judge is reasoning.[50]

How can we assist judges and all family court actors to hear the stories clients are telling? As we have described in Chapter 4, empathy is a critical component of narrative competence. Philip Genty discusses the magnitude of empathy.

> Part of this notion of empathy involves the lawyer's acquiring an understanding of the client's "social world" in order to appreciate the relationships, emotional demands and pressures that define the client's day-to-day life . . . . Peter Margulies has described this broad conception of empathy – which combines an appreciation

47 Philip N.Meyer, Storytelling for Lawyers 2 (2014).

48 Kathryn Hollingsworth & Helen Stalford, *Towards Children's Rights Judgments, in* Rewriting Children's Rights Judgments 53, 79 (Helen Stalford, Kathryn Hollingsworth, & Stephen Gilmore eds., 2017).

49 Kathryn Hollingsworth & Helen Stalford, *Towards Children's Rights Judgments, in* Rewriting Children's Rights Judgments 53, 80 (Helen Stalford, Kathryn Hollingsworth, & Stephen Gilmore eds., 2017) (footnote omitted).

50 Kathryn Hollingsworth & Helen Stalford, *Towards Children's Rights Judgments, in* Rewriting Children's Rights Judgments 53, 80 (Helen Stalford, Kathryn Hollingsworth, & Stephen Gilmore eds., 2017).

of the client's social and cultural world with an understanding of the client's perceptions of the legal world – as "empathic engagement."[51]

For Margulies, "empathic engagement posits that the micro version of empathy (involving interpersonal relationships) and the macro version (involving concern about conditions of political, social, and economic subordination in society) are complementary, not radically separate."[52] This depiction of the breadth and scope of empathy comports with the need for the ecological approach we prescribe to address families' legal problems.

Bruce Winick, the co-founder of therapeutic jurisprudence, defines empathy and emphasizes its relevance for judges:

> Empathy involves the ability to experience another person's feelings and to see the world through that person's eyes. Empathy has both cognitive and affective components. The judge should convey both an intellectual response to the individual, communicating that she understands the individual's predicament, and an emotional response, communicating that she shares the individual's feelings. The individual, after all, is a fellow human being with a human problem that the judge is attempting to help her deal with . . . . [T]he judge should communicate a sense of caring, sympathy, genuineness, and understanding. Just as physicians need to develop their "bed-side manner," judges need to develop what can be termed their "bench-side manner."[53]

Does empathy compromise the requirement of judicial neutrality, and does it create role confusion for judges? Judith Kaye, a former Chief Judge of the State of New York, responds. "A judge can be interested in the details of the parties' situation without crossing the professional divide between jurist and therapist. Hands-on justice doesn't have to mean hand-holding by the judge."[54] In focus groups with California and New York judges, the judges themselves have suggested they need more direct interaction with litigants, including asking more questions and seeking more information about each case, as well as exploring a wider range of possible resolutions and integrating social services interventions,[55] in line with the unified family court model. "[E]mpathy and mutual regard is [sic] difficult to foster through the infrequent contacts that judges and other professionals traditionally have . . . ."[56]

51 Philip M. Genty, *Clients Don't Take Sabbaticals: The Indispensable In-House Clinic and the Teaching of Empathy*, 7 Clinical L. Rev. 273, 275–76 (2000).
52 Peter Margulies, *Re-framing Empathy in Clinical Legal Education*, 5 Clinical L. Rev. 605, 615 (1999).
53 Bruce J. Winick, *Therapeutic Jurisprudence and Problem Solving Courts*, 30 Fordham Urb. L.J. 1055, 1069 (2003) (footnotes omitted).
54 Judith S. Kaye & Susan K. Knipps, *Judicial Responses to Domestic Violence: The Case for a Problem-Solving Approach*, 27 W. St. U. L. Rev. 1, 11 (1999–2000).
55 Raymond H. Brescia, *Beyond Balls and Strikes: Towards a Problem-Solving Ethic in Foreclosure Proceedings*, 59 Case W. Res. L. Rev. 305, 322, 346 (2009).
56 Pamela Casey & David B. Rottman, *Therapeutic Jurisprudence in the Courts*, 18 Behav. Sci. & L. 445, 453 (2000).

Active judicial intervention, a hallmark of the unified family court, is key to understanding the family's story and enabling the court to help people.

> The more judges intervene in individual lives, the more they may help the people into whose lives they intervene . . . . Acting for the betterment of families and society, unified family court judges intervene in personal lives in order to . . . help develop the sensibilities of family members so that they may solve their own legal, social, and personal problems.[57]

In addition to exhibiting compassionate caring, "[t]his is the most therapeutic endeavor of the unified family court."[58]

In order to develop empathy, family justice system actors, including judges, attorneys, court personnel, and service providers, must understand the client's story through the client's own eyes and must also account for as much of a holistic approach to the client's narrative as possible. Such empathic engagement is essential to caring and to appreciating the client's story. Jaycee Dugard, kidnapped at the age of eleven and held captive for eighteen years, targets the importance of this focused understanding, given the volume and diversity of family law cases coming before the courts, as we have discussed in Chapter 1.

> Families are like snowflakes: they come in many shapes and sizes and no two are the same. And like a snowflake, they are very delicate and must be protected and guarded from elements that threaten to destroy their precarious balance . . . . Unlike snowflakes, given the right tools, families can survive through the worst conditions.[59]

For the lawyer in telling a family's story and for the judge in retelling that story when rendering a decision, "[t]he events of stories must fit in the worlds (the settings, the descriptions, and the complete narrative environments) shaped around them and, in turn, these environments are developed only in tandem with the telling of the tale itself."[60] Employing an ecological approach on the part of all family justice system actors to facilitate their understanding of the family's situation aids in capturing the extent of the family's world, an approach that currently appears missing. "Many law stories discount the significance of settings and environments external to the various actors . . . ."[61]

Matthew Fraidin highlights the importance and power of narrative in the child welfare system, a part of the family justice system. He discusses the need at times to alter intentionally certain narratives. Fraidin focuses on the obligation to change

57 Stephen J. Cribari, *Unified Family Courts: Therapeutic Power and Judicial Authority*, Unified Fam. Chron, Spring 1999 at 8.
58 Stephen J. Cribari, *Unified Family Courts: Therapeutic Power and Judicial Authority*, Unified Fam. Chron, Spring 1999 at 7.
59 Jaycee Dugard, A Stolen Life: A Memoir 266–67 (2011).
60 Philip N. Meyer, Storytelling for Lawyers 156 (2014).
61 Philip N. Meyer, Storytelling for Lawyers 164 (2014).

"the narrative of child welfare, which describes children's parents as savages, beasts, and monsters . . . ."[62] Fraidin describes this reframing process:

> For the narrative to be remade, child welfare system actors must learn to listen for stories that would contribute to a new world-view. Lawyers, judges, and social workers are imbued with the overarching [negative] narrative, and operate in a world rigidly controlled by that narrative. System actors expect danger and harm and negativity, and reproduce it by focusing on the deficits and pathologies of families involved in the system. This self-perpetuating cycle can be overcome . . . by a more realistic assessment of the strengths and assets present in families. As system actors view child welfare differently, their stories about child welfare may change. Those stories, in turn, can rebuild a new narrative.[63]

To accurately frame the narrative and begin to empathically engage, how does one hear a family's story? Joan Tronto identifies "attentiveness" in her discussion of the elements of an ethic of care.[64] Attentiveness, or "noticing the need to care"[65] as Tronto defines it, routinely emerges in family court proceedings, where many urgent needs are apparent.[66] Family law matters and the court systems that address them demand our attention to determine how best to meet the family's needs. As Tronto observes, "We have an unparalleled capacity to know about others in complex modern societies."[67] The ethic of care mandates that in knowing, we simultaneously are compelled to respond.

As we have described in Chapter 1, the unified family court model is best suited to accommodate the requirement that the family justice system respond by

62 Matthew I. Fraidin, *Decision-Making in Dependency Court: Heuristics, Cognitive Biases, and Accountability*, 60 CLEV. ST. L. REV. 913, 970 (2013).

63 Matthew I. Fraidin, *Decision-Making in Dependency Court: Heuristics, Cognitive Biases, and Accountability*, 60 CLEV. ST. L. REV. 913, 971 (2013). *See, e.g.*, Aleza Freeman, *Negotiating a Child's Future*, UNIV. NEV. NEWS (April 6, 2018), https://www.unlv.edu/news/article/negotiating-childs-future (discussing the creation and implementation of a mediation program in child welfare cases designed to counteract potential negative effects resulting from an adversarial process); Candace L. Maze, Stefanie A. Klein, & Cindy S. Lederman, *The Use of Domestic Violence Advocates in Juvenile Court: Lessons from the Dependency Court Intervention Program for Family Violence*, JUV. & FAM. CT. J. 109 (Fall 2003) (identifying adult victims of domestic violence in child welfare proceedings and offering them a variety of services to help them achieve safe environments for themselves and their children).

64 JOAN TRONTO, MORAL BOUNDARIES: A POLITICAL ARGUMENT FOR AN ETHIC OF CARE 127 (1994).

65 JOAN TRONTO, MORAL BOUNDARIES: A POLITICAL ARGUMENT FOR AN ETHIC OF CARE 127 (1994).

66 *See, e.g.*, Barbara A. Babb & Judith D. Moran, *Substance Abuse, Families, and Unified Family Courts: The Creation of a Caring Justice System*, 3 J. HEALTH CARE L. & POL'Y 1 (1999) (describing the myriad nonlegal problems confronting family law litigants and one court system's attempt to address them).

67 JOAN TRONTO, MORAL BOUNDARIES: A POLITICAL ARGUMENT FOR AN ETHIC OF CARE 127 (1994).

hearing a family's narrative and developing the empathy that facilitates caring. The highest ranking family court judge in England and Wales, Sir James Munby, notes, "We should be treating . . . families holistically, but, too often, far too little time is spent identifying the underlying problem or, more typically, problems and then setting out to find a solution for the problems."[68] He believes that what "is so urgently required . . . is . . . engaging the therapeutic and other support systems that so many families, children and parents need if they are to achieve justice—both justice from the court and social justice."[69] The unified family court model encourages this dispensation of social justice.

> Unified family courts rely on compassion more than on coercion-based behavior modification programs frequently associated with probation, parole, and drug diversionary schemes. Unified family courts try to create conditions wherein compassionate people can connect with people who need the benefit of a compassionate response to their human situation.[70]

Is caring teachable?

The application of the ethic of care to the family justice system entails engaging judges, lawyers, and court staff in practices that are in harmony with and responsive to the plights and predicaments of families. In family courts, the interpersonal exchanges that occur between lawyers and their clients, in addition to those with judges and court personnel, are rife with complex and troubling stories.[71] The crux of creating a caring justice system hinges on meeting the challenges of providing both justice and care in a family legal forum.[72] Courts must hear the human need embedded in litigants' stories and must design effective strategies to respond.

We contend it is the people within the justice system who make the ultimate difference in caring. To that end, some state court systems have codified family court performance standards that explicitly define how court personnel must interact with court users.[73] For example, a Missouri juvenile justice performance

68 Nina Jacobs, *Munby Urges Holistic Family Court Reform*, CHILD. & YOUNG PEOPLE NOW (U.K.) (June 4, 2018), https://www.cypnow.co.uk/cyp/news/2005382/munby-urges-holistic-family-court-reform.
69 Nina Jacobs, *Munby Urges Holistic Family Court Reform*, CHILD. & YOUNG PEOPLE NOW (U.K.) (June 4, 2018), https://www.cypnow.co.uk/cyp/news/2005382/munby-urges-holistic-family-court-reform.
70 Stephen J. Cribari, *Unified Family Courts: Therapeutic Power and Judicial Authority*, UNIFIED FAM. CHRON., Spring 1999 at 7.
71 Judith D. Moran, *Families, Law, and Literature: The Story of a Course on Storytelling*, 49 U.S.F. L. REV. 1, 18 (2015) (explaining that family law cases are complex and emotionally laden).
72 *See, e.g.*, Victor D. Quintanilla, *Human-Centered Justice Design*, 121 PENN. ST. L. REV. 745, 745, 759–61 (2017) (noting the efficacy of this model to aid courts in formulating policies and procedures to advance a human-centered approach to justice).
73 *See* BARBARA A. BABB & JEFFREY A. KUHN, PERFORMANCE STANDARDS AND MEASURES FOR MARYLAND'S FAMILY DIVISIONS 6–7 (2002).

requirement states, "Personnel should be courteous and responsive to the public and afford respect to all with whom they come in contact. Sensitivity should be demonstrated towards all persons from different cultures, ethnic groups, and alternative lifestyles."[74] Although perhaps not designed for this purpose, we envision these standards as mandates for court actors to take a caring stance when interacting with families and children.

As discussed in Chapter 1, case management is a critical component of unified family court operations. While case management may appear as a purely administrative matter, it also contributes to caring.[75] The court system's early intervention in family law matters may avoid the possibility of festering acrimony between the parties and prolonged litigation, both of which harm families. The comprehensive nature of proactive case management, taking into account both legal matters and nonlegal problems, fulfills the heart of care ethics—a response to others that derives from the human context. A family court's service referral component, also discussed in Chapter 1 as a significant unified family court element, demonstrates that the court cares about the family in its totality and recognizes that legal solutions without more may not help parents and children.[76]

Aside from court performance standards, active case management, and the provision of relevant services, along with judges and attorneys responding to families' narratives, how does the family justice system cultivate an ethic of care? As we have stated in Chapter 3 in our discussion of the historical roots from which the ethic of care has sprung, for Aristotle, "[A] virtue is not something we start life with . . . . It is something we have to acquire."[77] This means that to imbue the family justice system with an ethic of care, family court actors must receive education and training in ethic of care practices, such as attentive listening, narrative acumen, and empathy. It requires an active commitment on the part of justice

74 MO. OFF. OF ST. CTS. ADMIN., REVISED MISSOURI COURT STANDARDS FOR THE ADMINISTRATION OF JUVENILE JUSTICE 6 (2004).

75 *See, e.g.*, Elayne Greenberg, *Bridging Our Justice Gap with Empathic Processes that Change Hearts, Expand Minds About Implicit Discrimination*, 32 OHIO ST. J. ON DISP. RESOL. 425, 431 (2017) (discussing court processes that include a "differentiated case management approach in which settlement conferences and dispute resolution processes are redesigned to maximize empathic opportunities for the parties."). *See also* Victor D. Quintanilla, *Human-Centered Civil Justice Design*, 121 PENN ST. L. REV. 745, 764–65 (2017) (explaining that research on procedural justice—how court processes "affect people's thoughts, feelings, and behavior . . . can be harnessed to advance human dignity as well as respectful and cooperative interactions between individuals and groups within society, and to nourish our democratic institutions and norms.").

76 *See, e.g.*, Barbara A. Babb & Judith D. Moran, *Substance Abuse, Families, and Unified Family Courts: The Creation of a Caring Justice System*, 3 J. HEALTH CARE L. & POL'Y 1, 23–24 (1999) (describing the court services component of the Circuit Court for Baltimore City's Family Division as essential). The authors state in that article, "The provision and unification of services enhance the court's effectiveness in resolving family matters . . . . [T]here are instances where court-connected services are the most appropriate remedy a judge has available." *Id.*

77 Daniel C. Russell, *Aristotle on Cultivating Virtue*, *in* CULTIVATING VIRTUE: PERSPECTIVES FROM PHILOSOPHY, THEOLOGY, AND PSYCHOLOGY 17 (Nance E. Snow ed., 2015).

system professionals to make caring an organizing principle and operational component of the court's functioning. The threshold question, then, is whether caring is teachable and, if so, how to teach it.

Once again, we turn to the medical profession. Successful initiatives launched in hospitals and medical schools teach doctors, nurses, and other hospital personnel how to extend an ethic of care toward patients.[78] Rita Charon has written extensively on her narrative medicine project, which instructs doctors, nurses, and allied healthcare professionals about the dimensions of caring that extend beyond traditional medical interventions.[79] Charon has taught her students to adopt the virtues of attentiveness and empathy for their patients' circumstances. She maintains that training is essential in healthcare settings, and the same holds true for the court system. It is uncomplicated to accept the premise that caring for families in court is necessary, but it takes an active commitment to make it an organizing principle and an operational component of the court.[80] It is illogical to expect an ethic of care to arise naturally from judges, lawyers, and court personnel without a proper introduction to and training about the concept. As Rita Charon has acutely observed,

> It is not enough to suggest that health care professionals have to bear witness to their patients' suffering [treat them with an ethic of care] on top of everything else they do. We cannot impose on our tremendously overworked and overburdened healthcare professionals to do that which they were never trained to do.[81]

The same holds true for those who work in the family justice system. Could we expect such a commitment to an ethic of care from our often overburdened family court judges, lawyers, and court personnel[82] without education and training to support them in such an endeavor?[83] We believe that is impractical.

78 *See generally* James R. Elkins, *An Argument Against Reticence in the Teaching of Virtue*, 21 Legal Stud. F. 221 (1997). *See also* Nel Noddings, *An Ethic of Caring, in* Ethical Theory: An Anthology 699, 711 (Russ Shafer-Landau ed., 2d ed. 2013) (explaining that educators are duty-bound to promote a caring ideal among their students).

79 *See, e.g.*, Rita Charon, Narrative Medicine: Honoring the Stories of Illness (2006); Rita Charon et. al., The Principles and Practice of Narrative Medicine (2016).

80 *See* Barbara A. Babb & Judith D. Moran, *Substance Abuse, Families, and Unified Family Courts: The Creation of a Caring Justice System*, 3 J. Health Care L. & Pol'y 1, 33–34 (1999) (describing the components of judicial training programs in the Circuit Court for Baltimore City's Family Division as a means to create a caring justice system).

81 Rita Charon, Narrative Medicine: Honoring the Stories of Illness 199 (2006).

82 Barry Sullivan, *Just Listening: The Equal Hearing Principle and the Moral Life of Judges*, 48 Loy. U. Chi. L.J. 351, 358 (2016) (noting the consequences of stress associated with "heavy caseloads and time constraints [that] may make it difficult for judges" to fully consider in decision-making the human beings before them, "their situations, their problems and their ideas").

83 *See* Elizabeth Fernandez, Jane Bolitho, Patricia Hansen, Myvanwy Hudson & Sacha Kendall, A Study of the Children's Court of New South Wales 45 (explaining that the paucity of instructional resources for court officers in "rural and remote communities" has caused them "stress . . . in dealing with social complexities for which they claim limited education and training").

The significant need for training in the virtues of empathy and attentiveness in law, as we have mentioned, stems from the fact that personal interactions comprise the reality and workings of the family justice system. These interactive experiences, between and among litigants and their lawyers, court personnel, service providers, and judges, are the foundation from which caring is conveyed. All of these court actors need to understand how to exhibit caring in a communicative milieu. For us, the art of listening and its companion, attentiveness, lie at the heart of caring endeavors,[84] as these facilitate understanding another's circumstances. Focused listening from a narrative perspective, or eliciting clients' stories, enables empathic regard for the person seeking help and provides insights for the listener about how to render effective assistance.[85]

Listening is a critical skill in professional practice. Rita Charon describes listening as a rigorous undertaking: "As the patient tells, I listen as hard as I can—I pay attention—as I sit there at the edge of my seat, absorbing what is being given . . . ."[86] For Charon, listening requires attention, or "the emptying of self so as to become an instrument for receiving the meaning of another."[87] Leonard Riskin has said that lawyers are hobbled by a purely analytical viewpoint which interferes with their ability to *listen* to their clients with the rigor to which Charon refers. Riskin believes that the lawyer's purely rational perspective interferes with "a lawyer's ability to see things broadly or deeply, to develop curiosity, to listen fully to clients and others, to learn about people's underlying interests, and to think creatively."[88] For us, the breadth and depth of inquiry and imagination Riskin envisions quite naturally fall within the realm of caring.

84 *See, e.g.*, Elayne Greenberg, *Bridging Our Justice Gap with Empathic Processes that Change Hearts, Expand Minds About Implicit Discrimination*, 32 Ohio St. J. on Disp. Resol. 425, 454–55 (2017) (describing an initiative to educate judges, lawyers, and court personnel about an empathic approach to resolving implicit discrimination cases: "Being educated about empathy will allow for enhanced perspective taking [understanding the point of view of each party] . . . . When judges are educated about empathy, they may find then that an empathic perspective helps them to better understand the dynamics and the context . . . .").

85 Rita Charon, Narrative Medicine: Honoring the Stories of Illness 66, 132 (2006).

86 Rita Charon, Narrative Medicine: Honoring the Stories of Illness 187 (2006). *See* Ben Brantley, *Beyond the Brutal Headlines on Race, Voices of Despair and Hope*, N. Y. Times, Nov. 3, 2016, at C2, for a theater critic's comments on the listening skills exhibited by a performance artist. The critic states, "[j]ust listen, if you would, to how she listens . . . . Ms. Smith talks practically non-stop in the show . . . . But Ms. Smith speaking is, implicitly, Ms. Smith listening [intently] . . . ." *Id.*

87 Rita Charon, Narrative Medicine: Honoring the Stories of Illness 132 (2006). *See also* Perri Klass, A Not Entirely Benign Procedure: Four Years as a Medical Student 105 (1987). Klass chronicles the difficulties she encounters as a medical student when she attempts to attend to her patients while she grapples with quieting the inner turmoil that diverts her attention. *Id.* Klass relates how she imagined her patients' negative judgments of her professional acumen as she tried to help them, thus interfering with her ability to listen to what they were trying to tell her. *Id.*

88 Leonard L. Riskin, *The Contemplative Lawyer: On the Potential Contributions of Mindfulnesss Meditation to Law Students, Lawyers, and Their Clients*, 7 Harv. Negot. L. Rev. 1, 14 (2002).

Judges, too, have the obligation to listen. According to Barry Sullivan, "[w]e should expect judges to listen and to listen in a particular kind of way."[89] He further remarks,

> By "listening," we mean something more than the physical act of hearing. We mean to say that judges should engage the litigants' arguments rigorously and respectfully, reflecting on the issues presented . . . . We expect a judge to try and see the parties' dispute, not solely from the judge's vantage point, but also from the perspectives of the parties and those of the individuals and institutions that may be affected by the judge's decision.[90]

Sullivan thus invokes narrative competency as a subset of listening—the expectation that the judge consider the presentation of the parties' narratives, which, in turn, helps the judge understand the issues before the court from the litigant's point of view.

Empathic regard, discussed earlier in this chapter, goes hand in hand with listening, as it allows the listener to *hear* and also to *imagine* another's circumstances. This facilitates the listener's ability to respond in a manner consistent with the situation described.[91] Robin West, in discussing the work of ethics scholar Martha Nussbaum, explains that judicial decision-making must include "infus[ing] legal and practical reasoning with both cultural knowledge and sympathetic listening."[92] Nussbaum asserts that one achieves empathic knowledge through the purposeful pursuits of narrative inquiry—listening for the story being told.[93] She also claims that empathizing is a muscular activity, which "atrophies unless it is constantly used."[94] This muscular activity is a necessary component of our vision of effective family court practice, as all family court actors must develop and maintain empathy. We believe the means to achieve this is through court-sponsored education and training initiatives focused on interpersonal skills.

As we have advanced, lawyers and judges must listen for stories. These stories arise from each client's point of view as she provides an account of her situation. We have emphasized that narrative skills enable judges to make more informed and effective decisions. These same narrative skills equip lawyers to become more client-centered advocates. The ability to listen for the client's point of view is critical, among other narrative skills, to devise a legal strategy and to facilitate the

89 Barry Sullivan, *Just Listening: The Equal Hearing Principle and the Moral Life of Judges*, 48 Loy. U. Chi. L.J. 351, 355 (2016).
90 Barry Sullivan, *Just Listening: The Equal Hearing Principle and the Moral Life of Judges*, 48 Loy. U. Chi. L.J. 351, 355 (2016).
91 *See, e.g.*, Atul Gawande, *Tell Me Where It Hurts*, New Yorker, Jan. 23, 2017 at 36.
92 Robin West, Caring for Justice 189 (1997).
93 *See, e.g.*, Atul Gawande, *Tell Me Where It Hurts*, New Yorker, Jan. 23, 2017 at 36.
94 Judith D. Moran, *Families, Law, and Literature: The Story of a Course on Storytelling*, 49 U.S.F. L. Rev. 1, 21 (2015) (citing Andrea McArdle, *Writing Across the Curriculum: Professional Communication and the Writing It Supports*, 15 J. Legal Writing Inst. 241, 248 (2009)).

making of a judicial decision that embodies care. If the litigant's point of view does not factor into these behaviors, the litigant is likely to experience a lack of care.[95] Further, while the lawyer or judge may intend to care, the person for whom the caring gesture is intended may not construe it as caring. Even a judge or lawyer who cares deeply may miss the mark for the lack of knowing the client's story—her point of view.

Conclusion

> What lies ahead [in family law] is something we cannot know; but eternal constant change seems to be the fate of this most vital and intimate branch of the law. Much has happened, in the course of the twentieth century. Is there a single theme, a single line of development, which ties the whole fabric together?[96]

For us, that theme, permeating the entire family justice system, is the need to care.

The application of an ethic of care to the family justice system involves a multi-layered enterprise, one that incorporates practical and theoretical approaches involving court structure and function. The structural aspect requires the adoption of a unified family court model. Principles from the ecology of human development and therapeutic jurisprudence must guide the operation of the family court. Narrative competencies that permeate the realm of court operations and how personnel within the family justice system conduct themselves, including the bench, the bar, and the administrative sphere of the courthouse, facilitate these principles.

In this chapter we underscore that caring is paramount to the operation of the family justice system. We address the need to teach judges, lawyers, and court staff how to care, and we discuss specific means to implement caring in court. We ground these activities in narrative practices, behaviors, and dispositions that engender and communicate caring: listening acutely and attending rigorously with an empathic regard for family law litigants. The ecology of human development and therapeutic jurisprudence, overarching principles to promote caring justice, frame the narrative practices. These theories and competencies enable the family to tell its story in court, and they equip the court to respond to the family's unique challenges in a manner that improves the lives of the family's members.

In our claim that court structural components enable caring, we advocate for the adoption of the unified family court model—a system which, among other

95 *See, e.g.*, Victor D. Quintanilla, *Human-Centered Civil Justice Design*, 121 PENN ST. L. REV. 745, 755 (2017) (commenting on the importance of "perspective taking"—eliciting a person's point of view—to engender empathy for that person and to use that empathy in developing "human-centered" solutions). *See also* Amy Coplan, *Understanding Empathy: Its Features and Effects, in* EMPATHY: PHILOSOPHICAL AND PSYCHOLOGICAL PERSPECTIVES 10, 13 (Amy Coplan & Peter Goldie, eds., 2011) (defining perspective taking with an other-orientation as that which allows one person to adopt the point of view of another relevant to the other's experience).

96 JOANNA L. GROSSMAN & LAWRENCE M. FRIEDMAN, INSIDE THE CASTLE: LAW AND THE FAMILY IN 20TH CENTURY AMERICA 22 (2011).

attributes, employs a holistic approach to family justice. Active case management, part of the unified family court blueprint, is especially relevant in a justice system that adopts a caring approach. Processing family court cases with an emphasis on early intervention, while addressing both legal and nonlegal matters, avoids festering acrimony and protracted litigation. This facilitates caring in court.

Our prescription for caring involves a commitment to pioneering practices and procedures, some of which may appear radical in the context of the family justice system. In discussing these novel approaches to instill caring in court, we point to instances of promoting caring in other fields. It is possible and necessary to build reservoirs of care among those who work within the family justice system. In the end, we hope this chapter provides those wishing to undertake family justice system reform projects with an appropriate perspective and the wherewithal to persevere.

6 Portraits of caring

Introduction

> Caregiving is not simply "another" moral activity, or indicative of another moral virtue, but rather, caregiving and the dispensation of justice are mutually dependent activities.[1]
>
> We need court leaders who understand the importance of anticipating and managing change, so that our courthouses are prepared to confront the challenges that millions of ordinary people bring into our courthouses every single day . . . These are people who are dealing with personal crises and [are] placing their hopes in the fairness and wisdom of judges and the legal system. And when we succeed in meeting these challenges, we send the message that our commitment as an institution is to serve the public in the best way possible and that our only agenda is to administer justice efficiently and effectively for the well-being of our citizens . . . . Court reform gives us credibility and strengthens our independence as a branch of government.[2]

In the preceding chapters, we have described theoretical foundations that contribute to fashioning effective family justice system reform: the unified family court, the ecology of human development, therapeutic jurisprudence, the ethic of care, and narrative theory and practice. We have discussed how these concepts combine to impact the structure and function of the family justice system.

This final chapter acknowledges and describes situations where an approximation of this approach is flourishing in the family justice system and its community partners both in America and abroad. Robin West has said, "For most of our history . . . our capacity to care has not been regarded as necessary to the capacity to do justice . . . ."[3] In the twenty plus years since West's statement, much about the justice system and the manner in which judges approach the work of doing justice has changed. We demonstrate that caring for court-involved families is possible, and we describe examples of its practice.

1 ROBIN WEST, CARING FOR JUSTICE 33 (1997) (footnotes omitted).
2 Judith S. Kaye & Susan K. Knipps, *Judicial Response to Domestic Violence: The Case for a Problem-Solving Approach*, 27 W. STATE U. L. REV. 1, 10–11 (1999–2000).
3 ROBIN WEST, CARING FOR JUSTICE 9 (1997) (footnotes omitted).

To highlight family court initiatives that advance caring, we have searched for documentation in news stories,[4] published reports,[5] scholarly articles,[6] accounts by judges about their demeanor on the bench and in their written opinions,[7] interviews and correspondence with judges,[8] and in other networks, such as listservs,[9] that track family law decision-making and family court structure and function.

We also reviewed data collected from our formal survey of a representative sample of family court systems across the United States and in other countries.[10] The survey contained a series of questions about court structures, policies, procedures, and services that indicate manifestations of caring in a court environment. The aspects of care featured in our findings included specifics about architectural and design features, specialty court programs, court-supplied services, court-community partnerships, and training programs for judges and court staff. In addition to the more formal aspects of our survey, we also interviewed judges who were gracious enough to impart relevant anecdotes about the family courts in which they preside.

Our search has yielded many examples of caring in family courts, reflected in court structural components, including courthouse design, and court policies, procedures, services, and perspectives on caring shared by family court judges. We shall discuss each of these aspects in the following sections of this chapter.

4 *See, e.g.*, Gaia Pianigiani, *Breaking Up the Family as a Way to Break Up the Mob*, N.Y. Times (Feb. 10, 2017), https://www.nytimes.com/2017/02/10/world/europe/breaking-up-the-family-as-a-way-to-break-up-the-mob.html?_r=0.

5 *See, e.g.*, Elizabeth Fernandez, Jane Bolitho, Patricia Hansen, Myvanwy Hudson, & Sacha Kendall, A Study of the Children's Court of New South Wales (2014).

6 *See, e.g.*, Barbara A. Babb & Judith D. Moran, *Substance Abuse, Families, and Unified Family Courts: The Creation of a Caring Justice System*, 3 J. Health Pol'y & L. 1 (1999) (describing elements of a caring family justice system).

7 *See, e.g.*, A (Letter to a Young Person), Re (Rev 1) [2017] EWHC (Fam) 48 (Eng.), *available at* http://www.bailii.org/ew/cases/EWFC/HCJ/2017/48.html.

8 *See, e.g.*, E-mail from Michael Keehan, High Court Judge, High Court of Justice of the Courts of England and Wales, Family Division, to Judith Moran, Adjunct Professor, Univ. of Balt. Sch. of L. (Aug. 31, 2017, 10:37 EST) (on file with authors).

9 *See, e.g.*, Posting of David Wexler, davidbwexler@yahoo.com, to tjlist@googlegroups.com (June 20, 2018) (on file with authors); Posting of Lisa Whittingham, rockyhorror1978@gmail.com, to tjlist@googlegroups.com (June 20, 2018) (on file with authors).

10 Survey Response, Stacey Marz, Director, Self-Help Servs., Alaska Court Sys., Anchorage, Alaska (Sept. 2017); Survey Response, Wiliam DeLisio, Manager, Family Law Program, State Court Adm'r's Office, Denver, Colo. (July 2017); Survey Response, Lillian Takaki, Law Clerk, Chambers of Hon. Catherine H. Remigio, Senior Judge of the Family Court of the First Circuit, Kapolei, Haw. (Aug. 2017); Survey Response, Janet Fink, Deputy Counsel, N.Y. State Unified Court Sys., N.Y.C. (July 2017); Survey Response, Ronald J. Pagliarini, Chief of Staff, R.I. Family Court, Providence, R.I. (June 2017); Survey Response, Despina M. Belle-Isle, Director, Court Improvement Program, Superior Court of D.C., and Lead Att'y Advisor, Family Court, Wash. D.C. (July 2017).

Court facilities and aesthetics

"The buildings we inhabit can change the way we feel."[11] Nevertheless, the physical aspects of the courthouse often are an overlooked yet important facet of implementing care.[12] The Report on Family Court Services, commissioned by the New York City Bar Association, Committee on Family Court and Family Law (hereinafter the Report) is illuminating in this regard.

The Report, aimed at highlighting much needed improvements to the New York City Family Court courthouses, was intended to shine a light on the physical aspects of family court courthouses in New York City and the effects of the physical structures on litigants and their families. The Report introduced its findings as follows:

> This report starts from the premise that courts can and should achieve justice not only through judicial decision-making, but also by creating *environments* in which all parties are treated with full respect and in which the best possible outcomes are facilitated. Family Courts strive to use conciliatory, child-focused, and family-friendly approaches in applying the law; it logically follows that their buildings and services should reflect these qualities.[13]

These remarks invoke the notion that the quality of the courthouse infrastructure matters in conveying care to litigants. The Report features a thorough examination of how to improve the courthouses[14] with an eye to making litigants feel cared for and cared about. It addresses four key areas: "Confidentiality, Access to Information, Accommodations and Childcare Services."[15] The recommendations

11 Fiona Pepper, *How Better Designed Therapy Spaces Could Improve Mental Health Treatment*, ABC (Austl.) (Aug. 27, 2017), http://www.abc.net.au/news/2017-08-28/better-designed-therapy-spaces-improve-mental-health-treatment/8836046 (reporting on research conducted in mental health facilities demonstrating that design features make a difference: patients interviewed spoke of "their own relationship to the environment, what was supportive and made them feel calm and reduced their stress and anxiety").

12 *See* Int'l Consortium for Ct. Excellence, http://www.courtexcellence.com (last visited June 1, 2018) (explaining that: "Excellent courts possess adequate court facilities," an endorsement of caring about courts' physical environments by an international consortium devoted to establishing standards for excellence in court systems worldwide).

13 Comm. on Family Court and Family Law, Ass'n of the Bar of the City of N.Y., Report on Family Court Services 42 (2006) (emphasis added). *See also* Alicia DeVault, Vanessa A. Helfrick, Shawn C. Marsh, & Katie M. Snider, *Environmental Considerations for Trauma-Responsive Juvenile and Family Courts: A Review of the Literature and Recommendations for Practice*, 69 Juv. & Fam. Ct. J. 5, 14–15 (2018) (discussing environmental recommendations for courts).

14 The courthouses surveyed included the five counties that comprise New York City: Queens County, Kings County, New York County, Richmond County, and Bronx County. Comm. on Family Court and Family Law, Ass'n of the Bar of the City of N.Y., Report on Family Court Services 3–4 (2006).

15 Comm. on Family Court and Family Law, Ass'n of the Bar of the City of N.Y., Report on Family Court Services 43 (2006).

under Confidentiality include designating private areas in proximity to courtrooms for litigants to meet with their attorneys.[16] Acknowledging the stress on litigants in navigating their way through family court both in terms of locating the appropriate courtrooms and understanding court protocols, the Report recommends a variety of interventions to provide access to information. These include posting clear directional signage, as well as establishing an information desk to explain court procedures and to answer other questions litigants may have about the court process and the courthouse environs.

The environmental enhancements recommended in the Report seek to make the court experience more welcoming.[17] In addressing courthouse accommodations, the Report recognizes the importance of clean and well-maintained facilities and amenities, such as food and drink machines, in addition to decorative touches, e.g., children's artwork posted in courthouse corridors.[18] Finally, the Report addresses the need for optimal childcare services in order to provide adequately staffed, well-appointed, and safe spaces for parents to leave children while they attend court hearings and related conferences.[19] The analysis and conclusions from the Report's findings represent a case study in how caring principles can enlighten family justice system reform initiatives that pertain to the physical structures of the court.

Another demonstration that court physical structures help to facilitate caring appears in the Performance Standards and Measures for Maryland's Family Divisions, where the document addresses the issue: "To provide a user-friendly court, the court must display adequate signage to direct family law litigants to appropriate destinations within the courthouse. Children must be accommodated in secure and family friendly areas staffed by childcare providers . . . ."[20] Maryland, in codifying expectations for courthouse facilities, has advanced the capacity of the

16 Comm. on Family Court and Family Law, Ass'n of the Bar of the City of N.Y., Report on Family Court Services 47 (2006). *See also* Fiona Pepper, *How Better Designed Therapy Spaces Could Improve Mental Health Treatment*, ABC (Austl.) (Aug. 27, 2017), http://www.abc.net.au/news/2017-08-28/better-designed-therapy-spaces-improve-mental-health-treatment/8836046 (noting that among the stressors associated with poorly designed institutional environments is the lack of "visual and audial privacy").

17 Comm. on Family Court and Family Law, Ass'n of the Bar of the City of N.Y., Report on Family Court Services 51 (2006). *See also* Elizabeth Fernandez, Jane Bolitho, Patricia Hansen, Myvanwy Hudson, & Sacha Kendall, A Study of the Children's Court of New South Wales 22–24 (2014) (noting the variability among parents and children in comprehending court processes, owing to cognitive ability, language proficiency, and socio-economic status, and the importance of providing clarification to compensate for the deficits). Further, the authors of this report have cited an interview with a court-affiliated support worker who remarked on the alienating effect on court users of being unfamiliar with "the layout of the court" and its policies and procedures. *Id.*

18 Comm. on Family Court and Family Law, Ass'n of the Bar of the City of N.Y., Report on Family Court Services 55 (2006).

19 Comm. on Family Court and Family Law, Ass'n of the Bar of the City of N.Y., Report on Family Court Services 57 (2006).

20 Barbara A. Babb & Jeffrey A. Kuhn, Performance Standards and Measures for Maryland's Family Divisions 12 (2002).

court to care beyond that which is aspirational in nature. By doing so, the state has demonstrated a model for conveying care to litigants that other jurisdictions may consider. For those jurisdictions contemplating family justice system reform, highlighting deficiencies in a report on courthouse facilities, as in New York, and codifying expectations for their implementation, as in Maryland, may present opportunities worth pursuing.

In addition to New York and Maryland, Colorado, Hawaii, and Rhode Island have made efforts to improve the court experience with both practical and aesthetic enhancements to court facilities. Children's artwork is on display in courthouses in these states.[21] Hawaii family courts also provide rooms for nursing mothers, and family-friendly bathrooms exist in both Hawaii and Colorado.[22] Hawaii family court courthouses contain designated areas for children adjacent to courtrooms. These spaces include children's book nooks and toys.[23] These accommodations convey to families that courts anticipate and care about their needs.

As explained at the outset of this section, physical spaces that project warmth have a beneficial effect on those who occupy them. The enhancements we have described diminish the sterile effect of institutional architecture that characterizes most courthouses and make the environs appear more comfortable to litigants and their children. Courthouses often are intimidating places to litigants and likely more so to a child. Decorative touches, such as colorful artwork, can make a difference and at minimal cost. A demonstration of caring in this regard is easy to implement.

Even the most well-designed courthouses, however, are not useful to litigants if they cannot access or attend court for some legitimate reason. To address the family court access issue, New York has experimented with Night Court, where the court operates a few nights each week.[24] Further, New York has established

21 Survey Response, Stacey Marz, Director, Self-Help Servs., Alaska Court Sys., Anchorage, Alaska (Sept. 2017); Survey Response, Wiliam DeLisio, Manager, Family Law Program, State Court Adm'r's Office, Denver, Colo. (July 2017); Survey Response, Lillian Takaki, Law Clerk, Chambers of Hon. Catherine H. Remigio, Senior Judge of the Family Court of the First Circuit, Kapolei, Haw. (Aug. 2017); Survey Response, Janet Fink, Deputy Counsel, N.Y. State Unified Court Sys., N.Y.C. (July 2017); Survey Response, Ronald J. Pagliarini, Chief of Staff, R.I. Family Court, Providence, R.I. (June 2017); Survey Response, Despina M. Belle-Isle, Director, Court Improvement Program, Superior Court of D.C., and Lead Att'y Advisor, Family Court, Wash. D.C. (July 2017).

22 Survey Response, Wiliam DeLisio, Manager, Family Law Program, State Court Adm'r's Office, Denver, Colo. (July 2017); Survey Response, Lillian Takaki, Law Clerk, Chambers of Hon. Catherine H. Remigio, Senior Judge of the Family Court of the First Circuit, Kapolei, Haw. (Aug. 2017).

23 Survey Response, Wiliam DeLisio, Manager, Family Law Program, State Court Adm'r's Office, Denver, Colo. (July 2017); Survey Response, Lillian Takaki, Law Clerk, Chambers of Hon. Catherine H. Remigio, Senior Judge of the Family Court of the First Circuit, Kapolei, Haw. (Aug. 2017).

24 Judith S. Kaye & Jonathan Lippman, *New York State Unified Court System: Family Justice Program*, 36 Fam. & Conciliation Cts. Rev. 144, 149 (1998).

satellite family court offices around New York City in locations that are distant from the actual courthouses.[25] Community Resource Centers have begun to offer assistance so that people can obtain information and assistance relevant to family law matters, including "hotline numbers . . . and addresses of service providers as well as a safety planning guide created by the New York State Office for the Prevention of Domestic Violence . . . ."[26]

Indeed, caring in court compels ensuring safety. In family courts, where cases frequently involve child custody and access issues, safety is especially important. Consequently, courthouse structures and procedures must adapt. One of the core concerns in child custody cases is the mechanics of arranging child access between the parents. Research confirms that the exchange of children can present high risks.[27] There are all manner of arrangements and locales for exchanging children for this purpose. In some clear cases, such as those where domestic violence is an issue, exchanges are monitored, and access itself may be supervised by a professional in a designated social service agency. An alternative is to provide a safe place within the courthouse to facilitate inter-parent exchange, as exists in one Maryland Family Division.[28] In such circumstances, courthouse security policies also must include measures that help to prevent, or at least diffuse, family violence. Providing secure spaces for families and children in courthouses, whether for child access or court appearances, requires specific training initiatives for security and administrative staff.[29] Educational programs to address this particular safety issue must include strategies used by community law enforcement in situations of intimate partner violence.[30] We address specific training initiatives in a subsequent section of this chapter.

25 Judith S. Kaye & Jonathan Lippman, *New York State Unified Court System: Family Justice Program*, 36 FAM. & CONCILIATION CTS. REV. 144, 149 (1998).

26 Judith S. Kaye & Jonathan Lippman, *New York State Unified Court System: Family Justice Program*, 36 FAM. & CONCILIATION CTS. REV. 144, 175 (1998).

27 *See, e.g.*, Barbara A. Babb & Judith D. Moran, *Substance Abuse, Families, and Unified Family Courts: The Creation of a Caring Justice System*, 3 J. HEALTH CARE L. & POL'Y 1, 28 (1999) ("The exchange of children is often a volatile event, as parents must confront one another during each scheduled visit.").

28 *See, e.g.*, Barbara A. Babb & Judith D. Moran, *Substance Abuse, Families, and Unified Family Courts: The Creation of a Caring Justice System*, 3 J. HEALTH CARE L. & POL'Y 1, 27–28 (1999) (describing the Neutral Drop-Off Center in the Circuit Court for Baltimore City's Family Division, which serves such a purpose).

29 Instances of violent episodes in and around the courthouse pursuant to domestic violence and child custody proceedings also appear in journalistic accounts of courthouse violence. In these instances, well-trained security personnel are necessary to ensure safety for litigants as well as for judges and court staff. *See, e.g.*, Cris Barrish & Melissa Nann Burke, *3 Dead, 2 Wounded in Del. Courthouse Shooting*, NEWS J. (Feb. 11, 2013), https://www.usatoday.com/story/news/nation/2013/02/11/delaware-courthouse-shooting/1909075/.

30 Zygmont A. Pines & Mary Beth Marschik, *Security Incident Reporting: An Essential Best Practice for All Courts*, 53 JUDGES' J. (2014) (discussing the best practice use of an incident reporting system developed in Pennsylvania).

Specialty court programs

Courts targeting young children

The concepts we advocate to ensure a family justice system that supports caring for families already have taken root both in states that have adopted in total or in part the unified family court concept, as discussed in Chapter 1, as well as in specialized programs that exist within family court domains.[31]

A recent example of a caring court, started in 2014, is the Family Resolutions Specialty Court in Massachusetts, where the goals include:

> to reduce conflict in cases involving children, to keep court proceedings child-focused, to give parents tools via mediation and the assistance of a clinically trained child specialist to address the problems facing their own family, and, finally, to increase all parties' satisfaction with the court process.[32]

Active judicial involvement and consistent case monitoring, coupled with the services of an interdisciplinary professional team, define this court, which suspends evidentiary rules and encourages information sharing. "Children have a voice from the very beginning, which focuses their parents on the primacy of continuing to raise healthy children despite the marital or relationship dissolution."[33] The ultimate objective of the court is to provide a system that is "more humane and more efficient than traditional family litigation, and ultimately give parents the ability to communicate well enough to obviate the need for repeated returns to court."[34] These therapeutic intentions are very consistent with our prescription for optimal family justice system functioning.

Other specialty court programs that highlight caring target particularized areas of need within the larger family court ambit. For example, acting upon research and advocacy begun in earnest in 2001;[35] a movement designed to target and improve the lives of the youngest children in the child welfare system has generated several new court projects. The Hawaii Zero to Three Court, for example, seeks to serve maltreated infants and toddlers within this age range who are the

31 *See, e.g.*, Hawaii Girls Court Program, http://www.girlscourt.org/aboutus.html (last visited June 1, 2018). *See also* Stephanie Johnston, *R.I. Judiciary Introduces New "Safe and Secure Baby Court,"* WPRI.com (Mar. 13, 2017), http://wpri.com/2017/03/13/dycf-introduces-new-safe-and-secure-baby-court/.

32 Linda S. Fidnick, *The Family Resolutions Specialty Court: A Community-Based Problem-Solving Court for Families in Conflict in Hampshire County*, Bos. Bar J., Fall 2017, at 3, 3.

33 Linda S. Fidnick, *The Family Resolutions Specialty Court: A Community-Based Problem-Solving Court for Families in Conflict in Hampshire County*, Bos. Bar J., Fall 2017, at 3, 5.

34 Linda S. Fidnick, *The Family Resolutions Specialty Court: A Community-Based Problem-Solving Court for Families in Conflict in Hampshire County*, Bos. Bar J., Fall 2017, at 3, 3.

35 Cindy S. Lederman, Joy D. Osofsky & Lynne Katz, *When the Bough Breaks the Cradle Will Fall: Promoting the Health and Well Being of Infants and Toddlers in Juvenile Court*, Juv. & Fam. Ct. J., Fall 2001, at 33. *See also* Cindy S. Lederman & Joy D. Osofsky, *A Judicial-Mental Health Partnership to Heal Young Children in Juvenile Court*, Juv. & Fam. Ct. J., Spring 2008, at 15.

subjects of child welfare proceedings.[36] Douglas County, Nebraska; Hennepin County, Michigan; and the Rhode Island Family Court have similar initiatives.[37] The goal of these courts is to expedite permanent placements for these very young children through the collaborative teamwork of court personnel, caregivers, and service providers. The guiding principles underlying this substructure of the family justice system emanate from child development theory. As one scholar has noted, research "has established that early childhood is critical to the development of a host of cognitive and non-cognitive skills, that the parent-child relationship is central to this development, and that disadvantages during this period"[38] are a significant factor in the lives of children. These specialized court programs aim to prioritize parents' and young children's needs that often are eclipsed by onerous court practices and procedures that cause delay and engender outcomes that may not take into consideration the goals of the child welfare system.

To correct the court processes that impede many child welfare cases, the Hawaii, Nebraska, Rhode Island, and Michigan strategies involve establishing long and short-term goals, expeditious court calendaring, and facilitating connections to appropriate services for parents. The court makes a concerted effort to interact with parents in meaningful ways by ensuring that parents understand expectations and take the required actions based upon the expectations. Court personnel serve as mentors who maintain frequent contact with the parents for whom they are responsible. The nature of these courts clearly is a system founded on intentional caring.

Girls court

The Hawaii Girls Court Program[39] targets the needs of female juvenile offenders. This innovative court project is one of the first nationally to incorporate a full range of gender-specific and strength-based programming for the very particular and critical needs of the female youth offender population. "The Hawaii Girls Court aims to hold girls accountable for their actions while

36 Survey Response, Lillian Takaki, Law Clerk, Chambers of Hon. Catherine H. Remigio, Senior Judge of the Family Court of the First Circuit, Kapolei, Haw. (Aug. 2017).

37 Douglas F. Johnson, *Zero to Three Family Drug Treatment Court and Other Musings for a Better Court Response to Infants and Toddlers*, Ct. Appointed Special Advocs. for Child. (Summer 2014), http://www.casaforchildren.org/site/c.mtJSJ7MPIsE/b.9167905/k.9B8D/JP4_Johnson.htm. *See also* Stephanie Johnson, *R.I. Judiciary Introduces New "Safe and Secure Baby Court,"* WPRI.com (Mar. 13, 2017), http://www.wpri.com/news/local-news/dycf-introduces-new-safe-and-secure-baby-court/1044390715; Kelly Smith, *Hennepin County Focuses on Infants to Break Child Protection Cycle*, Star Tribune (Aug. 7, 2017), http://www.startribune.com/hennepin-county-focuses-on-infants-to-break-child-protection-cycle/439097153.

38 Clare Huntington, *Early Childhood Development and the Law*, 90 S. Cal. L. Rev. 755, 761 (2017).

39 Hawaii Girls Court Program, http://www.girlscourt.org/aboutus.html (last visited June 1, 2018).

building on their strengths and reconnecting them to healthy peer, family, and adult relationships as well as to positive activities."[40] The program achieves these goals through a variety of interventions, which include "[t]herapeutic modalities and approaches (based upon relational theories) that address issues such as healing from physical, sexual and emotional abuse, family conflict, substance abuse, depression . . . ."[41] These interventions operate within a framework that emphasizes the female experience and its impact on the many issues affecting troubled girls.[42] As one psychiatrist, who has worked extensively with this population of youth offenders, has observed:

> Teen-aged girls in delinquent facilities often have cognitive, academic, and emotional deficits. Many describe physical and sexual abuse, and they often grow up in severely dysfunctional families. These girls improve when individual, family, and educational services are court mandated and closely monitored. Teenage girls respond well to social, therapeutic, and academic attention for their complex needs.[43]

Minors' court, Reggio Calabria, Italy

Caring in court also appears as an international phenomenon. News articles chronicling innovative practices in family justice systems in Italy, Brazil, and Australia demonstrate our caring approach. One article recounts a project in the minors' court in Reggio Calabria, Italy, in which Magistrate Roberto Di Bella, President of the court, "has decided to take a drastic step: separating children from their mob families and moving them to a different part of Italy to break a generational cycle of criminality."[44] Magistrate Di Bella has said that the impetus for his decision is concern for the welfare of children,[45] who inevitably follow their

40 Hawaii Girls Court Program, http://www.girlscourt.org/aboutus.html (last visited June 1, 2018).

41 Hawaii Girls Court Program, http://www.girlscourt.org/aboutus.html (last visited June 1, 2018).

42 *See, e.g.*, Dawne A. Mitchell, Letters, *Treating Traumatized Girls*, N.Y. Times, Dec. 12, 2017, at A30 (commenting on the importance of "wrap around services" to facilitate the development of "healthy long-term relationships and . . . transition to independent living.").

43 E-mail from Joan Gerring, M.D., Professor of Psychiatry, State Univ. of N.Y. Sch. of Med. at Syracuse, to Judith D. Moran, Adjunct Professor, Univ. of Balt. Sch. of L. (Dec. 7, 2017, 14:49 EST) (on file with authors). Dr. Gerring has served as a consulting psychiatrist for issues pertaining to delinquent girls housed in juvenile detention facilities. *See also* Julianne Hill, *Saving the Girls*, Nov. 2017, A.B.A. J. at 46 (advocating providing services to girls before they enter the juvenile justice system).

44 Gaia Pianigiani, *Breaking Up the Family as a Way to Break Up the Mob*, N.Y. Times (Feb. 10, 2017), https://www.nytimes.com/2017/02/10/world/europe/breaking-up-the-family-as-a-way-to-break-up-the-mob.html?_r=0.

45 *See, e.g.*, Alex Perry, *Letter from Calabria, Blood and Justice*, New Yorker, Jan. 22, 2018, at 36 (containing an account of the internecine web that binds women and children to the mafia enterprise known as the 'Ndrangheta and the dangers to mothers and children that accompany remaining within this criminal network).

fathers into a life of crime. "Sons follow their fathers . . . [b]ut the state can't allow that children are educated to be criminals."[46]

The program described by Magistrate Di Bella involves intensive oversight by psychologists and social workers who "work with the children constantly. . . . Most [children] stay in touch with the judges and their social workers even after the program ends."[47] The Italian Justice Ministry now is poised to standardize the procedure followed in the Calabrian minors' court in order to implement it on a regional and later national scale.[48] While this pioneering child welfare intervention on the part of the court system seems extreme, it undoubtedly is grounded in caring for children. "After children are moved to a different Italian region, the authorities can try to create the conditions for an ordinary childhood,"[49] where children are not pawns in a criminal enterprise and receive the care they deserve.

Aboriginal children's court program, Australia

This court program addresses a problem that has plagued the aboriginal culture in Victoria, northern Melbourne, Australia, where intra-familial violence has affected generations of children involved in the child welfare system. "For some of these children it has been their parents, grandparents and great grandparents,"[50] who also have been subjects of child protection cases. The initiative is similar in its mission to that of the Calabrian minors' court—to address an endemic cultural problem with a creative intervention on the part of the family justice system.

This pioneering court initiative, which operates within the Broadmeadows Children's Court, launched with the hope of bridging "the gap between indigenous

46 Gaia Pianigiani, *Breaking Up the Family as a Way to Break Up the Mob*, N.Y. Times (Feb. 10, 2017), https://www.nytimes.com/2017/02/10/world/europe/breaking-up-the-family-as-a-way-to-break-up-the-mob.html?_r=0.

47 Gaia Pianigiani, *Breaking Up the Family as a Way to Break Up the Mob*, N.Y. Times (Feb. 10, 2017), https://www.nytimes.com/2017/02/10/world/europe/breaking-up-the-family-as-a-way-to-break-up-the-mob.html?_r=0.

48 "The Justice Ministry in Italy has codified statutes so that Mr. Di Bella's innovation, so far limited to his corner of Calabria, can apply to fight mafias nationwide." Gaia Pianigiani, *Breaking Up the Family as a Way to Break Up the Mob*, N.Y. Times (Feb. 10, 2017), https://www.nytimes.com/2017/02/10/world/europe/breaking-up-the-family-as-a-way-to-break-up-the-mob.html?_r=0. The Magistrate acknowledges that removing children from their families is a "wrenching decision, and one [he] . . . does not take lightly." *Id.* The program has demonstrated that it provides children with a chance, as one imprisoned mafioso parent whose children were removed thanked Mr. Di Bella for the "'chance you gave to my children to live in a taintless environment and to live in legality[.]'" *Id.*

49 Gaia Pianigiani, *Breaking Up the Family as a Way to Break Up the Mob*, N.Y. Times (Feb. 10, 2017), https://www.nytimes.com/2017/02/10/world/europe/breaking-up-the-family-as-a-way-to-break-up-the-mob.html?_r=0.

50 Belinda Hawkins, *Children of the North*, ABC (Austrl.) (Dec. 20, 2017), http://www.abc.net.au/news/2017-12-19/what-can-a-kindergarten-teach-a-court/9164984.

Australians and the legal system."[51] The first step in establishing the program, designed to increase families' participation in child welfare proceedings, involved hiring a services coordinator with cultural roots in the community. One presiding Magistrate has commented on a chronic problem leading to an overabundance of children being removed from their parents.[52]

> The difficulty with Aboriginal families is that, for historical reasons, they don't like to come to court . . . . The history has been that they come to court and they either have children taken away from them, or they go to jail.[53]

In addition to partnering with a local early learning and family well-being center, the services coordinator also has connected personally with families to urge their participation in services and court-mandated appearances. This person-centered approach has increased parental involvement immeasurably, resulting in an increase in attendance at weekly hearings. "Aboriginal parents and grandparents turn up to court . . . ."[54] Instead of avoiding the court altogether or suffering fear and confusion in anticipation of the hearing, the parents' and grandparents' fear subsides at the sight of the coordinator. "He's been talking with them over the phone for weeks; he's gentle, he's glad to see them and he's one of them."[55] As a consequence of these efforts, this court has created a caring environment by making interpersonal connections with parents, which have led to improved child welfare outcomes.

A floating court on the Amazon, Brazil

In Brazil, while not a family court per se,[56] there exists a court that has adopted an inventive approach to meeting the needs of the community, which demonstrates a commitment to caring for families. The court in this case comes to the people in the form of a floating barge which trolls the Amazon and holds hearings in remote outposts along the river. The matters before the court have included non-payment

51 Belinda Hawkins, *Children of the North*, ABC (Austrl.) (Dec. 20, 2017), http://www.abc.net.au/news/2017-12-19/what-can-a-kindergarten-teach-a-court/9164984.

52 Belinda Hawkins, *Children of the North*, ABC (Austrl.) (Dec. 20, 2017), http://www.abc.net.au/news/2017-12-19/what-can-a-kindergarten-teach-a-court/9164984 (noting that "Aboriginal Victorian children are 15 times more likely to be removed from their families than non-indigenous children—the second highest rate in Australia . . . .").

53 Belinda Hawkins, *Children of the North*, ABC (Austrl.) (Dec. 20, 2017), http://www.abc.net.au/news/2017-12-19/what-can-a-kindergarten-teach-a-court/9164984.

54 Belinda Hawkins, *Children of the North*, ABC (Austrl.) (Dec. 20, 2017), http://www.abc.net.au/news/2017-12-19/what-can-a-kindergarten-teach-a-court/9164984.

55 Belinda Hawkins, *Children of the North*, ABC (Austrl.) (Dec. 20, 2017), http://www.abc.net.au/news/2017-12-19/what-can-a-kindergarten-teach-a-court/9164984.

56 *See* Simon Romero, *Justice and Care: A Floating Courthouse Takes Rule of Law to Brazil's Frontier*, N.Y. Times, Dec. 7, 2016, at A4. The matters presented for resolution and the services available include those that are specific to the needs of families. *Id.*

of child support and criminal cases,[57] but the court also dispenses other everyday items. "Some [who visited the court] sought the other services available on board, receiving social security cards, voting papers, and water purification tablets."[58] This is an example of court operations reflecting the heart of caring—that which takes into account people's circumstances as well as their legal issues and responds in kind to the evident needs of individual families and the community the court serves.

Court-supplied services

Another aspect of the family justice system and one that we have described in Chapter 1 as an essential ingredient of a unified family court model is court-supplied services. These services are designed to address the numerous nonlegal problems, such as poverty, substance abuse, and mental health issues, many families face. Court-based programs enable families to access services readily, as they often are located in the courthouse itself. It is generally more convenient for families to access the help they need in a centralized location.[59] Litigants often know where courthouses are and how to reach them via public transportation. Our survey has yielded examples of programs within courts that address a broad base of needs. We shall discuss examples of the many programs available across a variety of jurisdictions.

Court-based childcare programs

Childcare often is an impediment for parents to comply with scheduled court appearances. Court-based childcare centers spare parents the worry and expense of providing care for children while the parents attend court proceedings. A reliable childcare alternative that is readily available and conveniently located avoids the possibility that children are exposed to court proceedings, which are likely to cause undue stress for adults and children alike. Childcare centers exist in many family courts. In at least one jurisdiction, the state of Colorado, a statute mandates the provision of childcare centers.[60] The Colorado centers are provided at no cost to

57 Simon Romero, *Justice and Care: A Floating Courthouse Takes Rule of Law to Brazil's Frontier*, N.Y. Times, Dec. 7, 2016, at A4 (describing how mob justice is a recurring problem in the river towns, while the court has provided citizens with a reliable forum to establish and maintain law and order).

58 Simon Romero, *Justice and Care: A Floating Courthouse Takes Rule of Law to Brazil's Frontier*, N.Y. Times, Dec. 7, 2016, at A4.

59 Interview with Judith D. Moran, Adjunct Professor, Univ. of Balt. Sch. of L. (June 10, 2005). A former family court administrator has said that the courthouse is often a last resort for families troubled by many social problems that include legal issues, *but see* Jane C. Murphy & Jana B. Singer, Divorced from Reality (2015) (suggesting that community-based referrals are more appropriate for families).

60 *See* Family Friendly Courts Act, Colo. Rev. Stat. Ann. § 13-3-113 (West 2017) (providing for the establishment of children's centers in courthouses.) The Act also directs that courts must provide, as appropriate, referrals to programs for at-risk youth, employment counseling, financial management, education, mediation among other needs. *Id.*

parents and accommodate children from two through twelve years of age. In Oregon, CourtCare, a program supported by donations from judges, attorneys, and community members, offers free childcare to infants and children up to six years of age.[61] The New York City Family Court houses children's centers operated by a community-based agency in partnership with the Office of Court Administration.[62] Childcare is available for children up to twelve years of age, and the centers provide snacks and referrals for related services, such as early childhood education and child health programs. Staff in these centers receive training to identify child abuse and neglect, substance abuse, and household domestic violence.

Court-based family services

The Hawaii family justice system has incorporated an extensive array of specialized services for families. Two programs illustrate novel approaches to the needs of children and youth in foster care. Project Visitation is designed to maintain relationships between and among siblings who have been placed in separate foster homes. The project facilitates monthly visits for these otherwise disconnected children. Imua Kakou addresses an often neglected population—youth between the ages of eighteen and twenty-one who have aged out of the foster care system.[63] A voluntary program, Imua Kakou[64] makes available medical and dental care, rent stipends, and monthly mentoring for matters related to independent living and achieving personal goals.[65] These services are especially significant as the needs of youth emancipated from the state's protection are extensive and otherwise are likely unmet.

Translation services

Caring for family court litigants involves ensuring that the court both hears and understands their voices. The need for court translation services is critical, especially in jurisdictions where the population is culturally and ethnically diverse. Circumstances of diversity among family court users is a global problem, owing to vast numbers of refugee populations relocating to more stable political environments, such as countries in Europe and Scandinavia.[66] Given this population shift, translation services are

61 Comm. on Family Court and Family Law, Ass'n of the Bar of the City of N.Y., Report on Family Court Services (2006).

62 *See Children's Centers*, N.Y. State Unified Ct. Sys., https://www.nycourts.gov/courts/nyc/family/childservicecenters.shtml (last visited June 15, 2018).

63 *See, e.g.*, Lisa Rapaport, *Teens Leaving Foster System May Lack Needed Mental Health Care*, Reuters Health, Oct. 22, 2015, https://www.reuters.com/article/us-health-fostercare-teens-idUSKCN0SG2OX20151022.

64 Imua Kakou, a Hawaiian colloquialism meaning "before us." Google Translate, https://translate.google.com/#auto/en/imua%20kakou (last visited June 27, 2018).

65 Survey Response, Lillian Takaki, Law Clerk, Chambers of Hon. Catherine H. Remigio, Senior Judge of the Family Court of the First Circuit, Kapolei, Haw. (Aug. 2017).

66 *Refugee Population by Country or Territory of Asylum*, World Bank, https://data.worldbank.org/indicator/SM.POP.REFG (last updated 2018) (documenting the refugee population by country or territory of asylum).

a basic ingredient in caring for court-involved families. In Alaska, for example, court interpreters are available across case types. Parties, witnesses, and victims are entitled to translators; in certain circumstances, parents of juvenile defendants have access to them, as well.[67] The need for translation services in Alaska is particularly acute and challenging. Alaska provides an interesting counter-point to the conventional wisdom that diversity exists primarily in major cities.[68] Two Alaska counties rank first and second on a list of the five most diverse counties in the United States, which demonstrates the critical need for language translation.[69] The challenges with regard to translation services in Alaska are that the quality of court interpretation suffers from a paucity of state certified interpreters and that families often are unable to appear in person, given the state's rugged terrain and harsh climate. Alaska is attempting to overcome these obstacles and has achieved leadership status in the United States for its vanguard remote translation services achieved via telephone.

Court-community connections

The Hawaii Family Court, in partnership with the Hawaii Department of Human Services, EPIC 'Ohana, and Family Programs of Hawaii, has implemented a creative opportunity for judges to hear from foster youth during their review hearings. Teen Day, the name of the program, is a twice-yearly event designed to support youth about to become emancipated from foster care by providing information about community resources tailored to their needs. In addition to the involvement of community service providers, Teen Day is a unique occasion during which judges interact with the youth. The focus is on judges asking for and listening to the concerns of the young people who appear before them so that their stories emerge in the process. Family law scholars have commented that the court must hear the authentic voices of children.[70] In this case, the children receive a designated forum.

Other specialty programs designed to focus on the needs of children involve initiatives surrounding the collection and payment of child support. The goals of these programs generally involve removing barriers to co-parenting, fostering

67 *See* Telephone Interview with Stacey Marz, Director, Self-Help Services, Alaska Court System (Sept. 12, 2017) (noting that parents of youth who are subjects of delinquency cases have access to translation services).

68 Svati Kirsten Narula, *The 5 U.S. Counties Where Racial Diversity Is Highest—and Lowest: Why are Alaska's Aleutian Islands So Racially Mixed? And Other Questions From a New Map of U.S. Populations*, ATLANTIC (Apr. 29, 2014), https://www.theatlantic.com/national/archive/2014/04/mapping-racial-diversity-by-county/361388/.

69 Svati Kirsten Narula, *The 5 U.S. Counties Where Racial Diversity Is Highest—and Lowest: Why are Alaska's Aleutian Islands So Racially Mixed? And Other Questions From a New Map of U.S. Populations*, ATLANTIC (Apr. 29, 2014), https://www.theatlantic.com/national/archive/2014/04/mapping-racial-diversity-by-county/361388/.

70 *See, e.g.*, REWRITING CHILDREN'S RIGHTS JUDGMENTS: FROM ACADEMIC VISION TO NEW PRACTICE (Helen Stalford, Kathryn Hollingsworth, & Steven Gilmore eds., 2017) (explaining the components of judicial decision-making that ensure and illuminate a children's rights perspective). Among them is using child-friendly language, presumably that which embodies a child's voice. *Id.*

connections between parents and children, providing employment opportunities for financially unstable parents, and improving the payment and collection of support obligations.[71] These objectives often involve connecting with community agencies, with the intention to result in more positive outcomes for children and their parents than the traditional approach of punishing parents for nonpayment of child support. "In this approach, the court operates not as a social service provider, but rather as a portal through which families can connect with high-quality social services and more effectively benefit from the court's orders."[72]

Incarcerated parents often lose a connection to their children during incarceration and upon their release. The parole system does not address adequately the problems parents experience vis-à-vis their children upon reentry.[73] Many children often enter the foster care system due to these circumstances.[74] As a consequence, courts have begun to establish reentry courts and other programs to assist children of incarcerated parents. The general aim of these practices is to identify and address the barriers interfering with a positive parent-child relationship. To assist with this, courts often turn to community agencies and services, all in an attempt to improve the lives of children and their parents.[75]

Our research also has led us to examples of interdisciplinary partnerships between community health clinics and legal clinics that aim to create a practice model where lawyers and medical professionals work together to solve the often interconnected medical-legal problems facing family court litigants.[76] While these

71 *See, e.g.*, Matthew Hector, *New "Accountability Court" Helps Child-Support Obligors Keep Up Payments*, 104 Ill. B.J. 16 (2016); Laurie S. Kohn, *Money Can't Buy You Love: Valuing Contributions by Nonresidential Fathers*, 81 Brook. L. Rev. 53, 103 (2015); Milton C. Lee, *Fatherhood in the Child Support System: An Innovative Problem-Solving Approach to an Old Problem*, 50 Fam. Ct. Rev. 59 (2012); Sasha Aslanian, *Never-Married Parents Get Help from Special Court*, NPR, May 7. 2012, https://www.npr.org/2012/05/07/152157287/never-married-parents-get-help-from-special-court.

72 Ebony L. Ruhland, Alisha M. Hardman, Emily H. Becher, & Mary S. Marczak, *Co-Parent Court: A Problem-Solving, Community-Based Model for Serving Low-Income Unmarried Parents*, 54 Fam. Ct. Rev. 336, 337 (2016).

73 Erin McGrath, *Reentry Courts: Providing a Second Chance for Incarcerated Mothers and Their Children*, 50 Fam. Ct. Rev. 113, 114 (2012).

74 Myrna S. Raeder, "*Special Issue: Making a Better World for Children of Incarcerated Parents*," 50 Fam. Ct. Rev. 23, 23–24 (2012).

75 *See, e.g.*, Patricia Allard, *When the Cost is Too Great: The Emotional and Psychological Impact on Children of Incarcerating Their Parents for Drug Offenses*, 50 Fam. Ct. Rev. 48 (2012); Marguerite D. Downing, *Barriers to Reunification for Incarcerated Parents—A Judicial Perspective*, 50 Fam. Ct. Rev. 71 (2012); Philip M. Genty, *Moving Beyond Generalizations and Stereotypes to Develop Individualized Approaches for Working with Families Affected by Parental Incarceration*, 50 Fam. Ct. Rev. 36 (2012); Denise Johnston, *Services for Children of Incarcerated Parents*, 50 Fam. Ct. Rev. 91 (2012).

76 *See, e.g.*, Cheryl Brown-Irava, Miriam El-Chami, & Francisca Wong, *Health and Law: UC Health-Justice Clinic: Law Students Tackle the Intricate Interplay of Legal and Health Issues*, Ethos, Sept. 2017, at 43, 45 (Austl.) (describing an initiative under the auspices of a Health Justice Partnership that brings together law students from the University of Canberra's Law School with practicing lawyers and psychologists from the University's Medical and Counseling Service to help clients solve problems that

collaborations exist outside family court courthouses, they are instrumental in promoting caring for family law litigants. Medical-legal partnerships, also known as Health Justice Partnerships and Alliances, are a potent force to help families receive more effective medical treatment than that provided by healthcare professionals in community-based clinics.[77] In medical-legal partnerships, attorneys help doctors who often are stymied to provide sustainable relief from medical problems resulting from housing violations and other conditions for which there may be a legal remedy.

One example of an effective doctor-lawyer collaboration involved a physician who was frustrated by her inability to stabilize a patient's chronic asthma.[78] She learned that the root of the asthma problem stemmed from the failure of the patient's landlord to properly repair a broken window. The doctor's efforts to convince the landlord to fix the window were unavailing until she enlisted a lawyer friend to write a letter on the patient's behalf. That intervention prompted the appropriate window repair. "I figured out that we quickly needed a medical-legal partnership to take that whole, true care of the whole person, beyond my skill set, because that wouldn't have gotten the window fixed,"[79] the doctor said. The result was the creation of the Health Justice Alliance between Georgetown University's Medical and Law Schools, forging a link between "the medical center's focus on cura personalis, or care of the whole person, with the law center's motto 'law is but the means, justice is the end. . . .'"[80]

The mission of the Georgetown alliance, to meld justice with care, and similar medico-legal enterprises embodies the quality of care we advocate America's

highlight "the porous nexus between the client's nonlegal problems and those which are capable of a legal solution.").

77 *See, e.g.*, American Bar Association, *Medical-Legal Partnerships Pro Bono Support Project*, https://www.americanbar.org/groups/probono_public_service/projects_awards/medical_legal_partnerships_pro_bono_project.html. In 2007, the American Bar Association passed a resolution in support of a medical-legal partnership. *Id.* This resolution serves to encourage members of the legal profession to work with the healthcare profession and social service organizations to come together to identify and resolve legal issues that have detrimental effects on people's health and well-being. *Id.* In concert with the ABA resolution, the American Medical Association passed a similar resolution in support of such collaborative interdisciplinary efforts. *Id. See also*, National Center for Medical-Legal Partnership, *Celebrating the 10-year Anniversaries of AAP and ABA Medical-Legal Partnership Resolutions* (Nov. 22, 2017), http://medical-legalpartnership.org/celebrate-10-year-aap-aba-resolutions/.

78 Kat Zambon, *Doctors and Lawyers Speak Out for Health Justice Alliance*, Geo. Univ. Med. Ctr. (Sept. 22, 2017), https://gumc.georgetown.edu/news/Doctors-and-Lawyers-Speak-Out-for-Health-Justice-Alliance (reporting on an interdisciplinary collaboration dedicated to training future generations of lawyers and medical professionals to work together to improve the health and well-being of children and families).

79 Kat Zambon, *Doctors and Lawyers Speak Out for Health Justice Alliance*, Geo. Univ. Med. Ctr. (Sept. 22, 2017), https://gumc.georgetown.edu/news/Doctors-and-Lawyers-Speak-Out-for-Health-Justice-Alliance.

80 Kat Zambon, *Doctors and Lawyers Speak Out for Health Justice Alliance*, Geo. Univ. Med. Ctr. (Sept. 22, 2017), https://gumc.georgetown.edu/news/Doctors-and-Lawyers-Speak-Out-for-Health-Justice-Alliance.

family courts and their community partners adopt.[81] Incorporating interdisciplinary partnerships within the court's ambit enables a holistic and caring approach to family justice.

Court policies

Training for judges and court personnel

Training is an important facet of a caring justice system. It enables those who work in the family justice system to develop a basic understanding of the underlying issues in family law cases that complicate the legal matters before the court. As we have explained, family court litigants often are plagued with accompanying nonlegal issues relating to substance abuse, mental illness, and the problems associated with poverty. While these issues are prevalent, judges and court personnel may not understand their impact without training in these specific topics. In addition, other matters germane to families, such as child development and family dynamics,[82] have a bearing on family law decision-making. Curricular initiatives for all court actors must address these related subjects.[83]

Our survey of family courts has revealed some that have instituted training policies which reflect a dedication to caring for families. In Hawaii, the family

81 *See also* Karen Weintraub, *Using Medicine and Science to Improve the Quality of Life*, N.Y. TIMES, May 27, 2018, (Visionaries), at F4 (describing the non-profit organization *Health Leads* that "bring[s] together insurers, foundations, medical societies, state governments, community organizations and others who embrace" a more comprehensive view of healthcare). *Health Leads* was founded on the premise that "what is wrong with America's health care system [is that] . . . [i]t can be so focused on medicine that it misses the social issues that really drive health." *Id.* This vision is in line with our belief that rendering justice is also a complex enterprise and needs holistic approaches that leverage multiple partners and advocates.

82 *See, e.g.*, Clare Huntington, *Early Childhood Development and the Law*, 90 S. CAL. L. REV. 755, 761 (2017) (explaining that the parent-child relationship is central to "a host of cognitive and non-cognitive skills" that comprise the essential developmental tasks of early childhood). *See also* Douglas F. Johnson, *Zero to Three Family Drug Treatment Court, in* CLINICAL WORK WITH TRAUMATIZED YOUNG CHILDREN 269, 288 (Joy D. Osofsky, ed., 2013) (discussing a series of statewide trainings called "Helping Babies from the Bench" and focusing on the science of early childhood development).

83 *See, e.g.*, Natalie A. Knowlton, *The Modern Family Court Judge: Knowledge, Qualities, and Skills for Success*, 53 FAM. CT. REV. 203 (2015) (recommending an educational curriculum for family court judges that includes training in rules, statutes, and case law; evidence; ethics; trauma-informed decision-making; awareness of forensic trauma; child development and family dynamics; domestic violence; child maltreatment; substance abuse and addiction; mental health; cultural competence; understanding one's own biases; financial matters; resources available in the community for families; intervention strategies and processes, with an emphasis on knowing the standards for each; clarity and brevity in oral and written communications; listening skills; decisiveness; timeliness; dispute resolution techniques; humility and thoughtfulness; respectfulness and courtesy; stress management; administrative capacity; judicial leadership on and off the bench; and commitment to the family court bench).

justice system has established protocols for judges that involve weekly instruction on topics, such as domestic abuse, child sexual exploitation, and methods to understand and analyze custody evaluation reports.[84] Rhode Island has developed educational materials for its family court judges on mental health awareness, child development, and familial relationships.[85] The Rhode Island family court also has a training protocol for all court personnel, including sheriffs, service providers, clerks, and attorneys, that focuses on the intersection of trauma and family law matters.[86] The Maryland court system, in partnership with the University of Baltimore Law School Sayra and Neil Meyerhoff Center for Families, Children and the Courts, has developed and distributed a bench book on addiction and substance abuse, which is distributed to all family court judges and magistrates.[87]

We have concluded from a subpart of a National Assessment of Australia's Children's Courts[88] that the country has made a substantial commitment to improve its family justice system—one that highlights a dedication to training for court personnel. The Report demonstrates that caring for families and children is the animating principle of this systematic approach to court reform.[89] The published study itself is an act of caring simply by representing a deliberate attempt to identify areas in which to reform the court system from the standpoint of those who work within it. As the introduction to this report explains:

> While legislation frames the workings of the Children's Court, it is the professionals [judicial officers and service providers] attached to the court that interpret and implement these ideas on an everyday basis. For this reason, the perspectives of these professionals on the purpose, role, scope and effectiveness of the Children's Court of NSW [New South Wales] is critical to understanding the operation of this system in the current context and the areas that are in need of policy reform.[90]

Likewise, the concerns of and suggestions by the study participants themselves demonstrate a deep commitment to caring for Children's Court litigants. Among the perspectives shared by court magistrates and court professionals is the need for specific training in certain areas, including "the difficulties facing parents in

84 Survey Response, Lillian Takaki, Law Clerk, Chambers of Hon. Catherine H. Remigio, Senior Judge of the Family Court of the First Circuit, Kapolei, Haw. (Aug. 2017).
85 Survey Response, Ronald J. Pagliarini, Chief of Staff, R.I. Family Court, Providence, R.I. (June 2017)
86 Survey Response, Ronald J. Pagliarini, Chief of Staff, R.I. Family Court, Providence, R.I. (June 2017).
87 Barbara A. Babb, Gloria Danziger, & Judith D. Moran, Benchbook on Substance Abuse and Addiction for Family Courts (2010).
88 *See* Elizabeth Fernandez, Jane Bolitho, Patricia Hansen, Myvanwy Hudson, & Sacha Kendall, A Study of the Children's Court of New South Wales (2014).
89 Elizabeth Fernandez, Jane Bolitho, Patricia Hansen, Myvanwy Hudson, & Sacha Kendall, A Study of the Children's Court of New South Wales (2014).
90 Elizabeth Fernandez, Jane Bolitho, Patricia Hansen, Myvanwy Hudson, & Sacha Kendall, A Study of the Children's Court of New South Wales 16 (2014).

meeting restoration plans"[91] and "greater training on social welfare, child development and child psychology."[92] Judicial officers, noting the trauma underlying the cases in the Children's Court, have suggested that "collegial support" and "more opportunity to debrief" are needed.[93] The thoughts and remedies expressed by Children's Court judges indicate a court system with an interest in caring for families, judges, and court staff. The topics and opportunities identified by the respondents to this comprehensive survey of their needs are consistent with the prescriptions for caring in court that we have put forth. As we have mentioned, judges and court staff require specific training, as well as occasions to reflect with their colleagues on the challenges of working in a system that addresses the compelling, complex, and often heartbreaking issues facing families in crisis.

A similar training initiative, also nationwide in scope, has occurred in the United States. The National Council of Juvenile and Family Court Judges (NCJFCJ), "a professional organization with the mission of improving family courts' understanding of children's needs, [has] conducted the first nationwide survey of judges on the frequency of their contacts with military families and their perceived education needs,"[94] a growing subset of family law litigants. The NCJFCJ has embarked on this groundbreaking initiative in response to the "rising tide"[95] of cases involving military families and "with the implicit understanding that families who have endured multiple deployments and stress of more than a decade of war face a set of compelling and very unfamiliar life circumstances compared to civilian families."[96] As the concerns facing military families are unique to them, so, too, are the legal issues that drive them to the courthouse.[97] Judges and court staff

91 Elizabeth Fernandez, Jane Bolitho, Patricia Hansen, Myvanwy Hudson, & Sacha Kendall, A Study of the Children's Court of New South Wales 31 (2014). *See also* Larissa MacFarquhar, *When Should a Child Be Taken from His Parents?*, New Yorker, Aug. 7 & 14, 2017 (describing the child welfare conundrum facing judges and parents regarding compliance with court orders to remedy findings of child abuse and neglect). The article makes clear that child welfare policies may imperil the integrity of the family if perfection is the standard by which parents are judged. *Id.*

92 Elizabeth Fernandez, Jane Bolitho, Patricia Hansen, Myvanwy Hudson, & Sacha Kendall, A Study of the Children's Court of New South Wales 31 (2014).

93 *See* Elizabeth Fernandez, Jane Bolitho, Patricia Hansen, Myvanwy Hudson, & Sacha Kendall, A Study of the Children's Court of New South Wales 31 (2014).

94 Evan R. Seamone, *Educating Family Court Judges on the Front Lines of Combat Readjustment: Toward the Formulation and Delivery of a Core Curriculum on Military Family Issues*, 52. Fam. Ct. Rev. 458, 459 (2014).

95 Evan R. Seamone, *Educating Family Court Judges on the Front Lines of Combat Readjustment: Toward the Formulation and Delivery of a Core Curriculum on Military Family Issues*, 52. Fam. Ct. Rev. 458, 459 (2014) (citing a Memorandum from Janice M. Rosa, Justice (ret.), N.Y. Supreme Court, Supervising Judge, Family Courts in 8th Judicial Dist., to Judy Harris Kluger, Chief of Policy & Planning, N.Y. State Office Court Admin. 7 (Dec. 17, 2012)).

96 Evan R. Seamone, *Educating Family Court Judges on the Front Lines of Combat Readjustment: Toward the Formulation and Delivery of a Core Curriculum on Military Family Issues*, 52 Fam. Ct. Rev. 458, 460 (2014).

97 Evan R. Seamone, *Educating Family Court Judges on the Front Lines of Combat Readjustment: Toward the Formulation and Delivery of a Core Curriculum on Military Family*

who work with military families must confront an unfamiliar terrain of legal issues, complicated by the intersection of military regulations and laws, "all of which have a bearing on 'child support calculations,' 'parenting time,' and 'visitation.'"[98] One pioneering judge has acted upon this information and has created a family court special docket designed to address the unique needs of military families.[99] She asks and answers, "Why should the courts care? Simply put, we must. To ethically discharge our judicial duties, we must learn about and respond to this population and 'culture' in our midst."[100] Similar to other justice system initiatives, these efforts signify a concerted and deep dedication to caring for families.

Court procedures

Court procedures are essential to a caring court regimen. Case management is among the most salient. It involves multiple strategies, including centers to assist self-represented litigants, protocols that regulate trial processes, early settlement conferences, alternative dispute resolution, judicial case assignments, and parenting plan facilitation programs. The Alaska court system incorporates many of these procedural interventions, which, taken together, are demonstrable acts of caring for families.[101]

A substantial portion of Alaska court resources is devoted to providing assistance to self-represented family law litigants. Approximately seventy-five percent of Alaska's family law litigants represent themselves in court cases, demonstrating a great need for the court to function effectively when handling these matters. Alaska has created a Family Law Self Help Center and an Early Resolution Triage Program staffed with volunteer attorneys and mediators and overseen by a judge. While the goal of the triage program is to avoid a trial, among those cases that are not resolved without court involvement, the court determines eighty percent expeditiously in a single trial.[102] Alaska's parenting plan program aims to prevent post-judgment litigation of child custody and access matters. The initiative targets

Issues, 52. FAM. CT. REV. 458, 460 (2014) (explaining that "[n]ot since the Vietnam War have the American family courts witnessed so many combat readjustment issues.").

98 Evan R. Seamone, *Educating Family Court Judges on the Front Lines of Combat Readjustment: Toward the Formulation and Delivery of a Core Curriculum on Military Family Issues*, 52 FAM. CT. REV. 458, 460 (2014) (explaining that this is the most frequently cited issue by judges for which they needed specific training). Other training needs expressed by those surveyed were family violence and the "'effect of deployment on the soldier and family, specifically [PTSD] and other mental health issues as well as soldier reentry.'" *Id.*

99 Janice M. Rosa, *Mission Critical: A Call to Action for Juvenile and Family Courts, the U.S. Armed Forces, and Veterans Affairs*, 52 FAM. CT. REV. 511 (2014).

100 Janice M. Rosa, *Mission Critical: A Call to Action for Juvenile and Family Courts, the U.S. Armed Forces, and Veterans Affairs*, 52 FAM. CT. REV. 511 (2014) (footnote omitted).

101 Telephone Interview with Stacey Marz, Dir. of Self-Help Servs., Alaska Court Sys. (Sept. 12, 2017).

102 Telephone Interview with Stacey Marz, Dir. of Self-Help Servs., Alaska Court Sys. (Sept. 12, 2017).

uncontested cases and ensures that the parties have drafted feasible parenting plans. In cases where parenting plans are non-existent or otherwise problematic, program staff (social workers and psychologists) work with parents to create sustainable parenting plans. Finally, Alaska has instituted an alternative dispute resolution process in the form of neutral case evaluation in contested child custody cases. Evaluators review the facts pertinent to the case and work with parents to mediate an agreeable and viable resolution.

Alaska has undertaken these numerous preventive and early intervention strategies to avoid or temper inter-parental conflict and to limit the need to appear in court. These measures have special relevance for Alaskan parents because courts often are distant from where families reside, making it difficult for parents to return to attend court proceedings. This aspect of the Alaska court system, the disconnect between where families live and where courts are located, has a bearing on the processes the court implements.

The New York court system has adopted an innovative court procedure to help families overcome obstacles in navigating the court system that also demonstrates caring justice. Technological advances contribute to these efforts.[103] According to Chief Administrative Judge Lawrence K. Marks, "By expanding technology and modernizing our technology operations, we have made justice more accessible and more efficient."[104] While many, if not most, court systems have implemented technology to enable e-filings and electronic court calendars, family courts in New York are on the vanguard of a particularly unique practice. A sub-set of technological innovations in New York's family courts is designed to "shield victims of domestic violence from having to appear in court in the presence of their abuser."[105] A pilot program authorized by the state legislature in 2016 allows the family courts to accept e-filings for temporary orders of protection and affords the opportunity to hold initial court appearances via Skype. In addition, victims also obtain "a secure email account from which they can communicate and receive records regarding the case."[106]

103 *See* Lawrence K. Marks, *A Technology-Focused Approach to Administering Justice*, N.Y. L.J. (Jan. 19, 2018), https://www.law.com/newyorklawjournal/sites/newyorklawjournal/2018/01/19/a-technology-focused-approach-to-administering-justice/?slreturn=20180505181948 (describing, among the technological advances in the Family Court, one that "allows all parties to a case to sign in at a designated check-in desk, that then electronically alerts the courtroom when all parties are present and the case can be called"—avoiding the protracted wait-times that often characterize busy family courts and wreak havoc with parents' work and child care obligations).

104 Lawrence K. Marks, *A Technology-Focused Approach to Administering Justice*, N.Y. L.J. (Jan. 19, 2018), https://www.law.com/newyorklawjournal/sites/newyorklawjournal/2018/01/19/a-technology-focused-approach-to-administering-justice/?slreturn=20180505181948.

105 Lawrence K. Marks, *A Technology-Focused Approach to Administering Justice*, N.Y. L.J. (Jan. 19, 2018), https://www.law.com/newyorklawjournal/sites/newyorklawjournal/2018/01/19/a-technology-focused-approach-to-administering-justice/?slreturn=20180505181948.

106 Lawrence K. Marks, *A Technology-Focused Approach to Administering Justice*, N.Y. L.J. (Jan. 19, 2018), https://www.law.com/newyorklawjournal/sites/newyorklawjournal/2018/01/19/a-technology-focused-approach-to-administering-justice/?slreturn=20180505181948.

In another instance of a caring approach to resolving family law matters, Arizona has promulgated new rules of Family Law Procedure, which emphasize alternative dispute resolution and therapeutic jurisprudence.[107] Finally, we also mention multi-state reform efforts aimed at eliminating shackling of youth who appear before juvenile courts.[108] Although the practice is routine in many jurisdictions, a recent survey has yielded evidence that change is afoot, whether it is prohibitions or limitations executed via court rule,[109] state statute,[110] procedural methods,[111] or other avenues.[112] These reforms reflect jurisprudential interpretations that shackling violates due process.[113] They also reflect caring in juvenile court.

Caring judges

Judicial opinions

Our research has led us to a variety of formats indicating caring practices by family court judges. We feature a judicial opinion that embodies care.[114] The decision by a British High Court Judge, His Honor Justice Peter Jackson, presiding in The Family Court of England and Wales in the matter of the custody of a fourteen-year-old boy, is noteworthy.

The judge's decision accompanied his personal letter to the boy explaining the thinking framing the outcome.[115] The boy was the subject of a dispute about a change of custody from his mother, who lived in England with her second husband, to his father, who wished to relocate with his son to a Scandinavian country. The boy, through his solicitor, expressed his desire to make the move so that he could live with his father. The boy's mother and stepfather objected. The judge

107 *See* ARIZ. FAM. LAW R. 66–75 (emphasizing therapeutic jurisprudence).

108 Donna Quigley Groman, *Juvenile Shackling Reform: The Judicial Role in Ensuring Trauma-Informed Courts and Why States Are Rethinking Restraints*, 66 JUV. FAM. CT. J. 19 (2015) (noting that "[i]n most states, there are no statutory restrictions on shackling of young people in juvenile courts. The practice is commonplace.").

109 *See, e.g.*, ALASKA DELINQUENCY R. 21.5; WASH. JU. C. R. 1.6; PA. R. J. C. P. 139.

110 *See, e.g.*, 42 PA. CONS. STAT. § 6336.2 (2018).

111 *See, e.g.*, Memorandum Re: Restraints in Juv. Ct. from Michael F. Edgerton, Chief Justice, Commonwealth of Mass. Admin. Office of the Juv. Ct. (2010) (on file with authors).

112 *See, e.g.*, 10-223 N.M. R. A.; N.C. GEN. STAT. ANN. § 7B-2402.1 (West 2007).

113 Donna Quigley Groman, *Juvenile Shackling Reform: The Judicial Role in Ensuring Trauma-Informed Courts and Why States Are Rethinking Restraints*, 66 JUV. FAM. CT. J. 19, 20 (2015).

114 *See Judicial Decision Writing Can Improve Wellbeing (TJ Court Craft Series #10)*, INT'L SOC'Y FOR THERAPEUTIC JURIS. (Aug. 8, 2017), https://mainstreamtj.wordpress.com/2017/08/08/judicial-decision-writing-can-improve-wellbeing-tj-court-craft-series-10/ (detailing an opinion in which the judge, while following the law, "altered his approach in such a way as to maximize wellbeing of the parties and in particular the young person[,]" the subject of a contested custody case).

115 A (Letter to a Young Person), Re (Rev 1) [2017] EWHC (Fam) 48 (Eng.), *available at* http://www. bailii.org/ew/cases/EWFC/HCJ/2017/48.html.

asserted that remaining in England with his mother and stepfather was in the boy's best interest. The judge's decision included an explanatory letter to the boy:

> I realise that this order is not the one that you said you wanted me to make, but I am confident that it is the right order for you in the long run. Whatever each of your parents might think about it, I hope they have the dignity not to impose their views on you, so that you can work things out for yourself. I know that as you get older, you will do this increasingly and I hope that you will come to see why I have made these decisions. I wish you every success with your future and if you want to reply to this letter, I know that your solicitor will make sure that your reply reaches me.[116]

The fact that the judge took the time to write the letter and the words expressed within it undoubtedly represented a caring practice.

Another instance of a departure from normative standards of judicial decision-making also involved a letter, prompting a novel opinion in a child welfare matter. In this case, the judge received a letter written by a sixteen-year-old boy who, along with his three younger siblings, were separated from their mother owing to her prison sentence for "spreading Islamic State propaganda online."[117] The judge returned the children to their mother's care after the "judge was moved by a letter from her oldest son."[118] The judge told the mother, "In your exceptional case, the sooner you are returned to your children, the better for all concerned."[119] This opinion clearly embodied the caring stance we promote.

Judicial reflections

We have learned of a caring judge contained in an account sent to us by His Honor, Justice Michael Keehan, serving in The Family Division of the High Court of England and Wales.[120] This Judge writes about the care and concern with

116 A (Letter to a Young Person), Re (Rev 1) [2017] EWHC (Fam) 48 (Eng.), *available at* http://www. bailii.org/ew/cases/EWFC/HCJ/2017/48.html.

117 *See* Fiona Hamilton, *Extremists Should Lose Access to Their Children, Says Scotland Yard Chief*, TIMES (London) (Feb. 27, 2018), https://www.thetimes.co.uk/article/extremists-should-lose-access-to-their-children-says-scotland-yard-chief-wnrfjbnpq (describing controversy about the extent to which participation in terrorist activities rises to the level of child endangerment and abuse). Mark Rowley, the United Kingdom's "top counterterrorism officer" has recently exclaimed, "Courts should remove children from extremist families . . . [Rowley] claimed that exposing children to extremism was 'equally wicked' as exposing them to sexual abuse . . . ." *Id.*

118 Fiona Hamilton, *Extremists Should Lose Access to Their Children, Says Scotland Yard Chief*, TIMES (London) (Feb. 27, 2018), https://www.thetimes.co.uk/article/extremists-should-lose-access-to-their-children-says-scotland-yard-chief-wnrfjbnpq.

119 Fiona Hamilton, *Extremists Should Lose Access to Their Children, Says Scotland Yard Chief*, TIMES (London) (Feb. 27, 2018), https://www.thetimes.co.uk/article/extremists-should-lose-access-to-their-children-says-scotland-yard-chief-wnrfjbnpq.

120 E-mail from Michael Keehan, High Court Judge, High Court of Justice of the Courts of England and Wales, Family Division, to Judith Moran, Adjunct Professor, Univ. of Balt. Sch. of L. (Aug. 31, 2017, 10:37 EST) (on file with authors).

which he approaches some of the most difficult decisions he and his fellow judges on the High Court must make.[121]

> We, of course, deal with the most serious and the most tragic family cases. Telling parents that you are permitting the doctors to switch off their child's life support or that you are taking their children away from them for ever and placing them for adoption . . . .[122]

Justice Keehan's comments included narrative accounts of hard cases to which he devoted significant attention.[123] In one difficult matter, his concerns focused on how to avoid splitting apart two sibling groups to avoid a possible lifelong rift between two sets of children within the same family.[124] Further, Justice Keehan contemplated more generally on the finality of adoption cases: "I am increasingly questioning whether non-consensual adoption, with a plan to split the sibling group, is in the life-long welfare best interests of the children."[125]

In another case that demonstrated caring, Justice Keehan sought wisdom from narrative—a story told directly to him by a teenage girl "who had been sold by her mother and trafficked into this country for the purposes of domestic servitude."[126] The teen's mother had applied to have her daughter returned to her from the protective intervention of child welfare authorities, who had placed the teen in foster care. Hearing the girl's story prompted Justice Keehan to realize that she was capable of making a decision for herself. That insight supported denying the mother's application to have her daughter returned to her custody.

121 The judge at the same time acknowledges that the challenges "are similar to those faced by all levels of family judges and magistrates." E-mail from Michael Keehan, High Court Judge, High Court of Justice of the Courts of England and Wales, Family Division, to Judith Moran, Adjunct Professor, Univ. of Balt. Sch. of L. (Aug. 31, 2017, 10:37 EST) (on file with authors).

122 E-mail from Michael Keehan, High Court Judge, High Court of Justice of the Courts of England and Wales, Family Division, to Judith Moran, Adjunct Professor, Univ. of Balt. Sch. of L. (Aug. 31, 2017, 10:37 EST) (on file with authors).

123 E-mail from Michael Keehan, High Court Judge, High Court of Justice of the Courts of England and Wales, Family Division, to Judith Moran, Adjunct Professor, Univ. of Balt. Sch. of L. (Aug. 31, 2017, 10:37 EST) (on file with authors). *See also* Ian McEwan, The Children Act (2014) (describing a fictional account of an English family court judge who wrestled with whether a teenage boy was fit to make a potentially life-changing decision about his medical care). As in the case of the very real judge whom we have cited, the fictional judge pondered at length the vexed consequences of possible legal options at her disposal.

124 E-mail from Michael Keehan, High Court Judge, High Court of Justice of the Courts of England and Wales, Family Division, to Judith Moran, Adjunct Professor, Univ. of Balt. Sch. of L. (Aug. 31, 2017, 10:37 EST) (on file with authors).

125 E-mail from Michael Keehan, High Court Judge, High Court of Justice of the Courts of England and Wales, Family Division, to Judith Moran, Adjunct Professor, Univ. of Balt. Sch. of L. (Aug. 31, 2017, 10:37 EST) (on file with authors).

126 E-mail from Michael Keehan, High Court Judge, High Court of Justice of the Courts of England and Wales, Family Division, to Judith Moran, Adjunct Professor, Univ. of Balt. Sch. of L. (Aug. 31, 2017, 10:37 EST) (on file with authors).

Justice Keehan's musings clearly demonstrated factors we identified as hallmarks of caring. He gave thoughtful consideration to case narratives, listening acutely as they were told to him by the individuals appearing before him, while remaining mindful of the consequential effect of the law as it applied to the families.

We also read of a judge whose reflections of her own childhood prompted her to become a New York Family Court Judge. "Judge Lisa Friederwitzer's first experience in a courtroom was in 1979. She was 11 and it was brutal."[127] At the time, Judge Friederwitzer was the subject of a protracted and bitter custody dispute between her parents. She recalled that "testifying about which of her parents she wanted to live with left her feeling 'unprotected and vulnerable.'"[128] She said her desire to pursue a law degree and to become a judge was "'fueled by the desire to protect children from going through what I had to go through. . . .'"[129] This personal story as context for her approach to judging foreshadowed a commitment to caring for the children in the cases litigated in her courtroom.

Conclusion: Caring family courts

As mentioned in the Preface to this book, we have pursued the ethic of care as a guiding principle for family courts for over two decades. We have continued to think about ways in which this tenet can apply to family justice system reform efforts. Our work in developing one particular family court system has fueled our ongoing efforts over the years.[130]

We have provided in this chapter more recent initiatives taken by court systems that span the globe. While our overview is not exhaustive, it demonstrates the depth and breadth of practices that are possible avenues to facilitate caring. These examples include attention to court facilities and aesthetics—what environmental enhancements make litigants feel cared-for and cared-about. They showcase investments in safety protocols, specialty court programs, and court-based services. They illustrate cooperative efforts between courts and communities. They take account of court policies, especially those which address training for judges and court personnel—highlighting the importance of caring for the carers. Finally, we have discussed the evident care that judges have shown in crafting their decisions and reflecting on their work in the courts.

At its core, the family justice system is a distinctly human enterprise. The business of the court involves the most fundamental of human relationships—those which exist between and among the people who comprise a family unit—whatever that may be. In this way, the ethic of care, which is about human relationships and

127 Corey Kilgannon, *Years After Testifying, She Runs a Court of Her Own*, N.Y. TIMES, Mar. 1, 2018, at A20.

128 Corey Kilgannon, *Years After Testifying, She Runs a Court of Her Own*, N.Y. TIMES, Mar. 1, 2018, at A20.

129 Corey Kilgannon, *Years After Testifying, She Runs a Court of Her Own*, N.Y. TIMES, Mar. 1, 2018, at A20.

130 *See* Barbara A. Babb & Judith D. Moran, *Substance Abuse, Families, and Unified Family Courts: The Creation of a Caring Justice System*, 3 J. HEALTH POL'Y & L. 1 (1999).

the obligations that stem from them, is suited ideally as an overarching framework for thinking about families' stories, family courts, and how these courts can help most effectively the families and children who come to them and who need their assistance. Indeed, the family court must become a community care center, and we have supplied the essential elements with which to fashion this transformation.

Index

For Product Safety Concerns and Information please contact our EU representative GPSR@taylorandfrancis.com
Taylor & Francis Verlag GmbH, Kaufingerstraße 24, 80331 München, Germany

www.ingramcontent.com/pod-product-compliance
Ingram Content Group UK Ltd.
Pitfield, Milton Keynes, MK11 3LW, UK
UKHW011016180926
475701UK00004B/782

* 9 7 8 1 0 3 2 2 4 1 6 9 2 *